Holland

Holland

A Phaidon Cultural Guide

with over 275 colour illustrations
and 6 pages of maps

Phaidon

Contributors: A. A. M. van der Heyden, Dr Marianne Mehling, Dr Elisabeth Nowak, Rosella Richter

Photographs: A. A. M. van der Heyden

Maps: Herbert Winkler, Munich

Ground-plans: Karl Schneider, Solms

Phaidon Press Limited, Littlegate House, St Ebbe's Street, Oxford OX1 1SQ

First published in English 1987
Originally published as *Knaurs Kulturführer in Farbe: Holland*
© Droemersche Verlagsanstalt Th. Knaur Nachf. Munich 1985
Translation © Phaidon Press Limited 1987

British Library Cataloguing in Publication Data

Holland.—(A Phaidon cultural guide)
  1. Netherlands—Description and travel
  —1978- —Guide-books
  I. Heyden, A.A.M. van der II. Knaurs
  Kulturführer in Farbe, Holland. *English*
  914.92'0473   DJ16

  ISBN 0-7148-2394-5

Translated and edited by Babel Translations, London
Typeset by Hourds Typographica, Stafford
Printed in West Germany by Druckerei Appl, Wemding

Cover illustration: Windmills at Kinderdijk, near Rotterdam (photo: © Tony Stone Associates Ltd.)

Preface

The Dutch have an old saying that 'God created heaven and earth, but Holland is the work of man.' Indeed, from the time of the ancient Batavians many generations have laboured to tame the North Sea and to safeguard the hard-won soil and fertile pasturage where the broad ocean leans against the land. The flat countryside is criss-crossed by a network of canals with picturesque drawbridges and dotted with windmills: continuous drainage has remained vital to Dutch agriculture, and villages and whole towns have had to be built on piles.

In the sixteenth century the whole of the Netherlands came under the rule of the Spanish Habsburgs. Flanders and the other southern provinces, which now make up the kingdom of Belgium, continued in their allegiance to the Spanish crown and to the Catholic faith, whereas the northern Netherlands adopted Calvinist doctrines and embarked on a costly, long-drawn-out war of liberation. When it had gained its independence, Holland entered upon its Golden Age, characterized by maritime enterprise, by expanding trade and by colonial trading-posts in the East Indies, in southern Africa and in the Americas, where New Amsterdam was to become New York.

These geographical and historical facts and the country's comparatively small size gave the population a rare and enviable cohesion. The bourgeois culture of the seventeenth century was to burst into an efflorescence of the arts, painting above all. Well-to-do merchants both found and in turn stimulated a profusion of talent, indeed of genius, in painters' workshops of towns large and small. Thus bourgeois patrons took the place that prelates and noblemen were filling in countries remaining true to the Roman Church. They bought the multifarious pictures that make up the glory of the Dutch School of painting and its variety: landscapes, seascapes, quiet courtyards and views of sunlit interiors of elegant burghers' houses, music-making and other genre scenes, low life, still-lifes and portraits – all depicted with a loving brush that often imparts a moving poetry to the humblest subject. Most artists had a speciality; the towering genius of Rembrandt had several and he even painted scenes from the Bible, a rarity in a country that had banished embellishments from its churches.

The present book will introduce the traveller by word and picture to the cultural achievement of outstanding originality that he will encounter on his visit. It will guide him to the fine sober churches, to the great civic buildings in the cities and to the lovely high-gabled old merchant residences in towns large and small. It will guide him also to the pioneering work of modern architects, much of it commissioned to make good the ravages of the second world war. It will guide him to the great paintings from the Golden Age and to the collection of works by the country's best-known painter of more recent times, Vincent Van Gogh; to the collections of exotic artefacts from the former colonies; to the open-air museums of modern sculpture and of rural technology; to the museums of navigation and exploration, and to the museums of science, a field in which Holland has been prominent since a contemporary of Rembrandt, the great Leeuwenhoek, discovered the existence of bacteria, of red blood corpuscles, of spermatozoa and much else.

As with other guides in the series, the text is arranged in alphabetical order of place name for easy reference. The link between places which are geographically close but separated in the text because of the alphabetical arrangement is provided by the maps on pages 286–91. They show all the principal towns described in the text and also, in the same colour, those subsidiary places mentioned in the environs section at the end of each entry.

The heading to each entry gives the name of the town and, below, its geographical region and a reference to the map section, giving page number and grid reference. Within each entry the sights are printed in bold type: less significant objects of interest appear under the heading **Also worth seeing** and places in the vicinity under **Environs.** At the end of the book is an index of places mentioned in the text.

Aalten
Geldern   p.291☐N 6

Dutch Reform Church: 15C late Gothic basilica with ceiling paintings (some have yet to be uncovered) and a Romanesque tufa tower (*c.* 1200).

Aaltense oorlogs- en verzetscollectiv (7 Helfrischstraat): Exhibits of World War 2 documents and photographs of Aalten and Achterhoek. Visits by prior arrangement.

Museum Frerikshuus/Oudheidkamer Aalten (14 Markt): Old costumes, implements, engravings and photographs. Opening hours: 16 May–15 Sept. Tue., Wed., Thur., Fri. 10 a.m.–12 noon and Mon.&Sat. 2–5 p.m.; 16 Sept.–15 May: Mon., Wed. and Fri. 2–5 p.m.

Also worth seeing: There is a splendid panorama from the **Watertoren** (water tower) during the summer season (Tue., Thur., Sat. and Sun. 2–4 p.m. by prior arrangement). Craftsmen can be seen at work at the *Goud- en Zilversmeedatelier Elizeene* (36 Varsseveldsestraatweg). The *Wenninkmolen* (a corn mill in a wall) in the Gendringseweg was built in *c.* 1850 (visiting hours: Sat. 10 a.m.–12 noon and 1.30–5 p.m.).

Environs: Bredevoort (3 km. NE):

An old fortified town with a late Gothic *Dutch Reform church*, enlarged in 1639; tombstones and fine rococo pulpit. The timber framed farm, *'t Boerderij'ken* (Kerkstraat), still has original decorations (*c.* 1700). '*De Prins van Oranje*' (1884), a tall corn mill in a wall, is often operated today.

Aardenburg
Seeland   p.288☐D 8

This region was inhabited in the mid-Stone Age and in the Roman period. Aardenburg was a powerful trading town in the Middle Ages, from which time the remains of the fortifications date.

St.-Baafskerk: The original building which predated today's Dutch Reform church was founded in 959. The oldest part of the present church, the *nave* (*c.* 1220), is in Schelde-Gothic style. A larger choir was added to the nave some 100 years later. The W. portal dates from 1650. Resto-

Bredevoort (Aalten), Dutch Reform church

ration carried out after World War 2 revealed small tomb vaults with paintings; similar paintings in W. Zeeuws-Vlaanderen are 14C.

Gemeentelijk Archaeological Museum: Archaeological finds from the Stone Age and Roman period. Herb garden. Opening hours: Mon.–Fri., 10.30 a.m.–5 p.m.

Aarle-Rixtel

Nordbrabant   p.289☐K 7

Onze-Lieve-Vrouwekerk: Built in 1846 in Waterstaatsstijl; the carved pulpit is 23 ft. high.

Chapel of Onze-Liewve-Vrouw-in 't Zand: Early 16C. A *triptych* by the sculptor Jan Cornelisz van Oostzanen shows the Madonna and Child with St.John (1518).

Also worth seeing: A stone *hail cross*. In the Middle Ages hail crosses were set up at crossroads to guard against thunderstorms and showers of hail.

Environs: Kasteel Croy (2 km. SE): The N.–S. wing with round corner tower is the oldest section of the castle and probably dates from the first half of the 15C. Another wing and the eight-sided tower on the SE side were added *c.* 1500. The castle was built as a country residence rather than for purposes of defence. Surrounded by canals, it is a charming sight with its stepped gables, pointed arch niches and arch friezes. The castle derives its name from a former owner Jan v. Croy, canon of Cologne and Liège.

Aduard

Groningen   p.287☐N 2

History: A village in Groningen amid canals, with the important Bernardus abbey. Founded by Cistercians in 1192, the abbey was famous for its spiritual and secular treasures; wrecked by iconoclasts in 1580.

Dutch Reform Church: The rectangular hall (the present-day church) is all that remains of the monastery.

Aardenburg, St.Baafskerk

Aardenburg, town gate

Built in *c*. 1300 this Romanesque-Gothic building in Groningen brick was possibly originally the sick-bay. The walls inside are very finely worked; 18C decorations. The tombstone (*c*. 1570) to Bijter van Rees, sister of a prior, comes from the old abbey church. The original floor—flagstones with flower patterns—survives in the W. section.

Also worth seeing: The 17C *Steentil bridge*.

Environs: Fransum (3 km. N.): The *Dutch Reform church*, on a mound safe from flood waters, has a 13C nave and Gothic choir. The pulpit of natural stone and brick stands on an early Gothic capital. The church is now a branch of the Groningen museum. The *'Aeolus' water mill* dates from 1729.

Alkmaar

North Holland   p.286□H 4

History: First mentioned in 939. The

abbey of Egmond had the right to collect tolls; in 1248 this right passed to Count Willem II, who granted Alkmaar a charter in 1254. In 1573 the town withstood a siege by Spanish troops who had captured Haarlem. The old town still stands. The canals which have bulwarks, were dug in 1573–94 to the plans of Adriaan Anthonisz.

Grote or St.-Laurenskerk: This Dutch Reform church, a splendid late Gothic cruciform basilica, is a fine example of the Gothic style of Brabant. It was begun in 1470 on the site of a previous church which had been destroyed in 1468 when its unfinished tower collapsed. Anthonis Keldermans from Mechelen worked as architect from 1497–1501. The church was consecrated in 1512. The interior appears unusually broad and well-lit with a large Last Judgement, completed in 1519, in the choir vaulting. The late Gothic choir screen and choir stalls are of oak. A small, richly decorated organ by Hans of Koblenz (1511) is in the N. ambulatory. The splendid large organ (1641–3) was

Aduard, abbey ruins, gable

Alkmaar, weigh-house and bridge

Alkmaar, Grote or St.Laurenskerk

designed by Jacob van Campen. Boetius van Everdingen, an artist from Alkmaar, painted the majestic Triumph of David on the organ doors; inside there are hovering angels by Hendrik Gerbrandsz (1656). The pulpit dates from 1655. The pews opposite were designed by Jacob von Campens.

Kapelkerk (178 Laat): Founded by the Knights of Malta in the mid 15C, this church was originally single aisled. The interior was altered in classical style after a fire in 1760; the N. aisle dates from 1536–40.

Remonstrantse Kerk (37 Fnidsen): The church, which dates from 1658, stands in a courtyard with a gate dating from 1782. The church was formerly used as a place of refuge.

Stadhuis (97 Langestraat): A late Gothic town hall built 1509–20. The W. part was added in 1694; façade altered 1877–81. Inside the grisaille paintings are by Romeyn de Hooghe (1695).

Waag (Waagplein): Originally a single-aisled cruciform chapel, it was Converted into a weigh-house in 1582 when a rich façade was built where once the choir had stood. Since 1597–9 there has been a sturdy tower above the former crossing. Beneath the balustrade there is a carousel which is set in motion on the hour.

Stedelijk Museum Aklmaar (13 Doelenstraat): This museum occupies the house of the Sebastian hunters and dates from 1561. Exhibits include items from the siege of 1573, objects associated with the hunters' guilds, as well as old toys, tiles and gable stones. Museum opening times: Mon.–Thur.

10 a.m.–12 noon and 2–5 p.m.; Fri. 10
a.m.–5 p.m.;, Sat. and holidays 2–5
p.m.

Also worth seeing: The *Accijnshuis*
(Bierkade) is a tower-like building
(1622) with an eight-sided crown.
The warden's Room in the *Provenhuis
van Nordingen* (23 Lombardsteeg)
dates from 1656. The façade of the
charming *Provenhuis van Wildeman*
(87 Oude Gracht) dates from 1714
and has three interesting statues
depicting a wild man, poverty and old
age. The *Hof van Sonoy* (Nieuwes-
loot), formerly a foundation for old
men, is a picturesque group of buildings with attractive gables, delicate
gates and a slender octagonal early
17C tower. The *Hofje van Splinter* (2
Ritsevoort) was founded for needy
women in 1646. Its façade shows a
figure of mercy. The *Huis met de
Kogel* in the Appelsteeg is the only
wooden façade in Alkmaar; a bullet
from the siege of 1573 is still lodged in
the building on the side towards the
water. The broad sandstone façade of
the *house at 114 Langestraat* was built
in 1744 by François Absiel the architect, Asmus Frauen the sculptor and
Hermanus van Gorkum who worked
on the stucco. There are other interesting *façades* overlooking the charming canals and streets, particularly
*Bierkade, Oudegracht, Kraanbuurt,
Verdronkenoord* (the latter with '*De
Vigilantie*', *a warehouse* of 1665) and
Luttik Oudorp. The '*Van Piet*' *mill*
(1769) is the only corn mill still surviving on the ramparts.

Public events: The *cheese market* is
held in the weigh-house square 10
a.m.–12 noon every Friday mid-
April–mid-September.

Environs: Bergen Binnen (4 km.
W.): This handsome village has for
many years been a centre for painters,
writers, poets and architects. The 15C
Dutch Reform church was badly

Alkmaar, Stadhuis, tower ▷

damaged by fire in 1574 and only the choir was rebuilt (restored 1955–9). The N. chapel has the Nassau-Bergen family vault. The *Oude Hof*, the former residence of the v. Bergen noblemen, is a 17C town house. *'De Viaansche Molen'*, a water-mill (1564) is very attractive. The *'Het Sterkenhuis'* museum (21 Oude Prinsweg) occupies a house dating from 1655 and has exhibits of old furniture, pewter, linen and costumes. Opening times: May–15 Sept. Tue.–Sat. 10 a.m.–12 noon and 3–5 p.m., and July–15 Aug. also Tue. and Wed. 7–9 p.m.

Broek op Langedijk (8 km. NW): A picturesque town set in an area crisscrossed by drainage canals and ditches. The town has a late-Gothic *Dutch Reform church* with a 15C choir and an early-16C nave. The *Museum Broekerveiling* (20 Voorburggracht) occupies the former auction hall for fruit and vegetables which was built in the late 19C. Opening times: 1 May–1 Oct. Mon.–Fri. 10 a.m.–5 p.m.

Egmond Binnen (8 km. SW): The *Dutch Reform church* (1430) stands where Adalbert, a follower of St.Wil-

Alkmaar, Oude Gracht

librord, founded the first little church. The *Abbey of Egmond*, consecrated in 1143 and the oldest abbey in Holland has played an important part in history. Set on fire after a siege in 1573, the last surviving tower fell down in 1798 and the entire building was later torn down. The monastery was rebuilt in 1934 and raised to the status of an abbey in 1950, a thousand years after the first monk settled here. The *Museum Abdij van Egmond* (26 Abdijlaan; visits by prior arrangement) has a collection of prehistoric and Roman finds from the grounds of the former abbey and also documents relating to the monastery's history.

Egmond aan de Hoef (7 km. W.): Parts of the foundations are almost all that of the *castle* of the lords, later counts, of Egmond, which was damaged by fire in 1574. The oldest part was an irregular round keep with a four-cornered tower (probably 12C). The castle which was built later had a square main building and a lengthy barbican. The main castle tower is 13C, and the rest is 14C and early 16C. Lamoraal, Count of Egmond, was among those to live here. He became important after 1559 and was beheaded in Brussels in 1568 along with Count van Hoorne. The *Dutch Reform church* was probably founded in 1430. Formerly the castle chapel, it burned down in 1574. When it was rebuilt in 1633, the old choir section was retained.

Heiloo (2 km. S.): The whitewashed *Dutch Reform church* stands on the site where St.Willibrord founded a small church in the 8C. The 12C N. façade is Romanesque; the tower, also Romanesque, probably dates from *c*.1200. Beside the church is the *Willibrordus fountain* (probably *c.* 700).

Schoorl (10 km. N.): The **Dutch Reform church** (1783) is Gothic in style. The *former town hall* (1601) was rebuilt in 1931 a short way from the old site.

Uitgeest (17 km. S.): The tower of the *Dutch Reform church* dates from the first half of the 14C. The cruciform *church*, which is somewhat older, was enlarged in the 15C. The choir dates from *c.* 1500. Its S. façade has an attractive portal and a stepped gable (1635). The upper storey of the late-17C *former town hall* is reached by an external staircase.

Almelo

Overijssel   p.287☐N 4

Dutch Reform church: Originally the castle chapel, it was completely rebuilt about 1390; in 1733 most of this was torn down. The present building dates from 1738 with a sandstone choir which goes back to 1493; the unusual wooden roof of the tower was added in *c.* 1780. There is a fine *tomb* (1772) of the counts of Rechteren in the choir. The splendid *organ* has gilded decorations on a white ground.

Huis Almelo: Documented since 1318. The present building dates from 1662 but was altered considerably in 1883 when the central section

of the façade with pilasters and triangular gable was added.

Museum voor Heemkunde (24 De Waag): The museum in the former weigh-house and market hall has 17C flagstones, tiles, costumes, and exhibits relating to the town's tobacco and textile industries. Opening hours: Tue.–Sat. 1.30–5 p.m.

Environs: Geesteren (7 km. NE): '*Erve Brager*' is a farmstead with timber-framed barns and houses.
Hezinge (15.5 km. NE): In the town there are *timber-framed barns* with loam filling. Beside the Hooidijk there is an interesting old house in which men and animals shared a single room.
Rijssen (11 km. SW): Granted a charter in 1245. The *Dutch Reform church*, which has a 12C Romanesque N. façade, was enlarged in the 15,16&20C. Today this hall church has a nave and two aisles, stone vaulting and a sandstone font from *c.* 1200. A delightful pump with the town's coat-of-arms (1799) stands in the Plat Hogepad Muttewal. Some beautiful

Bergen Binnen (Alkmaar), Dutch Reform church

old houses stand in the Wierdensestraat and Haarstraat. The octagonal mill '*De Pelmolen*' dates from 1752.
Tubbergen (8 km. E.): The neo-Gothic *Roman Catholic church* was built by A.Tepe in 1897. The rather ponderous, unfinished tower dates from the first half of the 16C; the wooden spire was built in 1840 after the upper section had been torn down. The plain *Dutch Reform church* was built in 1810 and enlarged in 1931. The late Gothic sandstone pulpit dates from *c.*1500.
Vasse (12 km. NE): The '*De Mast*' water mill stands beside a deep pool. In the 17&18C Catholics held secret prayer meetings under the old oak tree near the chapel (75 Oldenzaalseweg).
Vriezenveen (6 km. N.): Originally a Friesian settlement. In the 18C it maintained trade in linen and associated products with Prussia, the Baltic countries and St.Petersburg. The *Oudheidkamer* (54 Westeinde), in a former merchant's house, has a Russian department. Opening times: 10 a.m.–12 noon and 2–5 p.m. daily. A few km. to the N. are the partly exca-

Rijssen (Almelo), pump

vated foundations of the *Cistercian monastery of Sibculo*, founded in the early 15C.

Alphen aan de Rijn
South Holland   p.289□G 5

The industrial community along the Oude Rijn comprises Alphen aan de Rijn, Aarlanderveen, Oudshoorn and Zwammerdam. The area has become famous for the *Avifauna bird sanctuary*. The charming polder countryside between Nieuwkoopse, Plassen and the Braassemer lake has a large number of fine *farmhouses* and *mills*, including the 'De Eentracht' corn mill and the four polder mills of Aarlanderveen, the only group of mills in the world still working as a unit. In Oudshoorn there is a pretty church (1665) by Daniël Stalpaert with original stained-glass windows.

Environs: Nieuwkoop (8 km. NE): A small settlement popular for its water sports. The former *town hall* (1628) is a rather simple building with a Renaissance façade decorated by pilasters and a figure of Justice; the gable is crowned by a lion with coat-of-arms.
Ter Aar (6 km. N.): The *town hall* (1969–70) a little way outside the centre is a fine piece of modern architecture. Built in limestone it consists of a central hall off which four wings extend.
Woubrugge (5 km. N.): The modern *town hall* is a small building which blends harmoniously in with the other buildings in the village. Traditional architectural elements such as an oriel window and a porch have been employed.

Ameland/It Amelân (I)
Friesland   p.287□L 1

Ameland, one of the West Friesian

islands, was formerly connected to Holwerd by a dyke which collapsed in 1883. Apart from gifts of property to Fulda, little is known of the history of Ameland before 1400. Treaties concluded after 1396 with Albrecht von Beieren and his successors stipulate neutrality and unconditional subjugation. Ameland paid taxes to Holland from about 1414 until 1808. Spain acknowledged the island's independence and neutrality in 1598 and religious freedom was assured. Ameland fell to Friesland in 1801.

Nes: The island's capital with a ferry service to and from Holwerd. All that survives from the 13C church is the *tower*, which was built in 1664 and increased in height in 1732. In this village, as in the three others on the island, there are the so-called *Commandeurshuizen* (houses belonging to the captains of whaling ships) many of which have parts of whale skeletons displayed in front of them. *Natural history museum and maritime aquarium* (16 Rixt van Doniaweg 16), opening times: 1 Jan.–1 Apr. Sat. 1–5 p.m.; 1 Apr.–1 July and 1 Sept.–1 Nov.

Mon.–Sat. 10 a.m.–12 noon and 1–5 p.m.; 1 July–1 Sept. Mon.–Fri. 10 a.m.–5 p.m. and 7–9 p.m., Sat. and Sun. 1–5 p.m.

Ballum (8 km. W. of Nes): This village full of trees has a free-standing **tower** with a saddle roof, which was probably part of the former castle chapel. The small *Dutch Reform church* has a fine pulpit (1604). The richly decorated *monument* to Wytso van Cammingha (d. 1552) in the graveyard chapel is by Vincent Lucas. The whaleboat captain's house was built in 1736.

Buren/Bûr (3 km. E. of Nes): The easternmost village on the island, it borders on the nature reserves which cover this part of the island. The *Het Oerd* nature reserve covers an area of 91 acres.

Hollum (12 km. W. of Nes): The most westerly village in the island, it has many 17C houses and a *17C Dutch Reform church*. The church was rebuilt in 1678 after being devastated by the Sea Beggars. The graveyard

Amerongen, Kasteel

has *stones* commemorating captains of whaling ships.

Amerongen
Utrecht   p.289☐K 5

Kasteel Amerongen: The imposing castle was burned down by the French in 1673 (one tower survived) and rebuilt in 1676–80 in Dutch classical style on the foundations of the medieval building (probably a keep). In 1879 it was taken over by Count Godard van Aldenburg Bentinck, who rebuilt the interior in splendid style, employing Petrus Josephus Hubertus Cuypers among other artists. Cuypers's best work here is the *ceiling decoration* in the upper gallery, which has splendid portraits of Amerongen noblemen and their wives. Cuypers also decorated the dining room and redesigned the Gobelin room where there are 18C *tapestries.* Today Kasteel Amerongen is owned by the 'Stichting Kasteel Amerongen', which maintains it as a museum.

Amerongen, Kasteel, half-tester bed

Opening hours: 1 Apr.–1 Nov. Tue.–Sat. 10 a.m.–5 p.m.; Sundays and holidays 2–5 p.m.

St.-Andrieskerk: This church of St.Andrew has a tall Gothic 15C choir and an enormous tower somewhat later in date. The inside of the nave was redesigned in 1661.

Environs: Leersum (3 km. NW): In 1810, B.W.H.Ziesenis, the Amsterdam city architect, redesigned *Broekhuizen* in the Empire style. The house was completely burned down in 1906 but restored to its appearance in 1810. A peristyle with four Ionic columns dominates the façade.

Amersfoort
Utrecht   p.289☐K 5

Mentioned as a settlement in 1028 and granted a charter in 1259. The first town fortifications date from 13&14C, when the Am Hof market square was the centre of the town. More walls were built 1450–1561.

Amersfoort, Waterpoort

The 'Muurhuizen' ('wall houses') which descend to the moat were built along the old town wall which by that time had lost its significance. The town flourished in the Middle Ages thanks to its breweries and clothiers. The beautiful old town centre with the double ring of canals still survives. The birthplace of Piet Mondrian (1872–1944).

Onze-Lieve-Vrouwentoren: St. Mary's tower (1471), almost 330 ft. high, is a splendid structure and one of the finest examples of late Gothic in Holland. The church was used as a gunpowder magazine in the 18C and most of the building had to be torn down after an explosion in 1787.

Grote or St.-Joriskerk: This large hall church dedicated to St.George lies on Am Hof. It has a nave and two aisles, a 13C Romanesque tower, a sandstone portal (*c.* 1500), and 14&15C vault and wall paintings.

Koppelpoort: This gate dates from the building of the second set of walls. Formerly both a water and land gate,

it still has the mechanism for lowering the watertight oak doors into the water.

Museum Flehite (50 Westsingel): A historical museum with documents relating to the town's history. Memorabilia of Johan van Oldenbarnevelt a famous citizen of the town (1547–1619).

Amsterdam
North Holland   p.286☐H 4

Amsterdam, the capital of the Netherlands, is among the world's finest cities. It derives its specific character from numerous canals and hence it is often known as 'Venice of the North'. The city also has about 7,000 houses classified as historical monuments. Most of these date from the 'Golden Age' of the 17C, when trade with India brought great affluence to the city. Trade is still very important today. Amsterdam is also the country's largest industrial city and ranks in fourth place among the world's cities as a financial centre.

Amersfoort, Koppelpoort

The city is of great cultural importance as well, being the seat of the Royal Dutch Academy of Sciences, two universities, numerous academies, two conservatories, 40 museums including the world-famous Rijksmuseum, many libraries, a city theatre, the Concertgebouw concert hall, and an international tourist centre and conference hall.

History: The old name of *Amstelledamme* was first mentioned in 1275 when Count Floris V granted the little fishing village the right to free travel and trade in its own goods all over Holland. The dam, probably built shortly before this, divided the Amstel from the IJ and the Zuiderzee, and favoured the rapid growth of trade. Amsterdam was granted a charter in *c.* 1300. The city became quite affluent in the 15C, mainly due to trade with the Baltic seaports. Economic growth was interrupted in the 16C when the Reformation began and Philip II of Spain ruled the Netherlands. The Duke of Alba occupied the city in 1567. However, prosperity increased again after the political revolution ('Alteratie') of 1578, when the reformed religion could be publicly practised, and also after the fall of Amsterdam in 1585. The population had doubled by 1595 thanks to the immigration of refugees fleeing from the Spanish regime—merchants from Flanders and Brabant, Jews from Portugal, and Huguenots from France. At the same time merchant shipping attained an undreamt-of success. The Mediterranean, Russia, the W. coast of Africa, the Cape Verde Islands, the West Indies, America and finally Indonesia were added to the Baltic, England and the W. coast of Europe, the traditional destinations for Dutch merchant ships. The powerful United Dutch East India Company was founded in 1602, and the world's first discount house was established in 1609. The West India Company followed in 1621. Developments were made in diamond trading and diamond grinding which had been introduced by the Portuguese Jews. The city systematically expanded from 1612 onwards, and at about this time the semicircular ring of three canals was built (the

Amsterdam, view of the city

Heren, Keizers and Prinsen canals). Amsterdam lost its leading position as a trading metropolis in the 18C with the ascendancy of London and Hamburg, which had been declared a free city. However, Amsterdam's trade and prosperity were not seriously disrupted until the fourth English war of 1780–4 and the French occupation of 1795. The city experienced an economic upswing in the second half of the 19C and when the North Sea canal was completed in 1876 the port became a centre for trade once again. Amsterdam was occupied by German troops in May 1940. Although the harbour and industrial district was destroyed during the war most of the city itself remained undamaged.

Religious buildings

Agnietenkapel (231 O.Z.Voorburgwal): The single-aisled chapel (1470), all that remains of the convent of St.Agnes, was restored throughout in 1919–20. The forecourt has a gate (1571; moved here in 1631) decorated in the Vredeman de Vries manner.

Begijnhof (between Kalverstraat, Spui and N.Z.Vorburgwal): Owned by the English Presbyterian community since 1607, it was consecrated in 1346. The late-Gothic *old church* has a 17C aisle. Opposite is the *Roman Catholic church of St.John and St.Ursula* (1671).

Nieuwe Lutherse Kerk (Singel): Built in 1668–71 to the designs of Adriaan Dortsmann. Rebuilt after damage by fire in 1822. Since 1935 it has not been used as a church. In 1975 the interior was rebuilt as a conference centre and concert hall.

Oude Lutherse Kerk (Spui): Late Gothic church built in 1632–3 on an irregular ground plan.

Mozes- en Aaronkerk (Roman Catholic church dedicated to St.Anthony of Padua, Waterlooplein): T.F.Suys was the architect of this most monumental church in the 'Waterstaatsstijl' style (1837–41). The façade has a temple-like portico and two wooden towers.

Nieuwe Kerk or **St.-Catharinak-**

Leeuwenburg and Oude Kerk

erk (N.Z.Vorburgwal/Dam): A late Gothic cruciform basilica. The choir and ambulatory are *c.* 1400; the sacristy dates from 1414–18. The nave was begun in *c.* 1435; other work including the side chapels and choir chapels probably dates from the late 15C to about 1540. After a fire in the church in 1645 work began on a W. tower, probably to a design by Jacob van Campen. However, only the substructure was completed by 1652 and part of this was torn down in 1785. The *interior* has windows which begin almost immediately above the nave arcades, and compound pillars. These decorations are later than the fire of 1645. The beautiful choir screen with its marble base is by Jacob Lutma (c. 1650); the splendid pulpit is the work of Albert Vinckenbrinck (1647–9). The organ was designed by Jacob van Campen and completed in 1670. The doors were painted by Jan van

Bronckhorst (1655). The lower half of the large window in the N. transept, depicting Count Wilhelm IV granting the city its coat-of-arms, is also by van Bronckhorst. There is a splendid *marble monument* to the famous Admiral Michiel de Ruyter (d. 1676), completed by Rombout Verhulst and assistants in 1681.

Noorderkerk (Noordermarkt): Ground plan in the shape of a Greek cross. The church was built in 1620–3, possibly by Hendrick de Keyser or Hendrick Staets.

Oosterkerk (Nieuwe Vaart): A Dutch Reform church built in 1669–71, probably to the plans of Adriaan Dortsmann, who may have been assisted by Daniel Stalpaert. Pillars divide the interior which has a Greek cross ground plan. All arms of the cross are roofed by wooden tunnel vaults, while lower sections have stone rib vaults.

Oude Kerk or **St.-Nicolaaskerk** (Oudekerksplein): This Dutch Reform church was originally a hall

Amsterdam, Oude Kerk **1** Tower from c. 1300, altered in 16C & 18C **2** Baptistery **3** Portal and 'Ijzeren Kapel' **4** Late Gothic portal

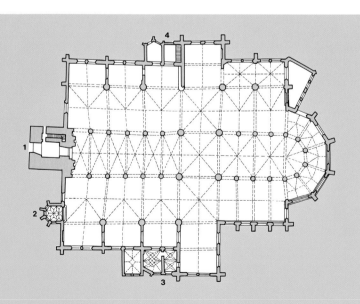

church but is now basilican in plan. The oldest section is the central part of the tower (*c.* 1300). Columns and arcades of the present nave come from the original church, which was built somewhat later than the tower on the site of an older building. The choir dates from *c.* 1370. Chapels were added to the crossing in the late 14C and to the aisles in the late 15C. The conversion of the church into a basilica began in the early 16C. The nave was increased in height in 1536, and the raised crossing was given a crowning tower in 1558. The tower received a new storey in 1564 and was completed in 1565. A portal and the 'IJzeren Kapel' followed in *c.* 1550 on the S. side and at the same time the baptismal chapel was built S. of the tower and a late Gothic portal and another chapel were added on the N. side of the nave. In the chapel of St.Mary (1553) N. of the choir there are three large *stained-glass windows* dating from 1555 and reworked in 1761–3; these show the Annunciation, the Virgin Mary visiting Elizabeth, the Adoration of the Child, and the Death of the Virgin Mary.

Oude Kerk

Oude Walenkerk (157 O.Z.Achterburgwal): A monastery was founded here 1409–15. Formerly a Paulusbroederen monastery church, altered into a late Gothic basilica in the mid 17C. The entrance gate in the Oude Hoogstraat is by Hendrick de Keyser (1616).

Westerkerk (Westermarkt): This Dutch Reform church, the largest and most monumental Renaissance church in Holland, was begun in 1620 to a design by Hendrick de Keyser. The tower was completed in 1638 with some alterations. Some 280 ft. high and the tallest tower in Amsterdam, it is topped by an imperial crown which also appears on the top of the city of Amsterdam's coat-of-arms; the right to bear this crown was conferred upon the church by Maximilian I of Austria. The church has a dignified and distinguished appearance both outside and in. Decorations in the main date from *c.* 1630. There are allegorical paintings by Gerard de Lairesse on the doors of the beautiful *organ* (1682). On 8 October 1669, *Rembrandt* was interred in the church

(beside the third marble column on the N. side) and a marble *memorial stone* commemorates this.

Vondelkerk (Vondelstraat): This Roman Catholic church (1870–80) by Petrus Josephus Hubertus Cuypers is among the most imaginative neo-Gothic churches, with an elliptical ground plan and a central tower. The layout of the surrounding streets was also designed by Cuypers.

Zuiderkerk (Zuiderkerksplein): This Dutch Reform church was the first such church to be founded in Amsterdam after the Reformation. Basilican in design, it was begun in 1603 to a design by Hendrick de Keyser and in use by 1611. The tower, completed in 1614, has a carillon by the Hémony brothers.

Synagogues: Of the synagogues in the Nieuwe Amstelstraat, J.D.Meyerplein and Mr.Visserplein, the Portuguese synagogue is the only one still in use. The *Grote* or *Hoofdsynagoge*, on the corner of the Nieuwe Amstelstraat, has a low porch and a sand-stone entrance and was built by Daniel Stalpaert in 1670–1.

Secular buildings

Accijnshuis (Oudebrugsteeg): This sandstone building with Ionic pilasters and sculptured decorations above the entrances was built in 1638.

Beurs (Damrak): The stock exchange building (1898–1903) by Hendrik Petrus Berlage (1856–1934) marks the monumental beginning of modern architecture. Play with the decorative possibilities of brickwork led to strange ornamental forms. The figures are by L.Zijl and J.Mendes da Costa, the painted tiles and stained-glass windows are the work of A.J.der Kinderen and R.N.Roland Holst, and the sgraffito is by J.Toorop.

Centraalstation: The main railway station (1885–9) is by Petrus Josephus Hubertus Cuypers. The façade is suggestive of classical castle architecture, with borrowed Gothic and Renaissance elements.

Concertgebouw (van Baerlestraat):

Nieuwe Kerk, angel on the organ

This concert hall (1888) in neo-Renaissance style was designed by the architect A.L.van Gendt.

Hoofdpostkantoor (N.Z.Voorburgwal): The main post office, neo-Gothic in design but with Renaissance ornaments, is by C.H.Peters (1895).

Koninklijk Paleis (Dam): Begun as a town hall in 1648 to designs by Jacob van Campen. Van Campen seems to have discontinued work on the building at a date no later than 1654 and Daniel Stalpaert, the city architect, then supervised the work until the building's completion in 1665. The city authorities had already moved into the building in 1655. The sculptures, which are mostly marble inside the building, were begun in 1650 by Artus Quellinus the Elder from Antwerp along with his assistants who included Rombout Verhulst. Work on the interior was still in progress in the early 18C. Louis Bonaparte fitted out the building as a castle in 1808. The early-19C alterations were removed in various

restorations between 1913 and 1968. The *exterior* has a plain lower storey and two upper storeys with pilasters and cornices. The corners of the building are accentuated while the front and rear façades are both emphasized by broad central projections with gables. The gable on the Dam side shows the patron saint of the city surrounded by sea gods. Above this there rises the bronze figure of Peace, flanked by Prudence and Justice. The patron saint, accompanied by the river gods of the Amstel and the IJ, is also seen in the gable facing the N.Z.Voorburgwal. Bronze figures depict Atlas between Temperance and Vigilance.

The *inside* of this immense rectangular building is symmetrically articulated. The court room immediately behind the entrance is succeeded (along the central axis of the building) by the citizens' hall and the jurors' hall. Courtyards surrounded by galleries, with more halls and rooms off them, are to be found on both sides of the citizens' hall. The *court room* is decorated with marble and on the rear wall there are three large reliefs

Westerkerk, organ

Westertoren with Emperor's crown

(showing the act of giving judgment) separated by caryatids. Bronze doors open into the *citizens' hall,* which is 112 ft. long, 55 ft. wide and 92 ft. high. The walls are articulated by pilasters, the lower ones of which are marble); the wooden barrel vault was painted in the early 18C. The groups of figures and the reliefs came from local workshops. The *galleries* have ornate sculptures, including Venus by Rombout Verhulst and Mars by Artus Quellinus the Elder. The paintings are mainly from the North Dutch school and mostly by pupils of Rembrandt, such as Ferdinand Bol, Govert Flinck and Jan Lievens, although some are by Jacob Jordaens from Antwerp.

's Lands Zeemagazijn (Kattenburg): This massive building (1656) with its projecting middle sections crowned by gables is by Daniel Stal-

paert, the city mayor. Completely burned down in 1791, it was later rebuilt. A poem by Joost van den Vondel relates that the gable sculptures are the work of Artus Quellinus the elder, although it is probably only the design that is his. (→Museums: Scheepvaart-Museum).

Oost-Indisch huis (24 Oude Hoogstraat): The S. wing (1606) is by Hendrick de Keyser; the courtyard façades of the N. wing (1633) and of the neo-Gothic E. wing (1890) were designed to be in keeping with the S. wing.

Oudezijds Huiszittenhuis (Waterlooplein): This elegant building (1654) is now the architectural academy. It has gables above the central projections on its front and rear sides. Peat storehouses (1610) adjoin the building.

Scheepvarthuis (Prins Hendrikkade/corner of Binnenkant): A shipping building (1913) by the architects J.M.van der Mey, M.de Klerk and P.L.Kramer in the expressive sculptural style of the Amsterdam school.

Stadhuis (O.Z.Voorburgwal): Originally a convent of St.Cecilia stood here but this was replaced after the Reformation by the Prinsenhof, which in turn was occupied by the admiralty in the 17C. Louis Bonaparte made the building his residence in 1808 and later the city authorities were housed here. This complex of buildings around a courtyard was altered several times between the 17C and 20C. The pilaster façade (1661) by Willem van den Gaffel survives outside the modern S. wing. Gable sculptures by Jan Gijseling. The massive block (1923–5) in the O.Z.Voorburgwal in the style of the Amsterdam school is by N.Lansdorp.

Stadsbushuis or Arsenaal (Singel): Today part of the university library. The façade with a cartouche is all that

Accijnshuis, town coat-of-arms

Koninklijk Paleis, tympanum, sculpture by Artus Quellinus the elder

survives of the original building
(1606), which was probably designed
by Hendrick de Keyser. Completely
rebuilt in 1970.

Stadsschouwberg (Leidseplein):
J.Springer was the architect of this
neo-Renaissance municipal theatre
(1892–4).

Tucht- or Rasphuis (Heiligeweg):
The prison has a gate (probably from
1603) attributed to Hendrick de
Keyser; the relief shows a cart drawn
by wild animals which the driver is
flogging.

Fortifications: Until 1481, when the
city wall was begun, there were only
earth ramparts between the gates and
towers. The **Schreierstoren** (a ponderous semicircular brick tower at the
corner of Prins Hendrikkade and Gel-
dersekade), the St.-Anthonispoort,
and the Munttoren, are surviving
remnants of the fortifications begun at
that time. An inscription on the N.
staircase tower of the *St.-Anthonis-
poort* states that it was built in 1488.
In 1545 Alexander Pasqualini and
Willem Dirksz proposed that this gate
should be bricked up, although it largely retained its old form. There are
round towers on both sides of the
main building. Two octagonal staircase towers stand on the side facing
the city. The first gate on the outer
side of the building has two corner
towers. The area between this gate
and the main gate was bricked up in
1617 when the building was converted into a weigh-house. The tall
spire was added to the main building
in 1691, when a dissecting room for
the surgeons' guild was built in the
gate. The *Munttoren*, one of the
corner towers of the former Regu-
lierspoort dates from *c.* 1490.
Increased in height in 1620 to a design
by Hendrick de Keyser, it received a
carillon by the Hémony brothers. The
Montelbaanstoren (early 16C) in the

◁ *Koninklijk Paleis, citizens' hall*

Oude Schans was built to defend the
shipbuilding wharfs. Its wooden roof
dates from 1606. Later gates include
the classical *Muiderpoort* (1770) by C.
Rauws and the more distinctly
classical *Haarlemmerpoort* (1840).

Walenweeshuis (Vijzelgracht): A
Walloon orphanage (1669–71) by
Adriaan Dortsman. The lower parts
in 1e Weteringdwarsstraat and Prinsengracht date from 1683 & 1726.

Wijnkopersgildehuis (10–12 Koestraat): This large house dating from
1611 was created by enlarging and
combining three houses dating from
1551. The oldest sections were converted in 1633 & 1655. The right half
has housed the vintners' guild since
1633.

**Residential houses and store-
houses:** Many of the city's houses are
older than might be supposed from
their façades which were frequently
rebuilt later. Some houses are still
basically Gothic timber-framed structures but only two also have a medieval exterior (*34 Begiynhof* with a
peaked gable, probably built shortly
after the city fire of 1453, and *1 Zee-
dijk*, which is probably mid 16C, with
eaves over the street). The oldest
stone façades date from *c.* 1600, and
most of them have richly decorated
stepped gables. Two of them, *142
Singel* (1605) and *57 O.Z.Voorburg-
wal*, are by Hendrick de Keyser. The
monumental *Bartolotti house* (170–
172 Herengracht) and *123 Keizersgracht* (1622) are also attributed to de
Keyser. The house at *177 Keizersgracht* (by Jacob van Campen, 1625)
has pilasters on each storey, and no
gable. *70–72 Herengracht* (1643), with
a central section topped by a gable, is
of livelier appearance. Playful elements in the manner of Hendrick de
Keysers became less frequent after
this, and the period dominated by
Philips Vingboons began. The oldest
house he designed is *168 Herengracht*
which dates from 1638. The houses

with the most elegant surviving façades are at *Nos. 364–370, 386, 412 and 450 Herengracht* dating from 1662, 1663, 1664 & 1665 respectively, *No. 319 Keizersgracht* (1639), *No. 460 Singel* (1662), *No. 145 Rokin* (1641), and *Nos. 77 & 316 Kloveniersburgwal* (1650 & 1655). The splendid façades of *257 Herengracht* and *401 Keizersgracht* are also attributed to Vingboons; *388 Herengracht*, with its rich pilaster façade (1665), may also be his work. His style in gables found many imitators. The impressive *Trippenhuis* (29 Kloveniersburgwal) was built by Justus Vingboons as a double residential house for Louis and Hendrik Trip; today it is the Royal Academy of Sciences (chimney pots in the shape of mortars are a reference to the gun foundries owned by the Trips). The influence of Jacob van Campen is seen in the façade, with Corinthian pilasters, at *No. 476 Herengracht* (*c.* 1670). An attic was added to this building in 1730. Pilaster orders became less common in the last quarter of the 17C, and a quieter and flatter treatment in the manner of Adriaan Dortsman and Steven Ven-

necool was now preferred. Some examples of this are seen in *436 Herengracht* (*c.* 1670), *446 Herengracht* (the house of mayor Andries de Graeff), *462 Herengracht, 216 Amstel,* and *Nos. 604, 672* and *674 Keizersgracht*. In the 18C the façades of the broad houses along the canals were built in this style although they were more lavishly decorated e.g. the following houses in Herengracht: *No. 284* from *c.* 1720–30 with good decorations, *No. 539, No. 475* (with stuccoes by Jan van Logteren), *No. 495* (a house by Jean Coulon, 1739), *No. 493* (1766), *No. 182* (1772), and *No. 40* from 1790. In the narrow houses of the 18C, the gable in all its variants (stepped gable, pointed gable, neck gable, bell gable) predominates.

Residential district in the style of the Amsterdam school: 1911–23, M. de Klerk built the houses around the *Johannes Vermeerplein*, the *Zaanstraat* and the *Henriette Ronnerplein*. The buildings of 1927 around the *Mercatorplein* are by H.P.Berlage, J.F.Staal, P.L.Kramer, H.T.Wijdeveld and others. H.T.Wijdeveld, D.Greiner,

401 Keizersgracht, gable

Herengracht, Bartolotti House

J.F.Staal, Margaret Kropholler and others had a share in many residential complexes in *W.* and *S. Amsterdam.*

Museums
Allard Pierson Museum (127 Oude Turfmarkt): A collection belonging to the Archaeological Institute of Amsterdam University. Antiquities from Mesopotamia, Egypt, Greece and Rome. Opening times: Tue.–Fri. 10 a.m.–4.30 p.m., Sat. and Sun. 1.15–4.30 p.m.

Museum Amstelkring (40 O.Z.-Voorburgwal): A house (1661–3) with a Catholic church in the attic (O.L.-Heer op Solder—Our Lord in the Attic) which formerly served as a refuge. Dedicated to St.Nicholas, it was in use until 1887. The former church was then set up as a museum. The museum has the church's original decorations and utensils from post-Reformation Catholic life in Amsterdam. Opening times: Mon.–Sat.: 10 a.m.–5 p.m., Sun. 1–5 p.m.

Amsterdams Historisch Museum (92 Kalverstraat): The Historical Museum in the former Burgerweeshuis (the 16&17C citizens' orphanage) has objects relating to the city's history, and a unique gallery of guns (in the roofed passage leading to the Begijnhof). Opening times: Mon.–Sat.: 9.30 a.m.–5 p.m., Sun. 1–5 p.m.

Anne Frank Huis (263 Prinsengracht): Anne Frank wrote her famous diary here when Amsterdam was occupied by German troops. Opening times: Mon.–Sat. 9 a.m.–5 p.m., Sun. 10 a.m.–5 p.m.

Architecturmuseum (1a Droogbak): A museum housing Dutch architectural documents, the archives of private architects from 1850 onwards and models of buildings. Opening times: Mon.–Fri. 10 a.m.–5 p.m., Sat. and Sun. 1–5 p.m.

Banketbakkersmuseum (220 Wibautstraat): A museum of bakery and pastry with an old bakery with shop, old implements, bread and cakes, old engravings and recipe books. Opening times: Wed. 10 a.m.–4 p.m. and by prior arrangement.

Keizersgracht, Huis met de Hoofden

Montelbaanstoren

Bijbels Museum (366 Herengracht): A bible museum with objects of biblical archaeology and utensils from the Middle East. Opening times: Tue.–Sat 10 a.m.–5 p.m., Sun. 1–5 p.m.

Bos-Museum (Amsterdamse Bos, Nieuwe Kalfjeslaan): A forest museum. Opening times: Mon.–Sat 9 a.m.–4 p.m., Sun. 10 a.m.–5 p.m.

Film-Museum (3 Vondelpark): Devoted to both Dutch and foreign films. Opening times: Tue. 1.30–5 p.m., Wed. & Thur. 9 a.m.–12.30 p.m. and 1.30–5 p.m.

Fodor-Museum (609 Keizersgracht): Founded by Carel Joseph Fodor, a coal merchant who left his collections of paintings, copper engravings and drawings to the city in 1860, on condition that his three houses be converted into a museum. Exhibitions of contemporary Dutch artists are held here. Opening times: Mon.–Sat. 9.30 a.m.–5 p.m., Sun. 1–5 p.m.

Vincent van Gogh Museum (7 Paulus Potterstraat): This museum opened in 1973 and has some 200 paintings and 400 drawings by van Gogh. Opening times: Mon.–Sat. 10 a.m.–5 p.m., Sun. 1–5 p.m.

Industrieel en Technisch Institut (224 Rozengracht): Institute of industry and technology with films, lectures and demonstrations. Opening hours: Mon.–Fri. 10 a.m.–4 p.m., Sat. and Sun. 1–4 p.m.

Joods Historisch Museum (4 Nieuwmarkt): Jewish History Museum with exhibits relating to Jewish culture, especially from the Netherlands; also documents relating to the persecution of the Jews in World War 2. Opening times: Mon.–Sat. 9.30 a.m.–5 p.m., Sun. 1–5 p.m.

Pijpenkamer ICON (16 Frederiksplein): Pipe Museum with 7,000 pipes from across the centuries. Opening times: Tue.–Sat. 10.30 a.m.–5 p.m.; closed on Sun., Mon. and holidays.

Rembrandthuis (4–6 Jodenbreestraat): Rembrandt lived here 1639–60. The house dates from 1606 and is one of the most splendid residential houses of the period. The collection has engravings and drawings by Rembrandt together with some of his personal belongings and paintings by his teachers and pupils. Opening times: Mon.–Sat. 10 a.m.–5 p.m., Sun. 1–5 p.m.

Rijksmuseum (42 Stadhouderskade): The Rijksmuseum has a classical ground plan and structure with Gothic and Renaissance style architectural sculptures. It was built in 1876–85 by Petrus Josephus Hubertus Cuypers and houses a comprehensive collection of 15–19C Dutch painting, with particular emphasis on 17C Dutch masters—the 'Night Watch' by Rembrandt is one of the best known of these paintings. The museum has a number of other departments, including a department of copper engravings, a department of sculptures and arts and crafts, a section devoted to the history of the Netherlands and a department of Asian art. Opening times: Mon.–Sat. 10 a.m.–5 p.m., Sun. 1–5 p.m.

Scheepvaart Museum (1–7 Kattenburgerplein): The 's Lands Zeemagazijn (17C) houses the Dutch shipping museum, with sea paintings, models of sailing ships and steamships, maps, globes, navigation instruments, and an extensive library. Opening times: Mon.–Sat. 10 a.m.–5 p.m., Sat. 1–5 p.m.

Spaarpotten Museum (20 Raadhuisstraat): The private collection of Ter Wolhaak has some 12,000 money

Tobias, Anna and the kid. Painting by Rembrandt in the Rijksmuseum ▷

boxes of different kinds from all over the world.

Stedelijk Museum (13 Paulus Potterstraat): Neo-Renaissance Museum building from 1892–5 by A.W.Weissman. Most of the exhibits are modern art works from 1850 to the present day.
Museum opening times: Mon.–Sat. 9.30 a.m.–5 p.m., Sun. and holidays 1–5 p.m.

Toneelmuseum (168 Herengracht): Theatrical museum with copper engravings, drawings, paintings, stage designs and costumes from the Dutch theatre. The house dates from 1638 and is by Philips Vingboons.
Opening times: 10 a.m.–5 p.m., Sun. and holidays 11 a.m.–5 p.m.

Tropenmuseum (2a Linnaeusstraat): Collection of interesting objects and utensils from the Tropics and sub-Tropics, including a mineral collection and information on developing countries in tropical areas.
Museum opening times: Mon.–Fri. 10 a.m.–5 p.m., Sat. and Sun. 12 noon–5 p.m.

Madame Tussaud (156 Kalverstraat): The Dutch counterpart of the English waxworks museum. The visitor can watch the waxworks being created in the studio. Opening times: 15 June–July: 10 a.m.–7 p.m., 11 July–31 Aug.: 10 a.m.–8 p.m., 1 Sept.–14 June: 10 a.m.–6 p.m.

Veiligheidsinstituut (22 Hobbemastraat): Demonstrations concerning safety at home and at work. Opening times: Mon.–Fri. 8.30 a.m.–12 noon and 1–4.30 p.m. Closed on Sat. and Sun.

Museum Willet-Holthuysen (605 Herengracht): History museum in a 17C residential house with a collection of furniture, glass, china, gold

◁ *Deutzenhofje (Prinsengracht)*

Detail of Rijksmuseum

Courtyard of Van Brants-Rushofje

and silver from the 16–19C, the whole collection contributing to give an insight into the life style of wealthy patricians in the 18&19C. Opening times: Mon.–Sat. 9.30 a.m.–5 p.m., Sun. and holidays 1–5 p.m.

Wijnkopsgildehuis (10–12 Koestraat): Vintners' guild. Opening times: Tue.–Fri. 10 a.m.–12 noon and 2–4 p.m.

Also worth seeing: The *Korenmetershuis* (grain measurer's house; 1620) in N.Z.Kolk and the *Saaihal* (the cloth hall; 1641), 7a Staalstraat both have good façades. The *Pakhuizen* (warehouses) of the Dutch East and West India Companies in Prins Hendrikkade date from the first half of the 17C and convey the impression of the wealth and power of these trading companies. *De Jordaan*, is the old popular quarter, lying between Prin-

sengracht, Westerkerk and Brouwersgracht. Planned in the 17C for workers, craftsmen and small traders, it attracted many French immigrants who settled here in the late 17C. The name 'Jordaan' (from the French 'jardin') may derive from the fact that most of the alleyways and canals bear the names of flowers. This picturesque quarter is very popular with young people today. Some charming 'Hofjes' lie behind mainly inconspicuous entrances and include the splendid *Claes Claesz, Anslo Hofje* (18–20 Egelantiersstraat) and *Suykerhofje* (149–163) by Pieter Jansz. Suyker (1670). The *Begijnhof* in Spui has an old church, and a Roman Catholic church as well as many interesting features. Attractive residential courtyards are also to be found E. of the Amstel: *Corvershof* (6–18 Nieuwe Herengracht) has a stately Louis XIV gable from 1721–3, *Hofje van Occo*

(94 Nieuwe Keizersgracht) dates from 1774, and *Van Brants-Rushofje* (28–44 Nieuwe Keizersgracht) was built in 1732–3 to the design of Daniel Marot. The *Deutzenhofje* (855–899 Prinsengracht) from 1695 and the *Huiszittenweduwenhof* (21–131 Karthuizerstraat) by Daniel Stalpaert (1650) are fine examples of residential houses with four wings around a courtyard. The *main building of Amsterdam University* (1754) was built by Pieter Rendorp as an Oudemannenhuis (home for old men). The Oudemanhuisport, a roofed passage, lies between Oudezijds Achterburgwal and Kloveniersburgwal. The house of the former *Felix Meritis society* (324 Keizersgracht), with a good façade, was built in 1778 to a design by Jacob Otten Husly. Interesting 20C buildings include the former building (1921–5) of the *Nederlandse Handel Maatschappij* (Dutch Trading Company) in Vijzelstraat by the architect K.P.C. de Bazel. The *Scheepvaarthuis* (house of shipping, Prins Hendrikkade) dates from 1911–16 and is the first example of the Amsterdam School. The *Openluchtschool* (open-air school, Cliostraat) by J.Duiker dates from 1930 and is an example of Neorealism. The *Werf 't Kromhout* (147 Hoogtekadijk) shows the appearance of an old wharf along with models of old ships; historic ships are also repaired and restored here. The *Magere Brug* over the Amstel is one of the few surviving bascule bridges. Painted white, it is raised by means of a simple chain hoist in the middle of the bridge. There are over 1,000 bridges in Amsterdam today. In the 17C there were 87 bridges of stone and 117 of wood. *Diamond cutting* has gone on in Amsterdam since 1586. Diamond cutters can be seen in action in the workshops of several companies, the addresses of which can be obtained from the tourist office (VVV), 10 Stationsplein. Many of the *windmills*, formerly city landmarks, have now disappeared. Surviving windmills include: *De Bloem* (465 Haarlemmerweg, visits arranged by telephone), *De Admiraal* (21 Noordhollandskanaaldijk), and the *Riekermolen* at the end of the Europa Boulevard along the Amstel. The *Artis* zoo at 40 Plantage Kerklaan was opened in 1838. Open to the public from 9 a.m.–6 p.m. from the beginning of May to the end of Sept., and from 9 a.m.–4.30 p.m. from the beginning of Oct. to the end of Apr.

Environs: Aalsmeer (17 km. S.): The mid-16C *Dutch Reform church* is an unusual single-aisled building with three transepts. '*De Leeuw*', an octagonal corn mill, was built in 1863; the water mill dates from 1742. Aalsmeer is an important horticultural centre; buildings in which the major flower auctions are held date from 1922 & 1928.

Broek in Waterland (10 km. N.): A picturesque village which flourished when people from Amsterdam moved here in the 18C. The late Gothic *Dutch Reform church* (probably *c.* 1425) has two aisles. Part of it burned down in 1573 and it was rebuilt over the following decades. A stained-glass window (*c.* 1640) shows the history of the building of the church. The carved pulpit (1685) has an hour-glass showing the maximum permitted length of the sermon. The village has a number of charming wooden 17&18C houses.

Durgerdam (8 km. NE): This village, with its 17C *wooden houses*, has retained the linear character of a typical dyke village. The *Dutch Reform* hall church dates from 1840; the former town hall of 1687 has a domed turret.

Ouderkerk aan de Amstel (10 km. S.): The large *Dutch Reform church* (1773–5) is attractively situated. There are some fine country houses along the Amstel between Oudekerk

Denial of Peter. Painting by Rembrandt Harmensz van Rijn in the Rijksmuseum ▷

and Amsterdam, e.g. *Oostermeer* (1728) with a fine entrance railing, *Wester-Amstel* and *Amstelrust* (1740). The *Portugees-Joodse Begraafplaats* (graveyard) has carved marble tombs and tombstones.

Ransdorp (9 km. N.): The Six villages of the Waterland, the region N. of Amsterdam, which united in 1619 to form the 'Unie van Waterland'. The large *church tower* (*c.* 1525), of an elaborate design but unfinished, dominates the village skyline. The *former village hall* (1652) can be seen near the tower.

Anloo
Drente   p.287☐N 3

Dutch Reform church: One of Holland's oldest churches, it stands in the middle of the village square, on a site occupied by previous wooden buildings. The 11C Romanesque tufa nave received a wooden barrel vault in the 18C. *Wall paintings* (13–17C) showing Saints and scenes from the life of the Virgin Mary were uncovered during restoration. Decorations

Anloo, Dutch Reform church

include a carved organ case and two pews with Louis XIV decorations. Above the bricked-up N. entrance a 12C sandstone sarcophagus lid has a relief of a man praying. The tower is later than 1150, the spire dates from 1757 and the stepped gables from 1895.

Pinetum ter Borgh (7 Anderenseweg): Exotic conifers, heather and rhododendrons.

Also worth seeing: *Farmhouses* of the Saxon-Drente type are found in and around Anloo. Many of these are hall farms, with a high entrance leading to the barn at the back with stables on both sides. Eight of the 52 *megalithic graves* found in Drente are in the Anloo area, mostly concealed in woods or cornfields. There are also a number of *burial mounds* dating from the Neolithic period (2100–1500 BC) to the Iron Age (650 BC).

Apeldoorn
Geldern   p.287☐L 5

Apeldoorn, founded by the Merovingians, was first mentioned in documents in 793. The settlement is made up of an urban centre (although it does not enjoy the status of a town) and several villages (Hoenderloo, Hoog Soeren, Loenen, Breekbergen, Kootwijk and Uddel).

Paleis het Loo: The *Nieuwe Loo*, the white residence at the N. edge of Apeldoorn, was begun in 1685 by Jacob Roman and Daniel Marot for William III of Orange. In the park there is also the 15/16C *Kasteel Oude Loo*, restored by Petrus Josephus Hubertus Cuypers in 1904. The castle was altered by King Louis Bonaparte during the time of French rule, at which time the gardens were made into the splendid French landscaped park which still survives today. The *Rijksmuseum Paleis het Loo* has interesting furniture and paintings, but the main feature is the collection of old coaches, sledges and cars belonging to the royal family. Opening times: 10 a.m.–5 p.m. daily, closed on 25 Dec.

Also worth seeing: *Grote Kerk* (1892) in the Loolaan. *Town hall* (1898). *Marialust historical museum. Van Reekum gallery. Berg en Bos nature reserve.*

Environs: Barneveld (30 km. SW): This agricultural town on the W. edge of the Veluwe is known for its various markets, including markets for calves, pigs, domestic animals, horses and ponies and eggs. A *statue of Jan van Schaffelaer* stands beside the 15C Gothic *hall church* in which there is a pulpit from 1654. The *Kasteel Jan van Schaffelaer* (1854) in Tudor style stands in a park open to the public. The *Veluws Museum Bairac* has historical and archaeological finds from the region—ceramics, coins and costumes.

Garderen (17 km. W.): A village on one of the highest ridges of the Veluwe. The *Dutch Reform church*

(1856) has a 14C Romanesque tower. The '*De Hoop*' *corn mill* (1855) can be seen in operation on Saturdays.

Loenen (10 km. S.): *Ter Horst*, a castle near Loenen was given its present appearance in the 16C. There is a classical stone pediment (1791–2) above the façade; rear and side façades are Renaissance. Traces of the rather severely designed 18C garden can be seen around the castle.

Vaassen (8 km. N.): The *Cannenburch* near Vaassen was mentioned in the 14C, its present appearance resulting from conversions and reconstructions carried out since the second half of the 16C. The window crests with their shell motifs, and the tower-like porch with its onion dome, are both Renaissance. A stone relief has the coats-of-arms, and the profiles of founders Hendrik van Isendoorn à Blois (d. 1594) and Sophie van Stommel (d. 1576). Maarten van Rossum, the general of Duke Karel van Gelre's army and also of Emperor Karl V's mercenaries, lived in the castle 1543–55. Since 1951 the Cannenburch has been owned by the 'Vrienden der Geldersche Kastelen' foundation and

Loenen (Apeldoorn), Ter Horst

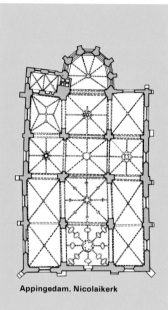

Appingedam, Nicolaikerk

first phase of expansion in the second half of 13C; the polygonal apse was added in the second phase—some 50 years later. Finally came the choir sacristy, chapels on both sides of the choir, and the tall aisles beside the nave, which are Gothic and late Gothic. *Paintings,* both decorative and purely ornamental dating from the different periods of construction, some in layers above one another, were uncovered during restoration work in 1948–54.

Stadhuis: This town hall was originally built as a courthouse (1630), with a weigh-house occupying the open colonnaded ground floor. The lively *façade* (restored in 1921) has stone Renaissance decorations, the Goddess of Justice and a pelican as a symbol of mercy.

Also worth seeing: *Damsterdiep* has a number of old *houses* with kitchens built out over the water.

Environs: Tjamsweer (at the edge of the town): The *Dutch Reform church* is a Gothic building from *c.* 1538, parts of which may be older. *Ekenstein castle,* rebuilt in neo-Gothic style in the 19C, has stones with carved coats-of-arms on the side and rear façades. Today the building is a hotel. Inside there are a neo-Gothic knights' hall and a painted room dating from the late 18C.

it is now a *museum* with furniture, portraits, porcelain, etc.

Appingedam
Groningen   p.287□O 2

Appingedam was on the sea and had a harbour until the 14C. Apart from Groningen it was the only town in this province to have surrounding ramparts. The defensive walls were razed after Emperor Charles V conquered the town in 1536, but the canals have survived.

Nicolaikerk: This fine Dutch Reform church, which has been extended several times, is now in the form of a hall church with a nave and two aisles. The nave still has the original 13C structure. A transept and a rectangular choir were built in the

---

Arnhem/Arnheim
Geldern   p.291□L 6

History: First mentioned in 893. In 1233, Count Otto von Geldern and Zutphen granted Arnhem a charter. Arnhem joined the Hanseatic League in 1443, and in 1514 Count Karl von Geldern freed it from Burgundian rule. Occupied by Spanish troops in 1546 and by the troops of Louis XIV in 1672, Arnhem became Dutch in 1813. The severe damage sustained in

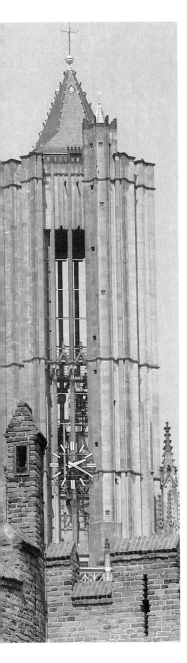

the Battle of Arnhem in 1944 has now been repaired but much of the old town was lost.

Grote Kerk or **St.-Eusebiuskerk** (Grote Markt): This parish church was built between 1452 and *c*. 1560 as a late Gothic basilica in the shape of a cross. It was carefully restored after devastation in World War 2, although the sculptures which were destroyed have not been replaced. Only the *Renaissance marble sarcophagus* of Karl von Egmont, Count of Geldern, survives. Opening times: 11 a.m.–4 p.m., Wed., Thur., Fri., Sat., end of May–15 Sept.

St.-Walburgiskerk (Grote Markt): The Roman Catholic church, a late Gothic building of the early 15C, still has the old pulpit of carved wood.

Duivelshuis (Grote Markt): This house, now part of the modern town hall, was built in 1540 for Maarten van Rossum, a military campaigner notorious for his brutality. The name of the house derives from the grotesque sculptures on the façade.

Provinciehuis (Grote Markt): The splendid local parliament building (the entrance, courtyard and Staten-zaal hall are the best features) was completed by J.J.Vegter the architect in 1954. The Provinciehuis has been joined quite skilfully to the *Sabelspoort* (1440), a gate in the old town fortifications.

Gemeentemuseum (87 Utrecht-seweg): The museum has a collection of works by Magic Realists (e.g. Carel Willink, Pyke Koch, Dick Ket); silver, Delft ceramics, and archaeological finds are also on display. Opening times: Mon.–Sat. 10 a.m.–5 p.m., Sun. and on holidays 11 a.m.–5 p.m.

Nederlands Openluchtmuseum (Rijksmuseum voor Volkskunde, 89

◁ *Arnheim, Grote Kerk*

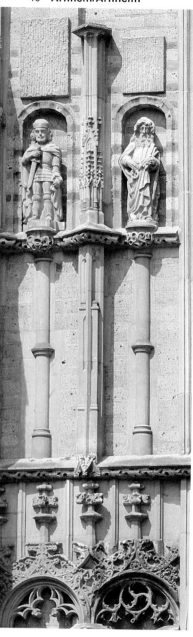

Schelmseweg): This open-air museum a little way outside the town, with farmhouses, residences, mills and craftsmen's workshops, gives the visitor a good idea of everyday life of former times. Opening times: 1 Apr.–1 Nov.: Tue.–Fri. 9 a.m.–12 noon and 12.30–5 p.m., Sat. and Sun. 10 a.m.–5 p.m.

Other museums: The *Historisch Museum Grenadiers en Jagers* and the *Museum Korps Rijdende Artillerie* are two museums devoted to army history. *The Museum Bronbeek* is devoted to the ethnography of what were the Dutch East Indies.

Environs: Aerdt (11 km. SE): The simple rectangular manor house dating from the mid 17C stands on the site of Ter Cluse, a medieval castle. Sash windows were re-installed during restoration work in 1964.

Elst (15 km. S.): Elst in the Over-Betuwe holds regular fruit and vegetable auctions. The foundations of two Roman temples have been uncovered beneath the 15C *Dutch Reform church* which has a Gothic tower.

Otterlo (15 km. NW): The *Hoge Veluwe National Park* 15,000 acres in area, is one of the great attractions in the Netherlands. Open to the public throughout the year from 8 a.m. until sundown, the park consists of a wild and varied landscape with woods and heaths, picturesque dunes and juniper trees in which roam stags, moufflons, wild boars and blackcocks. The land was once owned by the Rotterdam industrialist Kröller and his wife Kröller-Müller. The latter commissioned H.P.Berlage to build the St.Hubertus hunting lodge in the middle of the park in 1914–20. (Berlage also designed the Amsterdam stock exchange.) A museum for the Kröllers' extensive art collections was begun in 1938 to the plans of Henry van de Velde. The magnificent *Rijks-*

◁ *Arnheim, Grote Kerk*

Arnheim, Grote Kerk, marble sarcophagus of the Count of Geldern

museum *Kröller-Müller* (some 3 km. E. of Otterlo) has a fine collection of paintings and drawings by the Dutch painter Vincent van Gogh, along with many other works of modern art (by Léger, Mondrian and Picasso). In 1961 a statue park was set up next to the museum and this has an imposing selection of modern sculptures (works by Maillol, Giacometti, Fontana). Museum opening times: Mon.–Sat. 10 a.m.–5 p.m., Sun. and holidays 11 a.m.–5 p.m. (1 Nov.–1 Apr., 1 p.m.–5 p.m.), closed on 1 January. Statue park: 1 Apr.–1 Nov.: Mon.–Sat. 10 a.m.–4.30 p.m., Sun. and on holidays 11 a.m.–4.30 p.m. In Otterlo itself there is a *museum of tiles* (It Noflik Sté, 10 Eikenzoom) with old and new tiles, flagstones, and pictures on flagstones. Opening times: Tue.–Sat. 10 a.m.–12 noon and 2 p.m.–5 p.m., Sun. and on holidays 2 p.m.–4 p.m., closed on 1 Jan.

Zevenaar (9 km. SE): The house known as *Sevenaer*, a former medieval castle, has retained the character of a 17C lordly house. The 15C *Roman Catholic church* and the 17C *Dutch Reform church* have good decorations.

Assen
Drente   p.287☐N 3

History: The capital of the province of Drente was given a charter by King Louis Bonaparte in 1809 (partly because of its beautiful location), although at that time it was a village of less than 1,000 inhabitants. Assen developed around a Cistercian convent founded in 1257 and dissolved in the 17C. The Drente coat-of-arms, a Virgin Mary with a sceptre in her hand, indicates the former importance of convent.

Otterlo (Arnheim), hunting lodge of St.Hubertus

Dutch Reform Jozefkerk: A classical building (1848) with a projecting central section with colonnaded portal, pediment and a domed turret.

Former Provinciehuis (2 Brink): Occupies the 13C chapel which was part of the former Cistercian convent. Part of the cloister survives in the Rijksarchief built in 1902.

Automuseum (3 Rode Heklaan): This museum has interesting old cars and bicycles. Opening times: Apr.–Oct. 10 a.m.–6 p.m. daily.

Drents Museum en Ontvangershuis (1 and 5 Brink): This museum has archaeological finds from the Ice Age to the Middle Ages, the gold treasure of Beilen, finds from megalithic graves etc. The Ontvangershuis,

rebuilt after 1692 using old materials, was formerly a tax office and, from 1730–91, a prince's court. Today it has 18C panelling and a Louis XIV fireplace. Opening times: Tues.–Fri. 9.30 a.m.–5 p.m., Sat. and Sun. 1–5 p.m. (July and Aug. open on Mondays too).

Also worth seeing: 19C and early-20C buildings along the Anger. The *Paleis van Justitie* (4 Brinkstraat) is a classical building of 1840, and the *Huis van Bewaring* (9 Brink) at the rear dates from 1843. The *Rathaus* (8 Brink) occupies the so-called Huis Tetrode (1822). The former *Drostenhuis* (1 Kloosterstraat) was built in 1774–8 on the S. side of the former monastery. *Huize Overcingel* (27 Oostersingel), a country seat (1780), is situated in very beautiful surroundings.

building was enlarged several times in Gothic style. At the beginning of the present century part of the the Romanesque W. tower began to sink into the earth. This was, however, successfully stabilized by restoration work in 1943–58, at which time it also received a new spire, a copy of the former Saxon spire destroyed by lightning in 1911.

Environs: Noordwolde and **Zuidwolde** (5 and 7 km. S.): The *Dutch Reform church of Noordwolde* has a nave from the first half of 13C, a choir dating from *c.* 1300 and a 13C tower which formerly stood on its own but was heightened in 1639 and joined to the church. The sumptuous interior decorations include a richly carved pulpit of 1743. The tower of the *Dutch Reform church of Zuidwolde* dates from *c.* 1200 and was increased in height in 1638. The Romanesque tufa nave (possibly 11C) was altered in the 16C and plastered in the 19C.

Onderdendam (3 km. NE): The *Waterschapshuis* (water cooperative), with a classical entrance, was built in 1620 and considerably enlarged in 1660. Inside there are beautifully painted walls, fireplaces and tiles. Near the village is the octagonal '*De Zilvermeeuw*' mill (1870).

Assen, former Provinciehuis

Bedum
Groningen   p.287☐N 2

Dutch Reform church: An important cruciform church whose interior was badly damaged in 1851. The original 12C Romanesque tufa

Beetsterzwaag/Beetstersweach
Friesland   p.287☐M 2

Harinxmastate: A neoclassical country seat in a beautiful park. Part of the building is much older.

Lyndenstein: Dating from 1821 and later much altered. Landscape garden with busts.

Environs: Duurswoude/Duerswâld (10 km. E.): An old hamlet in the Opsterland. The old *church* (13C) is built of large, coarse bricks known as 'Friese moppen'.

Gorredijk/De Gordijk (8 km. SE):

A mid-17C village in the middle of heathland. There are old *gabled houses* in the Brouwerswal and in the main street. The *Opsterlân regional museum* (59 Hoofdstraat) has exhibits relating to marshland and the equipment used on it; there is also a model of the Gorrdijk entrenchment used during the war with Münster in 1673.

Bemmel

Geldern   p.291☐L 6

This village in the E. of the Betuwe gave its name to the district which includes the villages of Doornenburg, Angeren, Ressen and Halderen. The district administration has its offices in the remains of the medieval castle, *Kasteel Kinkelenburg*. Some attractive little medieval churches are to be found in *Bemmel* and *Ressen*. The *castle* in *Doorneburg* consists of the main keep and towers, barbican with gate, a wooden bridge over the surrounding moat, a chapel and a farm. The original 14C castle was destroyed

Bergen op Zoom, St.-Gertrudiskerk, tower

in 1945 but later restored to its former splendour. On display there are early-16C exhibits, old etchings of castles in Geldern and the area around Kleve as well as coats-of-arms. Guided tours: mid-Apr.—mid-May and Sept.: Sun. 3 p.m. Mid-May—mid-Aug.: Sun. 2.30 and 4 p.m. Summer holidays: Sun. 2.30, 3.30 and in case of demand also 4.30 p.m., and Tue.—Thur. 11 a.m., 1.30 p.m. and 3 p.m., Fri. and Sat. 1.30 and 3 p.m. Closed 1 Oct.—mid-Apr.

Bergen op Zoom

North Brabant   p.288☐F 7

History: Bergen op Zoom probably dates from the 13C. The town received its charter in 1287 and, being a border town, was much reinforced in the late 16C. The town successfully withstood sieges by Parma in 1588 and by Spinola in 1622.

St.-Gertrudiskerk: Originally a simple church, it was enlarged by the Antwerp architect Everaert Spoorwater (d. in Bergen op Zoom in 1474) in the 15C. In 1489 Anthonis Keldermans from Mechelen continued the expansion on a grand plan, and this work was almost finished in the following century. The cruciform basilica, at the time much deteriorated, was much damaged in a bombardment by French troops in 1747. When rebuilt on a smaller scale in 1752, the former wooden spire was replaced by an octagonal dome popularly known as 'Peperbus' (pepperpot). The interior damage caused by a fire in 1972 has now been repaired.

Markiezenhof (Steenbergsestraat): A late Gothic house belonging to the Marquis of Bergen op Zoom and built in 1485–1512 by Antonis Keldermans and his son Rombout. Buildings surround three courtyards, two of which have open galleries. The cast-iron window bars date from the time of the building's original construction. A statue of St.Christopher occupies an arched niche above the entrance. The building has been under restoration since 1963 and most of it is now open to the public as a *museum*—the largest cultural museum in the three southern provinces. Opening times: Tue.—Sun. and on holidays: 2–5 p.m.; mid-June—mid-Aug.: Tue.—Fri. 10 a.m.–5 p.m., Sat. Sun. and holidays 1–5 p.m.

Stadhuis: The Bergen op Zoom town hall occupies three buildings: the Schepenhuis, the old town hall built after the town fire of 1397; the Leeuwenborgh to the right of this, a centre for English merchants; and, to the left of the Schepenhuis, the 'De Olifant' house with a gate on the St.-Annastraat. Both the Schepenhuis and Leeuwenborgh were given their present façade in 1611.

Lieve-Vrouwepoort: This early-14C white stone gate is also known as the prisoners' gate and was once part of the town's defences. The two massive towers have firing slits and machicolations. The brick structure with two bartizans is of a later date.

Also worth seeing: The statue of the *Virgin Mary* at the corner of Grote Markt and Kremerstraat. The house at No. 35 Zuidzijde Haven has a *stone relief* of the Three Wise Men on its façade.

Environs: Halsteren (2.5 km. N.): This village has an attractive old centre. The small Renaissance *town hall* with a stepped gable (1633) has kept its charm despite the extensions at the back which date from 1917. At the peak of the gable there is an enthroned lion with coat-of-arms. *St.-Martinuskerk* (1457) behind the town hall was built on top of older masonry.

Roosendaal (10 km. E.): Only a few historical buildings have survived in this modern shopping and industrial centre. *St.-Janskerk* (1839) in 'Waterstaatsstijl' has a colonnaded portal with pediment. The *old town hall* (1 Markt) dates originally from 1534 and was restored in 1975. There is now a *regional museum* in the *Tongerlohuis* (2

Bergen op Zoom, St.-Gertrudiskerk 1 Tower (c. 1350) **2** Nave (1752) **3** Choir begun in 1443

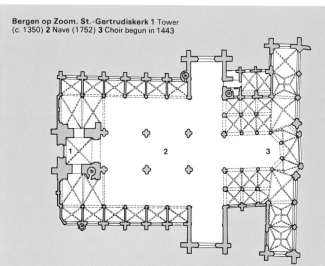

Molenstraat), a former priest's house (1762).

Wouw (5 km. E.): The Gothic 15C *St.-Lambertuskerk* was almost completely destroyed in 1944; church and tower have been restored as far as possible. The wooden statues which survived can be seen in the choir.

Bergum/Burgum
Friesland   p.287☐L 2

Dutch Reform church: This 13C Romanesque-Gothic church was originally a parish church with only a nave. It was later expanded into a monastery church with a nave and two aisles; the 12C tower was increased in height at the same time. Inside there are a fine 17C pulpit, a large organ (1788) and two 17C pews.

Also worth seeing: The restored *De Pleats farmstead* (80 Schoolstraat) dating from 1733 is now a cultural centre.

Environs: Eestrum/Jistrum (7 km.

NE): This village has a beautiful little 13C *Romanesque-Gothic church* with a saddle-roofed tower the top half of which has niches and friezes of round arches.

Bierum
Groningen   p.287☐O 2

Dutch Reform church: The finest part of this single-aisled 13C Romanesque-Gothic church is the somewhat older W. part which includes the saddle-roof tower and which consists of a low, crypt-like lower storey above which there is a storey vaulted like a dome and open towards the nave of the church. The choir was built on the site of a former 14C apse. *Vault paintings*, which came to light in restoration work, include Christ Enthroned, the Virgin Mary between symbols of Evangelists, St.Catherine and the Coronation of the Virgin Mary and fabulous beasts. A rococo mourning panel (1795) is particularly interesting among the fine decorations.

Bergen op Zoom, Stadhuis

Environs: Godlinze (5 km. SW): The Romanesque-Gothic *Dutch Reform church* is rendered on the outside. Of interest inside are a tabernacle and remains of 15C vault paintings. The lower outer part of the tower is 12C; the upper section dates from 1554. The village has a permanent exhibition of the work of the Italian sculptor Bruno Santera.

Holwierde (5 km. S.): The monumental *Dutch Reform church* is the result of several phases of expansion on an essentially 11C tufa nave. Small Romanesque windows were rediscovered. Ornamental paintings and paintings of figures (of various dates) were uncovered in the crossing vault. The baroque pulpit now stands in front of the late-Gothic wooden choir rails.

Krewerd (5 km. S.): The organ (1631) in the modest but beautiful Romanesque-Gothic *Dutch Reform church* is one of the oldest functioning organs in the Netherlands.

Losdorp (2 km. W.): The *Dutch Reform church*, a hall church from the 13C, was much altered in 1775–6.

Spijk (3 km. NW): The 13C *Dutch Reform church* occupies a charming location in the middle of this village which is part of the municipality of Bierum. The church was rebuilt in 1676 and again in 1902.

Blokzijl

Overijssel   p.287☐L 3

This unique little town was founded by Dutch merchants in the 15C. It was fortified in 1581 and granted a charter in 1672.

Dutch Reform church: Originally a small hall church built in 1609 as one of the first Protestant churches in the country. Alterations from 1630 to 1662 made it into a cruciform church. Fine Renaissance decorations include a *pulpit* (1663) and a 17C *model of a warship*.

Havenkolk: The harbour in the middle of Blokzijl is surrounded by fine *houses* which are very similar to 17&18C houses found in Amsterdam. e.g. houses at *6, 7 & 8 Bierkade*. During the 17&18C Blokzijl was still a port exporting products like turf, reed mats and timber.

Also worth seeing: In *Kerkstraat* there are some more good 17&18C *houses*, with various different types of gable.

Environs: Kuinre (10 km. NW): A little old harbour town at the mouth of the Linde which lost its function when the Zuiderzee was drained. The *town hall* dating from 1776, was built on a weigh-house dating from 1648. Other *houses*, bear witness to the town's former prosperity.

Bolsward/Boalsert

Friesland   p.286☐K 2

History: In *c.* 715 a settlement was established on a terp and by 870 there

Blokzijl, Dutch Reform church

Bolsward, St.-Maartenskerk, tower (left), pulpit (right)

was a 'stins' or residential tower. The town was an important maritime centre during the late Middle Ages. In 1422 Emperor Sigismund made Bolsward a member of the Hanseatic League. The town was granted a charter in 1455. Bolsward was well known for its cloth.

Grote Kerk or St.-Maartenskerk: This massive Gothic building (1446–66), visible from afar with a tall saddle-roofed tower, is one of the finest churches in Holland. The nave is 200 ft. long and has mighty columns between the aisles. In the N. aisle there are *vault paintings* (*c.* 1500) of scenes from the life of the Virgin Mary. The 15C choir stalls are richly carved with Biblical images. The organ (1775–81) was built by A.A.-Hinsch, the famous organ builder from Groningen. The beautiful carved pulpit dates from 1622. The

church is open to the public at the following times: Mon.–Fri.: 10 a.m.–12 noon and 1.30–5 p.m. During the holiday season it is also open on Saturdays 10 a.m.–1 p.m. and 2–4 p.m.

Stadhuis: The town hall (1613–17), possibly the best example of 17C Friesland architecture, was built by local craftsmen and artists, e.g. Jacob Gijbertsz, who was also mayor. The front has a fine, carved *baroque gable* above the door and an *external staircase* (1768) in rococo style. The lower floor was a weigh-house. Inside there is a central hall with a fine council chamber and old furniture, Bolsward silver and paintings. Opening times: 1 Apr.–31 Oct: Mon.–Fri. 9 a.m.–12 noon and 2–4.30 p.m.

Also worth seeing: The Romanesque-Gothic *Broerekerk*, founded in

1270, was formerly part of the Franciscan monastery destroyed in 1580. The inside was devastated by fire in 1980. The town has a large number of 17&18C *houses with gables*, especially in *Dijlakker, Groot Zand, Nieuwemarkt* (St.-Anthoniegasthuis with a fine classical façade), *Dijkstraat* and *Jonemastraat*. The *Monsmastate country house* with a pilastered façade (1709) and a *polder mill* (1824) can be found in Franekerstraat outside the town.

Environs: Burgwerd/Burchwert (7 km. N.): This *Dutch Reform church* is basically a well-preserved Gothic building whose outer walls were rebuilt in the 17C using old materials. The pulpit, font rails, and heavy brass hour-glass holders are the best of the decorations.
Witmarsum/Wytmarsum (6 km. NW): This village is the birthplace of Menno Simonsz, leader of the Mennonites. The late Gothic *Dutch Reform church* (1633) has pretty decorations and 17C pews.

Bolsward, Stadhuis, portal

Borger
Drente   p.287☐O 3

Hunebed (on the way to Bronneger) is the largest megalithic tomb in Drente. 69 ft. long, it is quite well preserved although two roof stones have subsided. 47 stones survive, some of which weigh 20,000 kg.

Hunebedmuseum "t Flint 'n hoes' (12 Bronnegerstraat): This *museum devoted to Megalithic tombs* occupies the former orphanage. Opening times: Easter–Sept.: Tue.–Sun., 10 a.m.–5 p.m.

Also worth seeing: The *Dutch Reform church* dates from 1826 with a massive brick tower which is probably 14C. Outside the church there is a grating above a square opening. Popular belief has it that the grating

was intended to prevent the Devil from disturbing the peace of those buried in the graveyard.

Environs: Drouwen (2.5 km. N.): A *megalithic tomb* from the Neolithic period (2700–2400 BC). The *National History Museum Drouwenerzand* (5a Gasselterstraat) exhibits both indigenous and exotic flora and fauna. Opening times: Apr.–Sept.: 10 a.m.–5 p.m. daily; May–Aug.: 10 a.m.–6 p.m.; Oct. and Mar.: Sun. only 10 a.m.–5 p.m. Fossils are on display in the museum known as *Versteend Leven* (7 Alinghoek). Opening times: Apr.–Sept., 10 a.m.–6 p.m. daily.

Bourtange
Groningen   p.286☐P 3

History: Bourtange fortress (1580–3)

was built by order of William of Orange on a sandy ridge (tange) in the Bourtange moorland. It was further reinforced by Prince Maurice in 1605 to defend it against the troops of the Bishop of Münster.

Museum Vesting Bourtange: Star-shaped fortress around a central courtyard. With ramparts, bastions and cannons, it gives the visitor a good idea of its former appearance. The information centre is open daily 9 a.m.–5 p.m.; Easter–1 Oct.

Boxmeer

North Brabant   p.291 □ L 7

Traditionally the site of a miracle in *c.* 1400, this village on the left bank of the Maas became a place of pilgrimage.

Kasteel Boxmeer: Founded probably *c.* 1200. Only the medieval foundations survive today. Large parts of the castle were devastated in 1572 under the Duke of Alba's leader-

ship; in 1576 it withstood a siege by Count Willem van den Bergh. The castle was later rebuilt, although part of it was torn down in 1806. The surviving part is 17C with a corner pavilion which was added in 1782.

Also worth seeing: The *Carmelite monastery* was founded in 1653. The gate bears the founders' coats-of-arms with Renaissance ornaments. A small *chapel dedicated to St.John Nepomuk* dates from 1739.

Boxtel

North Brabant   p.290 □ I 7

Situated on the Dommel, Boxtel is now an industrial town. Formerly the village was a place of pilgrimage as the result of a miracle said to have occurred in the town and the procession of the Holy Blood still takes place on Trinity Sunday.

Kasteel Stapelen: First mentioned in 1293 as the castle of the former barons of Boxtel. Today the building is a somewhat fantastic collection of

Borger, Hunebed (megalithic grave)

battlements, towers and stepped gables mostly dating from the second half of the 19C.

Also worth seeing: *St.-Pieterskerk*, a 15C late-Gothic cruciform basilica with a 16C chapel. The *Kannuniken-huis* (4 Duinenwaal) is 17C; the *Vrouwengasthuis* (35 Markt) was founded by Magdalena van der Stappen in 1646.

Environs: Esch (3 km. NW): Prehistoric objects and Roman tombs were discovered in this district and finds are on display in the Noordbrabants Museum in 's-Hertogenbosch. Little else has survived from former times. The only part of the Roman Catholic church not to have been pulled down is the 15C brick tower, which has tympana and a frieze of arches below the crooked spire. 15C *Oude-mannenhuis*.

Breda

North Brabant   p.290☐H 7

History: Breda, important for its wool and cloth trade, received a charter in 1252. During the following century it became the main town of the barony of the same name and the seat of the house of Nassau. Spaniards occupied both castle and town in 1590. Prince Maurice of Orange recaptured the town by a ruse, smuggling 70 of his soldiers hidden under a layer of turf, into the town by boat. The castle was recaptured by the Spanish general Spinola in 1625; the town's surrender is recorded in the painting 'Las Lanzas' ('The Surrender of Breda') by Velásquez (Prado, Madrid). Breda subsequently declined in importance and it was only after the ramparts were razed in the 19C that it began to expand and grow stronger economically.

Grote Kerk or **Onze-Lieve-Vrouwekerk** (Grote Markt): This fine cruciform Gothic church dedicated to the Virgin Mary has a tower 322 ft. high, and a choir begun in 1410. Nave, transept and tower followed in 1468. The tower's wooden spire burned down in 1694 and was replaced by the present structure in

Boxmeer, castle

Boxmeer, Carmelite monastery, founder's coat-of-arms in cloister

1702. The ambulatory and the chapel to the Virgin Mary were built in *c.* 1526. Interesting features include the richly-carved *choir stalls* (mid 15C), the *pulpit* (*c.* 1640), and the *Renaissance mausoleum* to Engelbert of Nassau (d. 1506) and his wife Cimburga of Baden (d. 1501). This black marble monument, built on the orders of Hendricks III of Nassau, has alabaster figures of the count and his wife (attributed to Jan Gossaert). Four kneeling alabaster figures at the corners support a black marble slab on which the count's armour is displayed. The church is open to the public May–Sept.: Tues.–Sat.: 10 a.m.–5 p.m.; Mon. & Sun.: 1–5 p.m.

Begijnhof (Catharinastraat): The buildings of the Beguine convent, said to have been founded in 1240 by Machteld van Diest, wife of Godevaert van Breda en Schoten, are grouped around an elongated courtyard. The new chapel (1837) is in Waterstaatsstijl. The Beguines lived in rather austere communities although they had many freedoms not usually associated with life in a sisterhood.

Kasteel Breda (Kasteelplein): The 'Koninklijke Militaire Academie' has been housed in this castle since 1826. The castle, in existence at the beginning of the 15C, was extended in 1536–8 by the Italian architect Thomas Vincidor to form the residence of Hendrick III of Nassau. Its present appearance dates from 1668–81, and was designed by Jacob Roman for the future later king and governor William III. The castle can be visited during the tour of the town organized by the VVV (tourist office).

Hofhuys (14 Catharinastraat): A 16C

Breda, Kasteel

house with a very atmospheric court-yard. Michiel van Piggen, William of Orange's counsellor, lived here from 1552–84.

Oud-Mannenhuis (Boschstraat): This former almshouse for old men (1643), with a brick façade and a stone portal, is the De Beyerd cultural centre today. The courtyard is sur-rounded on two sides by a colonnaded passage.

Spanjaardsgat: A water gate (1610) between the two seven-sided rampart towers (Duiven and Granaat towers).

Stadhuis: In 1766–8, Philip Willem Schonk, the military architect, incor-porated the former town hall and the house called Vogelsanck into a single building with a simple façade. There is a good copy of the Velázquez paint-ing 'Las Lanzas' ('The Surrender of Breda') in the hall. The stairwell and council chamber have stained-glass paintings from 1926 by Joep Nicolas which show important events from the town's history.

Vismarkt: The fish market by the harbour is an open hall with late 18C Doric columns.

Stedelijk en Bisschopelijk Museum (19 Grote Markt): This museum occupies the former meat hall of 1614 (gables added in 1772). On exhibit are numerous religious works of art, etchings and coins. Opening times: Tues., Sun. and holi-days: 1–5 p.m., Wed.–Sat. 10.30 a.m.–5 p.m.; closed on 1 Jan., 25 Dec. and Rosenmontag.

Volkenkundig Museum Justinus van Nassau (13 Kasteelplein): Devoted to Dutch-Indian folk art.

Breda, Grote Kerk, tower

Opening times: Mon.–Fri. 10 a.m.–5 p.m., Sun. and holidays 1–5 p.m., closed on 1 Jan. and Rosenmontag.

Events: The *Nederlands Kunsten Antiekbeurs* is held in the congress centre every year around Easter time. An *art and antiques market* is held in the harbour market from early May to late Sept. The *Oude Stijl Jazzfestival* is held in the town on Ascension Day every year.

Environs: Chaam: (12 km. SE): The tower of the 16C *church* was destroyed in 1944; surviving sections have been restored.

Etten (13 km. W.): The *Grote Markt* is famous for its double row of linden trees planted in the 18C. Only the central choir section of the early 16C *hall church* survives. It was attached

◁ *Breda, Grote Kerk, organ*

Breukelen, Oudaen country house

to the present parish tower (1771) by the architect Philip Willem Schonk. In 1776 Schonk also built the classical *town hall*. The *weigh-house* has open arcades and a low roof. *St.-Paulus-hofje*, founded by Justus de Nobelaer in 1681, consists of a courtyard (with water pump) surrounded on three sides by small, low houses. Today it houses the Jan Uten Houte museum.

Ginneken (1 km. S.): This former village, now part of district of Breda, has a 14/15C *Dutch Reform church*, which was rebuilt some time after 1648. *Huis Bouvigne,* an elegant 17C summer house has a hexagonal tower.

Breukelen

Utrecht   p.289☐l 5

Kasteel Gunterstein: Dating from 1681 with an unusually tall chimney and figures in niches.

Kasteel Nijenrode: Built in 1270, probably as a residential tower—the large tower visible today dates from 1917/18. In 1860 the outside of the castle was dramatically altered in Tudor style; at the beginning of the present century the height of the castle keep was increased in Renaissance style.

Landhaus Oudaen: This castle-like country house was originally the seat of a medieval knight when it consisted of a residence and two towers. Another building was added in the 17C when the towers were partially torn down and converted into bartizans.

Environs: Kockengen (5 km. SW): In 1353 Charles V granted this village the right to conduct trials with a court of lay assessors, which had the effect of raising Kockengen to the status of

town. Dykes were built and the area was drained. Two *water mills*, the 'Spengen' mill in the N. and the mill belonging to the Kockengen water federation in the S., were built in the first half of the 17C. Their 19C successors continued to operate until 1961. The pretty late Gothic *Maria-Hemelvaartkerk* was a pilgrimage church before the Reformation; today it is a Dutch Reform church.

Brielle
South Holland   p.288□F 6

Brielle or Den Briel, the main town on the island of Voorne, was the birthplace of the nautical hero Maerten Harpertzoon Tromp (b. 1598, d. 1653 in the battle of Terhijde). It was important in the Eighty Years' War when the Sea Beggars took the town from the Spaniards. Originally a fortress town it protected the mouth of the river Maas until the mouth was dammed in 1952.
Some foundation walls of the medieval defences have been excavated; the 18C fortifications are in the main intact.

St.-Catharijnekerk: An unfinished late Gothic cruciform basilica (1417) with fine tomb monuments. The bells (1660) in the tower are by F.Hémony.

Stadhuis: The town hall, originally 14C, received a Louis XIV gable façade in 1792.

Trompmuseum: This museum houses objects of artistic interest, particularly from the 16&17C when the town was at its most prosperous. Opening times: Mon. 10 a.m.–12 noon, Tue. 9–11.30 a.m. and 12.30–5 p.m., Wed.–Sat. 9 a.m.–5 p.m.

Environs: Abbenbroek (8 km. SE):

◁ *Kockengen (Breukelen), Dutch Reform church*

The choir (*c.* 1300) of the famous *Dutch Reform church* was the model for the Flemish-Zeeland brick Gothic style. Nave and two aisles dates from *c.* 1500; the tower is early 15C.

Heenvliet (7 km. SE): The town was originally 17C. The *Ravenstein* ruins include a rather unusual residence; instead of the usual square tower, there is an area bounded by four round corner towers (restored in 1960), in the garden of the former bailiff's house. Angelus Merula, a local priest 1530–3, was held prisoner in Ravestein after he adopted the Reformed service.

Hellevoetsluis (9 km. S.): A little old fortified town and formerly an important naval harbour. The harbour was closed down in 1935 and converted into a centre for water sports. The *former admiralty building* from the mid 17C, today's town hall, is by Pieter Post. Neo-Gothic *water tower* (1896). *Nationaal Brandweermuseum* (5 Gallasplein), a museum devoted to the fire brigade. Opening times: Mon.–Sat. 10 a.m.–4 p.m., Sun. and holidays 11 a.m.–4.30 p.m.

Oostvoorne (5 km. W.): Documented since 1105, Oostvoorne lies within the line of the dykes near Brielse lake and Oostvoornse Meer. The originally medieval *Dutch Reform* church was rebuilt in *c.* 1627 after a fire. The tower with a fine onion dome survives from the 13C. The foundations of the *castle*, which belonged to the rulers of Voorne, were excavated in 1935. This once massive castle may have had a tower dating back to *c.* 1100. In the middle of a field there is a *Kogelgloeioven*, where bullets were made.

Brielle, St.Catharijnekerk

1890–1. Arches above the windows are decorated with coats-of-arms. A statue of the goddess of Justice stands above the entrance and there are also statues on top of the gables. The double staircase is decorated by lions bearing the Zeeland and Brouwershaven coats-of-arms. A staircase tower divides the older brick section at the rear and the new front section.

Also worth seeing: The predominantly 14C *Dutch Reform church* in the attractive market square was originally founded in 1293. A *statue* of Jacob Cats, poet and statesman (b. in Brouwershaven in 1577), also stands in the market square. The *mill in the rampart* dates from 1724.

Brouwershaven
Zeeland   p.288☐E 6

Stadhuis: The town hall's attractive, narrow gable façade (originally dating from 1599) received its stone facing when the building was restored in

Environs: Dreischor (7 km. SE): The particularly beautiful 14&15C *church* is surrounded by a moat. A *Museum of agriculture* can be found at

5 Moggestraat. Opening times: 1 June–1 Sept.: Mon.–Sat. 1.30–4.30 p.m.

Buren

Geldern   p.289☐I 6

Dutch Reform church: This spacious late Gothic building has a nave and two aisles. Its exterior is rendered except in the W. section. Alexander Pasqualini may have been responsible for increasing the height of the church's tower in Renaissance style in the 16C. In 1665, Pieter Post added the fine storey with clock to the latter's octagonal storey.

Stadhuis: The building was acquired in 1554 to serve as the town hall. It was rebuilt in 1608 and again in 1739–40. Interesting external features include the tall roof with 17C turret, the Louis XIV entrance and the cornice.

Fortifications: The ramparts around the town, dismantled to some extent in the 19C, have survived in good condition. There are 'Muurhuizen' (wall houses) along the town wall, which were altered by Alexander Pasqualini in 1554. The only gate to have survived on the W. side is the *Huizer-* or *Kuilenborgse Poort,* enlarged by Willem van Soelen in 1630.
Nothing survives of the former *castle.*

Koninklijk Weeshuis: Maria of Nassau ordered this elegant structure to be built by van Oudendijck in 1613 to the plans of Adrian Fredericksz, sculptor and architect.

Boerenwagenmuseum (4 Kornewal): This museum has a collection of old peasants' wagons and carts from Geldern. Opening times: 1 May–30 Sept.: Tues.–Sun. 1.30–5.30 p.m.

◁ *Buren, Dutch Reform church*

Also worth seeing: The *weigh-house* has an early-19C wooden colonnaded gallery. In the *Rode Heldenstraat, Herenstraat* and *Voorstraat* there are some roughcast *houses,* which are

possibly 16C and have stepped gables at the sides and cornices along the street front. The *'De Prins van Oranje' windmill* standing on the rampart was built in 1716.

Coevorden
Drente   p.287☐O 4

This charming old fortress town was laid out in the form of a seven-pointed star by Count Willem Lodewijk. Built 1597–1607, it was redesigned and extended by Menno van Coehoorn in 1700. The town's former layout can now only be seen in the plan of the streets.

Kasteel: This was the only castle in the province of Drente. Its surviving

Coevorden, Kasteel

Culemborg, Stadhuis

NW wing is today part of the town hall. The foundations date back to *c.* 1100, but the walls have been much altered over the centuries. The low, round corner tower and the S. staircase tower have been rebuilt. The façade has a stone dated 1527 showing the coat-of-arms of Karel van Egmond, Duke of Gelre. Opening times: Mon.–Thur. 9 a.m.–12 noon and 1.30–5 p.m., Fri. 9 a.m.–12 noon.

Gemeentemuseum 'Drenthe's Veste' (5 Haven): The town museum, contained in three attractive 17C houses which were part of the former arsenal, has prehistoric exhibits and historic documents relating to the area.
Opening times: Mon.–Fri. 10 a.m.–12.30 p.m. and 1.30–5 p.m., Sat. 2–5 p.m.; Apr.–Sept.: Sun. 2–5 p.m.

Also worth seeing: The *Dutch Reform church* (*c.* 1641) has a dome above the crossing. The light interior has a column which bears the coat-of-arms of the Protestant Bohemian emigrant Karel Rabenhaupt, baron of Sucha. When the Bishop of Münster invaded in 1672, Rabenhaupt defended the N. of the town and as a reward was made governor. The upper part of the *façade* of the house at 9 Friesestraat dates from 1631 and is richly decorated in the Flemish-North German Renaissance style. *De Catshaar* (1797), a square redoubt with outworks on both sides lies in the Vlieghuizer heath on the way towards Schoonebeek.

Culemborg
Geldern   p.289☐I 6

This town on the left bank of the Lek has been the centre of the region from early times (it was granted a charter in 1318). From the 17C onwards it was an industrial centre as well. The picturesque town centre is partly surrounded by remains of the 14C fortifications.

Grotekerk or **St.-Barbarakerk:** This magnificent 14&15C church has splendid interior decorations.

St.-Elisabeth's orphanage: Today the town's *museum of antiquity* is housed in the former girl's wing of this building dating from 1559.

Stadhuis: The 14C late Gothic town hall has a tribune overlooking the market. Part of a pillory survives in the SE corner.

Also worth seeing: The house where *Jan van Riebeeck*, the explorer, was born. The classical hall housing the *fish market* dates from 1787. The *Lanksmeer-* or *Binnenpoort*, an inland harbour is 14C.

Delden, Kasteel Twickel

Dalfsen
Overijssel   p.287□M 4

Dalfsen, one of the oldest villages in Salland is beautifully situated on the Overijsselse Vecht.

Dutch Reform church: This late Gothic church (probably second half of 15C on the site of an earlier building) is basilican in form with a tall choir. The massive, unfinished tower is older and has a low spire.

Huis Rechteren: This old castle is skirted by the River Vecht. The various phases of its construction can be clearly distinguished. The tall round keep is 14C, the rear section with its tall roof is late medieval and the front including the entrance dates from 1726 and 1898 when the middle section was increased in height. This is one of the few castles in the Netherlands which is still occupied by descendants of the founder family whose name they still bear. The Van Rechterens have collected a large number of objects of artistic interest, including family portraits and old furniture.

Also worth seeing: *Huis Den Berg,* an elegant early-18C mansion which has preserved its old character surprisingly well. The *Huize De Aalshorst (c.* 1700) is an elegant country house built to look like a farm. The attractive *Huize De Leemcule* (1823) stands on a site formerly occupied by a knight's residence. Other attractive *country houses* include *De Horte* (18C) and *Hessum* (19C). The octagonal *'De Westermolen'* corn mill dates from 1818.

Delden
Overijssel   p.287☐O 5

The centre of this old fortified town is still enclosed by almost circular ramparts.

Grote or St.-Blasiuskerk: A late Romanesque cruciform basilica altered in the 15&16C to form the Dutch Reform hall church with nave and two aisles visible today. The pillars between the aisles, and also a window on the E. wall of the N. aisle,

Delden, St.Blasiuskerk

date from the Romanesque structure. The vault of the third bay of the nave has a Last Judgement which is possibly late 15C. The *early Renaissance memorial* with its relief of Frederik van Twickelo (d. 1545) came from Hengelo and may formerly have been the topmost stone of a tomb.

Kasteel Twickel: Founded in 1347, the present building surrounded by ditches and tall trees dates from 1551. Despite later alterations the elongated front section has survived in early Renaissance style. A stone coat-of-arms, tree of knowledge and a relief of the Adoration of the Magi, decorate the entrance; columns on both sides of the door have figures of Adam and Eve. New sections were added to the back of the building in the early 17C, in 1692 and in 1847.

Delft
South Holland   p.289☐G 5

Delft is the birthplace of Hugo de Groot (1583–1645) who, under the name of Grotius, is remembered for his writings on international law. The painter Jan Vermeer (1632–75), founder of the Delft school, was also born here.

History: Delft was granted a charter in 1246 and later developed into a flourishing commercial town thanks to its cloth trade, breweries and shipping. In 1389, the 'Delfshavense Schie' linked the town with the mouth of the River Maas further to the S; today the outer port of Delfshaven is part of the city of Rotterdam. Large parts of Delft were destroyed by a fire in 1536. The first potteries date from the 16C and 'Delft Blue' was produced by a flourishing ceramics industry until the late 18C; the industry was again prosperous in the second half of the 19C, although not

Delft, Stadhuis ▷

Delft, Oostpoort and tower of Nieuwe Kerk

as economically important as in the 17C. Delft was one-time residence of the Stadholder of Orange. In 1584, William of Orange was murdered in the Prinsenhof on the orders of Philip II of Spain.

Nieuwe Kerk (Markt): A Gothic building (1384–1496) with a carillon (1663) by the Hémony brothers; the tower is 355 ft. tall. The choir has the sumptuous *tomb of William of Orange* in black and white marble. This monumental Renaissance structure was begun by Hendrick de Keyser in 1614 and completed by his son Pieter in 1622. 41 princesses and princes of the house of Nassau-Orange are buried in the crypt beneath. The monument to William I (d. 1843 in Berlin) can be seen in the ambulatory, where there is also Canova's tomb relief for Willem George Frederik of Orange (d. 1709). The N. wall of the choir has a marble monument to Hugo Grotius, whose bronze statue (1886) stands in the middle of the market square. Opening times: 1 Apr.–1 Oct. Mon.–Sat. 9 a.m.–5 p.m.; 1 Oct.–1 Apr. Mon.–Sat. 10 a.m.–12 noon and 1.30–4 p.m.

Oude Kerk (Heilige Geestkerkhof): The Old Church built 13–15C has a tower dating from *c.* 1300 and inclining slightly towards the Oude Delft canal. Two famous Dutch admirals, Piet Hein (d. 1629) and Maarten H. Tromp (d. 1653) are buried here, as are the painter Jan Vermeer and the scientist Antony van Leeuwenhoek (1632–1723). The pulpit was carved in 1548. Opening times: 1 Apr.–1 Oct. Mon.–Sat. 12 noon–4 p.m.

Armentarium: The arsenal beside the Oude Delft canal was built in 1601 and enlarged in 1692 by order of the states of Holland and West Friesland. The large relief above the entrance has Mars, the Roman god of war.

Begijnhof (215 Oude Delft): The Beguine convent in Delft has a late Gothic gate with a relief of St.John the Evangelist. The Oud-katholieke Schuilkerk, built in 1743 by the architect Daniel Marot has surprisingly fine baroque decorations.

Gemeenlandshuis van Delfland (167 Oude Delft): Originally built in *c.* 1520 as a residence for Jan de Huyter, dyke master of Delfland and mayor of Delft. It was rebuilt in 1620 and since then has been the Gemeenlandshuis (administrative office overseeing the dykes). Fine stone gable.

Hofje van Gratie (3 Van der Mastenstraat): This picturesque charitable foundation dates from 1575 and is composed of seven houses and a charming courtyard.

Hofje van Pauw (154 Verwersdijk): Charitable foundation built in 1707 for unmarried women; fine warden's room.

Kruitmagazin: The powder magazine on the W. side of the Schie, S. of the town. Built in 1660 to the plans of Pieter Post after the powder magazine within the town walls had exploded, it consists of two large gunpowder towers and an attractive gatehouse.

Oostpoort: The E. gate and the only one to have survived from the old fortifications. Built in *c.* 1400 it is flanked by two round towers with slender helm roofs from the early 16C.

Prinsenhof (1 Agathaplein): Originally the convent of St.Agatha it dates from *c.* 1400. From 1573 it was the residence of Prince William of

Gemeenlandshuis, portal with coat-of-arms ▷

Orange, and it later became the centre for the Delft cloth trade. Today it is occupied by a *museum* (Stedelijk Museum Het Prinsenhof), chiefly devoted to the Eighty Years' War (1568–1648) between the Netherlands and Spain. William I of Orange was murdered on the stairs on 10 July 1584. The museum also has exhibits relating to the house of Orange-Nassau, portaits of Hugo Grotius and his family, Delftware and paintings by artists from Delft. Opening times: Tues.–Sat. 10 a.m.–5 p.m.; Sun. and holidays 1–5 p.m.

Stadhuis: The Delft town hall stands oposite the Nieuwe Kerk in the SE of the Markt. Fires in 1536 and 1618 destroyed much of the original building (*c.* 1300) and all that remains is *Het Steen*, a tower with lower storeys of brick; upper storeys are late 15C. The building was rebuilt in 1618 in Dutch Renaissance style to the plans of Hendrick de Keyser. The *council chamber*, the *assembly hall*, and the *Oranje gallery* with its 16–18C paintings are of interest inside. Open to the public Mon.–Fri.

Museums
Stedelijk Museum Het Prinsenhof (see Prinsenhof).

Rijksmuseum Lambert van Meerten (199 Oude Delft): Tiles and tile decorations, lace and silver. The rooms have Renaissance furniture. Opening times: Tues.–Sat. 10 a.m.–5 p.m.; Sun. and holidays 1–5 p.m.

Museum Paul Tétar van Elven (97 Koornmarkt): The house of the painter of the same name (1823–96) with rooms in 18&19C styles. Opening times: end of Apr.–end of Oct. 11 a.m.–5 p.m.

Volkenkundig Museum Nusantara (4 Agathaplein): Ethnographical museum with Indonesian exhibits. Opening times: Tues.–Sat. 10 a.m.–5 p.m.; Sun. and holidays 1–5 p.m.

Armentarium (1 Korte Geer): Since the beginning of 1986, this has housed collections devoted to the Dutch army, including the 'Generaal Hoefer' weapon museum.

Also worth seeing: The old art of manufacture of delftware is still practised by three *workshops* which are open to the public. *I. De Porceleyne Fles* (196 Rotterdamseweg): 1 Apr.–31 Oct. Mon.–Sat. 9 a.m.–5 p.m., Sun. 10 a.m.–4 p.m.; 1 Nov.–31 Mar. Mon.–Fri. 9 a.m.–5 p.m., Sat. 10 a.m.–4 p.m. *II. De Delftse Pauw* (133 Delftweg): 1 Apr.–30 Sept. 10 a.m.–4 p.m. daily; 1 Oct.–31 Mar. Mon.–Fri. 9 a.m.–4 p.m., Sat. and Sun. 11 a.m.–1 p.m. *III. Atelier de Candelaer* (13 Kerkstraat): 1 Apr.–30 Sept. Mon.–Fri. 9 a.m.–6 p.m., Sat. 9 a.m.–5 p.m., Sun. 10 a.m.–6 p.m.; 1 Oct.–31 Mar.: Mon.–Fri. 9 a.m.–12.30 p.m. and 1.30–6 p.m., Sat. 9 a.m.–5 p.m.

Delfzijl
Groningen   p.287☐O 2

A 13C fortress situated at the mouth of the Ems which was important from the beginning of the Eighty Years' War. Delfzijl attained international importance as a harbour in the late 19C and it is now the third largest harbour in the Netherlands. It is also a modern industrial town thanks to its salt production and natural gas deposits.

'Adam' mill: A timber mill dating from 1795, it was transferred from Bedum and rebuilt in the centre of Delfzijl in 1875. Now an art centre.

Geologisch Museum Het Flinthok (11 Kustweg): Geological finds from the provinces of Groningen and Drente. Opening times: 15 May–15 Sept. Sun.–Fri. 1–5 p.m.

Also worth seeing: The rear façade (1752) of the *Zijlvesthuis*. The *whipping post* in the *Pijpplein*.

Environs: Termunten (7.5 km. E.): The *Dutch Reform* church which stands on a knoll, has 12C foundations. The choir is a fine example of the richly articulated 13C Romanesque-Gothic style found in this province. Part of the tower was restored after severe war damage.

Termunterzijl (7 km. E.): The village now has the second largest shrimp harbour in the Netherlands. The *sluice bridge* has a monumental parapet of 1724, richly decorated with coats-of-arms and cartouches.

Denekamp

Overijssel   p.287□O 4

Roman Catholic church: Single-aisled 13–15C church built in stone from Bentheim. The tower was built in the second half of the 15C. The E. section was built by W. te Riele in 1911. Bells date from 1436, 1518 & 1530.

Kasteel Singraven: Documented

since 1381. The right side of the present house (18–20C) has an unusual tower (1661) with Ionic pilasters and a richly framed entrance. A double mill in the grounds combines a corn and oil mill with a sawmill for wood. First mentioned in 1448 it has been rebuilt several times since. Two paintings by Meindert Hobbema depicting the mill can be seen in the Louvre in Paris and the National Gallery in London.

Deventer

Overijssel   p.287□M 5

History: The town, probably Carolingian in origin, was an important trading centre from the 9C onwards and a member of the Hanseatic League, whose ships sailed up and down the IJssel. At that time Deventer maintained relations with Denmark and W. Germany. Deventer was granted a charter before 1230. It was also an important intellectual centre in the Middle Ages. Geert

Deventer, Grotekerk, fresco

Deventer, Grote Kerk, interior

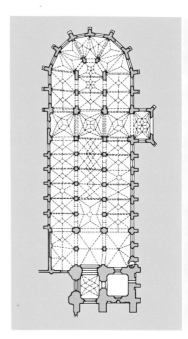

Deventer, Grote or St.Lebuinuskerk

Grote (1340–84), the founder of the 'Modern Devotie' (a community similar to a monastery), was born here. Erasmus of Rotterdam spent some time at the chapter school. The town is also known as 'Koekstad', from the spiced cakes baked here. Today an industrial town, parts have preserved their medieval character.

Grotekerk or **St.-Lebuinuskerk:** Former collegiate church founded in *c.* 1046 by Bernoldus, bishop of Utrecht, who retreated here when the Normans threatened Utrecht. The present late Gothic hall church is the result of alterations made to the unusually large early Romanesque basilica from the 11C, considerable parts of which have survived, e.g. the rib-vaulted crypt with two rows of columns and cushion capitals and the tall brick choir and E. transept. The most radical changes began in the second half of the 15C when the S. aisle and tower were built. These were followed by the ambulatory and Raadskapel and, in the 16C, by the N. aisle. The whole church was given new rib, stellar and net vaults in the 15&16C. In 1612–13, the tower was increased in height and crowned with an open dome to a design by Hendrick de Keyser. The carillon (1654) was in the main the work of François Hémony. Inside the building, there are attractive decorative paintings and paintings of saints (*c.* 1500) on the vaults. St.Michael and St.Quirinus on the walls behind the ambulatory date from the same time. Opening times: Mon.–Fri. 10 a.m.–5 p.m. Sat. 1.30–5 p.m.

Bergkerk or **St.-Nicolaaskerk:**

Deventer, Penninckshuis, façade detail

This cruciform Romanesque basilica is the main church of the Bergkwartier district. It was built in *c.* 1200, from which time the two towers on the W. side also date. A new choir was built in the first half of the 15C and this was followed by a new basilican nave with broad aisles; the transept chapels were added in *c.* 1500. The towers were increased in height (probably late 15C) and given slender spires. The round-arch niches deriving from the Romanesque transept contain the figure of a bishop and an early-13C figure of Christ. There are paintings on the vault and on the walls (damaged; late 15C and early 16C). The church is now a cultural centre.

Broerenkerk: This Roman Catholic church dedicated to St.Lebuin was formerly part of the Minderbroedersklooster (founded 1335). The two-aisled hall church with stone

vaulting is mainly 15C. The *ivory chalice* said to have belonged to the Anglo-Saxon apostle Lebuin has an early-16C silver frame. Visits by arrangement with the verger (19 Smedenstraat).

Mariakerk: Picturesque remains of the former 15/16C parish church—partly torn down in the 17C—in the NW corner of the Grote Kerk. The building was formerly an arsenal and military store; now a cultural centre.

Penninckshuis (89 Brink): The splendid Renaissance *façade* (*c.* 1590) has figures symbolizing the Virtues. A statue of Albert Schweitzer stands outside the house.

Stadhuis (Grote Kerkhof): The town hall is a conglomeration of different building styles. The monumental sandstone façade (1693–4) facing the Grote Kerkhof is by Jacob Roman. The side wing, which has pilasters and faces on to the Polstraat is by Philips Vingboons (1662). Inside there are good decorations, a painting (1667) of the councillors of Deventer by Gerard Terborch, and a painting (1621) of the four Evangelists by Hendrick Terbrugghen. Opening times: Mon.–Fri. 9 a.m.–12 noon and 2–4 p.m.

Landshuis: Built in 1632 on the site of an older house. Today the Landshuis is part of the town hall. It has a fine gable façade in a somewhat provincial Renaissance style.

Waag (57 Brink): Splendid late Gothic building (1528) with a staircase tower, three bartizans and a wooden roof turret. A sandstone external staircase dates from 1643.

Museums
Atheneumbibliotheek (12 Kloosster): A library founded in 1560 with important old manuscripts and early printed books. Opening times: Mon. 1–5 p.m., Tues. 10 a.m.–9 p.m., Wed.

1–5 p.m., Thur. 1–9 p.m., Fri. 10 a.m.–5 p.m.

Burgers Fietsenmuseum (58 Kolkweg): A collection of some 200 models of bicycles. Visits by prior arrangement (not more than three persons at a time).

Ruimtevaartcentrum Deventer (1 Muntengang): An exhibition in this former mint illustrates the development of space travel. Opening times: Mon.–Sat. 10 a.m.–5 p.m.

Speelgoed en Blikmuseum (47 Brink): This museum, occupying two 15C houses, has toys and objects made from pewter. Opening times: Tues.–Sat. 10 a.m.–12.30 p.m. and 2–5 p.m., Sun. 2–5 p.m.

Also worth seeing: *In de drie Haringen* (55 Brink), a house built in the style of Vredeman de Vries in 1575. The *Bergkwartier* district is so called after fishermen on their way to fish off Bergen in Norway. It was awarded the European Prize for the Preservation of Monuments in 1975. The

Deventer, copper kettle by weigh-house (left), Landhuis portal (right)

Buiskensklooster, a former house of the Devotio Moderna, was founded in 1394; its S. section, restored in 1972, contains the *town archive* (Mon.–Fri. 9 a.m.–12 noon and 1.30–5 p.m., Tues. also 7–9 p.m.). The *Atheneumbibliotheek*, a library occupying the N. part, was restored in 1978.

Environs: Bathmen (7 km. E.): The choir and tower (with a saddle roof, unusual for Overijssel) have survived from a 15C structure which occupied the site of the present *Dutch Reform church* (1870). The *'De Leeuwe'* corn mill (1830) stands on the way to Holten.
Diepenveen (4 km. NW): The *Sion Cistercian abbey* was the first community to be built for monks in the N. of the country after the Reformation. The *Dutch Reform church* survives from the Augustinian monastery founded in 1409. The church went over to the Reformed divine service in the mid 17C. Rebuilt in 1720. The large cross (1493) in the Boxbergerweg commemorates Johannes Luekens.
Olst (8 km. NE): Documented in 974

as belonging to the Essen foundation in Westphalia. The tower of this charming *Dutch Reform church* is Romanesque in its lower part. Gothic nave and a modest, somewhat older choir. *Huis Boksbergen*, a late Gothic country house, was altered in the 17C. *Huis Hoenlo*, possibly dating from the 13C, has a 15C main building and two 18C wings.
Wesepe (7.5 km. NE): The *Dutch Reform church*, is single-aisled with a squat tower, both of which may be 14C. The choir dates from 1503.

Diepenheim
Overijssel p.287☐N 5

Dutch Reform church: Built in 1679 in Gothic style. Tower and single aisle with square apse. The pulpit dates from 1690.

Huis Diepenheim: Mentioned in 1330 as belonging to the Bishop of Utrecht. The elegant mansion visible today dates from 1648 and occupies the site of an old castle built for Ber-

Diepenheim, Huize Warmelo

end Bentinck. A monumental sandstone gate of 1685 opens into the forecourt.

Het Nijenhuis: A simple mansion documented since 1457. Rutger Jan Schimmelpenninck lived here. Its present form is mid 17C with 19&20C corner towers.

Also worth seeing: The *Huize Warmelo* from the mid 17C (later altered) and still surrounded by a moat. Princess Armgard, mother of Prince Bernhard, lived here. The *Huize Westerflier*, documented from 1046, was given its present form in 1729. *'Den Haller'* a wooden corn-grinding water mill, originally dating from 1237 has been rebuilt several times.

Diever

Drente   p.287□M 3

Dutch Reform church: The Pancratiuskerk by the common has a 9C Romanesque tower. The tufa substructure was later increased in height with the addition of a brick storey. Choir rebuilt in the 14C; nave and two aisles altered in the 15C. Gothic niches above the arcades of the nave. The village church has a very spacious interior with a pulpit from *c.* 1765.

Museum Schultehuis (7 Brink): The building dates from 1604 and was formerly occupied by the Ketel family who provided many of the town's mayors; the family's coat-of-arms can be seen above the door. The museum mainly displays old furnishings. Opening times: May–Sept.: Mon.–Sat 10 a.m.–12 noon and 2–5 p.m.

Glasmuseum-Glasblazerij 'De Spiraal' (6 Moleneinde): An exhibition of glass and glass-working throughout history. Opening times: July and Aug. Mon.–Fri. 10 a.m.–12 noon and 1.30–5 p.m., Sat. 10 a.m.–5

p.m.; Sept.–June Tues.–Fri. 1.30–5.30 p.m., Sat. 10 a.m.–5 p.m.; closed in Jan.

Also worth seeing: Behind the church stands the *Franze huizen,* where French emigrants lived after the revocation of the Edict of Nantes. By the common the old *smithy* is still in operation. In the NE of the village there is a *megalithic tomb* and *neolithic burial mounds.* An octagonal *upright mill* stands in the nearby village of *Oldediever.* Attractive *farms.*

Events: *Performances of Shakespeare* are held in the open-air theatre in July and Aug.

Doesburg

Geldern   p.287□M 5

This little town, formerly a member of the Hanseatic League, stands at the confluence of the Oude and the Gelderse IJssel. It received a charter in 1237 and has preserved its attractive historical town centre despite industrialization and the devastation of World War 2.

Grote Kerk or **St.-Martinuskerk:** 15C church in the town centre with 308-ft. tower.

Gasthuiskerk: The chapel (probably 14C) of the former hospital with a small 15C tower.

Stadhuis: The town hall (originally *c.* 1400) has a collection of antiquities. Like the late Gothic weigh-house, it is a typical 16C Geldern brick building.

Museum De Roode Toren: Devoted to local history and prehistory. Opening times: Tues.–Fri. 10 a.m.–12 noon & 1.30–4.30 p.m., Sat. 1.30–4.30 p.m.

Also worth seeing: In the De Lage Linie recreation area, a walk can be taken along the (restored) 17C *fortifications*, which were built by Menno van Coehoorn, the fortress architect.

Doetinchem

This former Hanseatic town on the Oude IJssel is the cultural and economic centre of Achterhoek. Much devastated in 1945, it was rebuilt as a modern business centre.

St.-Catharinakerk: A large 16C Gothic hall church with a 14C choir.

Museum 't Gevang: This former 17C prison houses documents and objects of local interest.

Environs: Huiz Slangenburg (4 km. E.): A 17C mansion built from the remains of a medieval castle, which is most clearly visible in the two round towers at the back. The hall has a stuccoed ceiling and mythological *wall paintings* (c. 1700). The house was taken over by the State in 1945 and it is now the guest house of the nearby Benedictine monastery.
Hummelo-Keppel (5 km. NW): A parish made up of Hummelo, Laag-Keppel, Hoog-Keppel, Drempt and the hamlet of Eldrik. The small *church* (12–15C) in *Drempt* has wall tapestries which the local inhabitants wove to a Scandinavian design. *Hoog-Keppel* has a late-14C *church* with a tufa tower. The late 16C/early 17C *Kasteel Keppel* and a 14C *water mill* stand by the Oude IJssel in *Laag-Keppel.*
's-Heerenberg (15 km. S.): The castle of the van Berg family who later became counts. The square brick residence (15C), still the dominant feature, developed from a round 12C keep, a fragment of which can be seen on the wall of the main building. The building was probably originally circular; today's polygonal shape probably results from later enlarge-

Doesburg, Grote Kerk, portal, detail

ments. Restored after fires in 1735 and 1939. Good art collections in the castle. Guided tours: Mar.–May and Oct.–Nov. Sun.2.30 p.m.; June–Sept. 2.30 p.m. daily. Late Gothic *town hall* (1528). The former *mint* (15C).

Dokkum

The most northerly town in the Netherlands, it has many interesting monuments.

History: Old sources relate that St.Boniface, one of the most important European missionaries, was murdered near Dokkum in 754, as a result of which the town thus became a place of pilgrimage.

Dutch Reform church: Built on a

Dokkum, canal with Stadhuis

knoll above the flood water in the 14C and altered in the 15&16C. Today the W. façade of the church bears the stepped gable visible in 18C drawings. The organ dates from 1688, the pulpit from 1751. Many tombstones.

Stadhuis: Part of the town hall visible today is 16C; the building is documented as being a town hall in 1608 and another part dates from 1762. Both sections were given a classical façade in 1834. There are gilded and painted 18C wallpapers in the rich interior.
Opening times: Mon.–Fri. 9 a.m.–12 noon and 2–4 p.m.

Admiraliteitshuis: The office of the admiralty of Friesland and Groningen has been in Dokkum since the early 17C. The house was built in 1618 and restored in 1963 since which time it has housed a *regional museum* with

Frisian costumes, folk art, silver and ancient objects. Opening times: 1 Apr.–30 Sept. Mon.–Sat. 10 a.m.–5 p.m.; 1 Oct.–1 Apr. Mon.–Sat. 2–5 p.m.

Also worth seeing: Along Diepswal, Zijl, Vleesmarkt, Halve Maans and Hogepol fine *houses* have stepped gables and good façades. The *weigh-house* in Breedstraat was built as a butter weigh-house in 1752. Dokkum has two *mills:* 'Zeldenrust' (restored in 1969) and 'De Hoop' (1849), both on the former ramparts.

Environs: Hantumhuizen/Hantumhuzen (6 km. NW): The 13C *church* is one of the finest examples of Romanesque-Gothic architecture in Friesland. The three domed vaults in the nave are supported on pillars and have painted ribs and decorations.
Holwerd/Holwert (8 km. W.): This

Veenwouden (Dokkum), Schierstins

village is situated on a terp amid mud flats and is the departure point for ferries to Ameland. The 13C *Dutch Reform church* has a massive tower with an extraordinarily tall spire (1729). Two small ashlar portals have delicate sculptures. The white *Doopsgezinde Kerk* is a Mennonite church.

Lauwersoog (17 km. NE): The village stands at the centre of the area of mud flats drained in 1969. The 'Lauwersmeer', formerly a bay and now a lake, is used for a variety of water sports. '*Expozee*' is an exhibition centre which documents the development of the Lauwersmeer and reclamation in general. Opening times: Apr.–Sept. Tues.–Fri. 10 a.m.–5 p.m.; Sat., Sun. and holidays outside the holiday season 2–5 p.m. The industrial harbour of Lauwersoog is also the departure point for the ferry to Schiermonnikoog.

Metslawier/Mitselwier (7 km. N.):

The *Dutch Reform church* (1776) in the middle of the attractive village centre has a plaque in memory of All Saints' flood of 1 November 1570, when large sections of Friesland and Groningen were under water.

Moddergat/It Moddergat (13 km. N.): A former fishing village in the mud flats. The '*Fiskerhûske*' museum, which has old furniture and models of ships, is actually three 18C fishermen's cottages. Opening times: Mar.–Oct. Mon.–Sat. 10 a.m.–5 p.m.

Veenwouden/Feanwâlden (10 km. S.): The *Schierstins* of Veenwouden is surrounded by a ditch. Before 1439 it belonged to the monks of the Klaarkamp monastery. Originally a defensive tower, this structure is the only surviving building of its kind in Friesland. The tower, the surrounding houses, and the *Dutch Reform church* (1648) with its saddle-roof tower, make Veenwouden a most attractive and unique tourist resort. This part of Friesland differs greatly from the rest of the area having a sandy soil and consisting of mainly excavated moorland.

orangery houses a *biological museum* documenting the natural history of Zeeland. Opening times: 10 a.m.–5 p.m. daily; closed on 25 Dec. and 1 Jan.

Domburg

Zeeland   p.288☐D 7

The oldest and most important seaside resort on the NW coast of Walcheren it was already very popular in the 19C. Attractive churches are to be found in Domburg and the surrounding villages of Aagtekerke and Oostkapelle. Domburg *town hall* has a fine gabled façade and two stepped gables at the sides.

Environs: Grijpskerke (9 km. SE): The *Munnikenhof*, a mansion with a 14C octagonal tower, was once the home of Jacob Cats, the poet and statesman.
Kasteel Westhove (3 km. E.): This medieval castle (originally 12C) stands in the middle of a small wood a little way outside Oostkapelle. The

Doorn

Utrecht   p.289☐K 5

Huis Doorn: This castle was originally a knight's estate, from which time a surviving corner tower dates. The building was redesigned in classical style in the 18C. 1920–41 it was owned by Wilhelm II, the last German Kaiser. After this it was opened to the public as museum devoted to the Kaiser. Opening times: 15 Mar.–1 Nov. Mon.–Sat. 9.30 a.m.– 5 p.m., Sun. 1–5 p.m.; closed on Easter Day and Whitsuntide.

Church: The church in the village square is in part Romanesque; rebuilt in 1888.

Environs: There are many castles to the S. of Doorn around the villages of

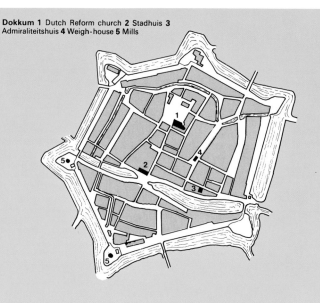

Dokkum 1 Dutch Reform church **2** Stadhuis **3** Admiraliteitshuis **4** Weigh-house **5** Mills

Cothen, Nederlangbroek and Overlangbroek.

Kasteel Hardenbroek (5 km. SW): The present Louis XIV appearance of this castle near Cothen dates from 1762. Nothing survives of the previous medieval structure, a tower built by a younger son of the van Wulven family. With one interruption (1686–1748) Hardenbroek has been continuously inhabited by the van Wulven family (who then called themselves van Hardenbroek).

Kasteel Hindersteyn (4 km. S.): Also founded by the van Wulven family. An annex with a stepped gable, battlements and neo-Gothic windows was added some time after 1847 to the original tower which dates back to *c.* 1300. Neo-Gothic windows were installed in the thick walls of the old tower.

Kasteel Lunenburg (4 km. S.): Thoroughly restored under the supervision of E.A.Canneman the architect, the castle now appears a typical example of a free-standing medieval residential tower dating from about 1300. The house added in the 19C, and much damaged by Allied bombs in 1944, has been torn down and replaced by a residence and stables built outside the moat (based on an 18C drawing).

Kasteel Moersbergen (2 km. SW, very near to Doorn): Redesigned in neo-Gothic style; in 1927 largely restored to its 17C state.

Kasteel Sandenburg (3 km. S.): A large square tower with four storeys and a pointed roof stood here in the late 18C. The residential wings with their battlemented turrets were added in *c.* 1850. This large white building looks especially imposing in summer against its background of dark green trees.

Kasteel Sterkenburg (4 km. SW): Beside the little river Langbroeker. Residential wings were rebuilt on the old foundations in *c.* 1850. The round medieval tower is probably the oldest part of any of the castles in the area. This building was founded 1250–1300 by a member of the van Wulven family.

Kasteel Walenburg (4 km. S.): The Walenburg castle was probably built at about the same time as the Lunenburg. The building lay forgotten for a

Doorn, Huis Doorn with bust of William II

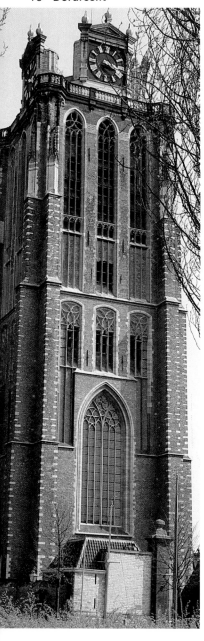

long period, and as a result the medieval tower has survived almost undamaged; only a small residence has been added.

Kasteel Zuylenburg (5.5 km. SE): A simple rectangular house in Overlangbroek (it may originally have been a tower house). One of the first family seats of the van Zuylen family.

Maarn (4 km. N.): Maarn and Maarsbergen formed a community in 1000 (at the time they were known as Manderen and Merseberck). *Kasteel Maarsbergen,* which was originally late medieval, was taken over in 1656 by Samuel de Marees, the son-in-law of Trip, the mayor of Amsterdam. It was restored to its old appearance in 1930.

Dordrecht
South Holland   p.290□H 6

The town of Dordrecht is on the island of the same name, which is linked by several road and railway bridges to the island of IJsselmonde and to W. North Brabant. In 1421 the flood of St.Elizabeth separated the town from Brabant. In 1572 it became a base for the Sea Beggars in the liberation struggle against Spain. Dordrecht was at its zenith in the 13C and received a charter in 1220).

Grotekerk or **Onze-Lieve-Vrouwekerk:** Built at various different periods, this magnificently located church of the Virgin Mary is one of the finest in the Netherlands, and it is the only one to have a nave vaulted entirely in stone. Probably begun in the 1280's, sieges, fires and the flood of St.Elizabeth delayed completion until the second half of the 15C. The late medieval carved wooden *choir stalls* are by Jan Terwen, a Flemish artist. The splendid *choir* is by Evert Spoorwater, also Flemish. The large *organ* dates from 1671. The *brass choir*

◁ *Dordrecht, Grotekerk*

screen (1743) is marble in the lower sections. The *marble pulpit* has a richly decorated abat-voix (1765). The sturdy tower was left incomplete at a height of 230 ft; the superstructure with its four clock housings is baroque. The church is open to the public May–Sept. Tues.–Sat. 10 a.m.–12 noon and 2–4 p.m.

Groothoofdspoort: This large gate (formerly the main gate) is all that remains of the medieval town walls; redesigned in baroque style in 1618 and 1692. A richly framed relief of the town's patron saint faces the river.

Stadhuis: Originally built in 1544, it was altered 1835–42 in the style of the time. Classical gabled façades were added, and the portal was given four Ionic columns in colossal order. The town coat-of-arms, flanked by two gryphons, occupies the gable panel. A square bell turret rises above the central section.

Dordrechts Museum (40 Museumstraat): The main emphasis here is on paintings by artists from Dordrecht, including 17C sea- and riverscapes, and modern Dutch art. Opening times: Mon.–Sat. 10 a.m.–5 p.m., Sun. and holidays 1–5 p.m.; closed on 25 Dec. and 1 Jan.

Museum Mr.Simon van Gijn (29 Nieuwe Haven): Today the district museum, it was acquired by Mr.Simon van Gijn, a banker and art collector, in 1864. Rooms in Louis XIV style, a collection of silver, glass and earthenware, old toys, and historical engravings. Opening times: Mon.–Sat. 10 a.m.–5 p.m., Sun. and holidays 1–5 p.m., closed on 25 Dec. and 1 Jan.

Also worth seeing: *Arend Maertenshof* (38 Museumstraat) built in 1625, with a monumental wrought-iron fountain. *De Gulden Os* house (43 Groenmarkt). *Beverenburg* house (81 Wijnstraat) with stone window frames

Dordrecht, Stadhuis

(1556). House at *79 Wijnstraat*, built in 1650 to a design by Pieter Post. House at *10 Korte Engelburgkade*, with pilaster façade and sculptured garlands of flowers below the windows.

Environs: Maasdam (14 km. W.): The countryside around this town is typically Dutch in appearance with many watercourses and white willows. The *Dutch Reform church* , a small hall church, has a tower from *c.* 1650.

Drachten

Dutch Reform church: The entrance of this church completed in 1743 is crowned by the founders' coats-of-arms surrounded by foliage.

The pretty pulpit (1745) is decorated with allegorical figures.

Streekmuseum Smallingerland 'It Bleekershûs' (14 Moldeneind NZ): This regional museum has prehistoric finds, ceramics, costumes and a room decorated in the style of about 1900. There is also a Dada archive with works by Theo van Doesburg and Rinsema. Opening times: Tues.–Sat. 10 a.m.–5 p.m.

Environs: Kortehemmen/Koarte Himmen (2 km. S.): The *Dutch Reform church* (c. 1300) now stands amidst large trees. The large wooden belfry is free standing.
Rottevalle/De Rottefalle (3 km. N.): The village inn has a well-preserved old *taproom,* decorated in appropriate style.

Dwingeloo

Dutch Reform church: Single-aisled Gothic St.-Nicolaaskerk (15C) has a spire, which is unusual for the area and probably dates from 1631.

Huize Oldengaerde: An elegant country mansion dating from 1717. The classical façade has Ionic pilasters, festoons and a triangular gable.

Also worth seeing: The *Batinger Schut*, a ruined wooden weir in the River Beiler, was built for Batinge farm.
Other interesting old *farms* include Nos. 11, 13 and 51 Westeinde dating from 1711, 1825 and 1838 and Nos. 14, 14 and 17 Lheebroek.

Edam, Stadhuis, entrance

Edam
North Holland   p.286☐I 4

A pretty little town built in the late 12C near the dam on the River Ee. The town was granted a charter in 1357 and a new harbour was built which gave the town the right of free passage between the Zuiderzee and Purmermeer. Edam then developed into a prosperous port. Economic decline began in 1565 when lock gates were built to counter the danger of flooding. Edam cheese has made the town world famous.

Grote or St.-Nicolaaskerk: This very large late Gothic Dutch Reform church was rebuilt with a cruciform ground plan in the 15C. The 15C tower is probably the oldest part; the choir section is 16C. The spacious interior has good proportions and a pleasing appearance which is heightened by the 17C *stained-glass windows* which survive almost in their entirety. The decorations are also mainly 17C, but there are some late Gothic pews (*c.* 1500).

Speeltoren: The Onze-Lieve-Vrouwekerk or Kleine Kerk was torn down in 1883, although the mainly-15C tower survives. The tower's octagonal top (1568–9) was probably built for the carillon cast by P.van der Gheys from Mechelen in 1561.

Stadhuis: Built in 1737, the elegant façade has carved sandstone frames around the entrance and central window above it. The roof has a domed wooden turret. In the council chamber the walls (1738) are decorated with Biblical scenes.

Damsluis: The iron railing of the lock-gate bridge opposite the town hall is essentially Gothic with later alterations.

Edams Museum (8 Damplein): This museum in an attractive gabled house (1550) displays furniture and paintings, some of which are most unusual: 'The Fat Man' (said to have weighed over 440 lb.), 'The Man with the Long Beard', and 'The Tall Maid' (8 ft. 2 in. tall), each of whom lie buried in the Grote Kerk.

Also worth seeing: In the *Grote*

Edam, Speeltoren ▷

Kerkstraat, by the *Voorhaven* and in the *Lingerzijde,* there are a large number of *dwelling-houses* which are bear witness to the town's former prosperity.

Environs: Volendam (2 km. S.): Many of the houses in this well-known fishing village on the IJsselmeer still have their wooden gabled façades. The *Dutch Reform church* (1685) is somewhat reminiscent of a farmhouse.

Eindhoven
North Brabant   p.290☐K 7

Today this is the fifth largest town in the Netherlands. It was only of slight importance in the Middle Ages, and later suffered greatly from fires and war damage. Eindhoven's growth into an important industrial town began in 1891 when the brothers Anton and Gerard Philips set up a light-bulb factory. Today this 'town of light' is at the very centre of the international Philips concern, which employs some 40,000 people in Eindhoven alone.

St.-Catharinakerk (Kerkstraat): A cruciform neo-Gothic basilica built by P.J.H. Cuypers in 1860–7 (amongst his best works). The two towers are different and are crowned with a lily and a cross respectively.

St.-Joriskerk by the architect H.J. van Tulder and **St.-Lambertuskerk** by Wolter ter Riele are both 19C.

Stadhuis (Stadhuisplein): The town hall is a modern building (1965–9) with good interior decorations. In front of it stands a monument to freedom by P.Gregoire in memory of World War 2.

Evoluon (1a Noord Brabantlaan): A mushroom-shaped structure built in 1966 for the 75th anniversary of Philips. The building is devoted to science and technology and visitors can themselves take part in experiments. Opening times: Mon.–Fri. 9.30 a.m.–5.30 p.m., Sat. 10 a.m.–5 p.m., Sun. and holidays 12 noon–5 p.m.; closed on 25 Dec. and 1 Jan.

Stedelijk van Abbemuseum (10

Geldrop (Eindhoven), Kasteel

Bilderdijklaan): A museum founded in 1936 by Henri van Abbe, a cigar manufacturer, and built by the architect A.J.Kropholler. It is famous for its collections and exhibitions of 20C art (Cubism, Constructivism, De Stijl, École de Paris, Cobra, Zero, Post Painterly Abstraction, Minimal Art, Conceptual Art, etc.). Opening times: Tues.–Sat. 10 a.m.–5 p.m., Sun. and holidays 1–5 p.m.; closed on 25 Dec. and 1 Jan.

Also worth seeing: The remains of the *former Augustinian monastery of Marienhage* (17C). A 15C *church tower* by the graveyard.

Environs: Asten (24 km. E.): The massive 19C church of *Onze-Lieve-Vrouw Presentatie* has a fine carillon, stained-glass windows by Landij and a richly carved pulpit. The attractive *upright mill* (1506) in Molenstraat was restored in 1975. There are three museums at 23 Ostaderstraat: the *Nationaal Beiaardmuseum* (a bell museum, open from 10 a.m.–5 p.m. daily except Mon.), a *nature studies centre* and the *Museum Jan Vriends*

(natural history collection). The *De Grote Peel nature reserve* to the S. of Asten is in a strangely monochrome moorland which can be traversed on log bridges such as were used by the ancient Romans. The history of peat-cutting is depicted in the Mijl op Zeven visitors' centre.

Bergeyk (15 km. SW): Village in the Kempenland amidst pine woods, rye fields and moors. Bronze Age *burial mounds*. The *former Roman Catholic church* has one of the oldest bell towers in the Netherlands. Next to it there is a small *Dutch Reform church* of 1812. A *windmill* dates back to 1363 in its original form.

Eersel (14 km. SW): One of the oldest villages in the Netherlands; it is also one of the eight villages whose names end in '-sel', which thus became known as 'The Eight Delights'. The other seven are Duizel, Hulsel, Knegsel, Netersel, Reusel, Steensel and Wintersel (Wintelre). The *Mariakapel* (1464), used as town hall until 1957, stands in the Kempen (market place) which has old linden trees and a stone pump. The *Roman Catholic church* has a

Eindhoven, Evoluon

splendid tower (*c.* 1400) with diagonally matched arched buttresses.

Geldrop (6 km. E.): The *Kasteel Geldrop*, in the Mierloseweg, stands in the middle of a landscaped English garden which is open to the public. The castle (1616) is partly surrounded by a moat. *St.-Brigidakerk* (1891) by the architect C.Weber has a large dome and two towers. The *local museum* has prehistoric utensils and objects. The *windmill* (1864) was restored in 1969/70.

Heeze (10 km. SE): The oldest section of the *castle*, a long building with stepped gables, was built in the 16C on older foundations. The main building is by Pieter Post (*c.* 1665). The rooms have attractive wall tapestries and other decorations. Guided tours are held at 2 p.m. on Wed. and Sat. from Mar. to Oct.

Nuenen (7 km. NW): Vincent van Gogh (1853–90) lived here from Dec. 1883 to Nov. 1885. A memorial stone by the sculptor Hildo Krop was set up here in 1932 in memory of Van Gogh's stay. The *Van Gogh study centre* was opened in 1976. Van Gogh's father preached in the simple

Dutch Reform church (1824). The priest's house behind it, particularly van Gogh's studio, has been restored to its state of about 1884.

Oost-, West- and Middelbeers (15 km. W.): A 14C *tower* is the only remnant in *Oostelbeers* of the former village. *Westelbeers* has a small *chapel of the Virgin Mary* (1637), built to offer prayers against the plague. The *Romanesque-Gothic church* in *Middelbeers* has been completely restored.

Weert (29 km. SE): Archaeological finds have proved that this region in the Limburg province was settled at an early date, although Weert was not mentioned in documents until 1062. It is still possible to see where the former ditches around the town lay. The tomb of Count van Hoorne, the ruler of Weert, who was beheaded in Brussels in 1568 together with Count van Egmond, can be found in the late Gothic *St.-Martinuskerk,* a 15&16C hall church. The *Franciscan monastery* church was consecrated in 1526. Most of the monastery buildings are 18C. The 15C *castle* was damaged in 1702 in the War of Spanish Succession and only ruins survive.

Elburg, Vischpoort, fishermen's gate

Emmen, Dutch Reform church

The *Museum De Tiendschuur* has objects associated with the town's history.

Elburg
Geldern   p.287☐L 4

A town on the Veluwesee lake with a rectangular grid of streets. Formerly a Hanseatic port, it was rebuilt further inland in 1396 after repeated flooding.

St.-Nicolaaskerk: Probably early 15C. Inside there are wall paintings and a pretty choir screen. 16C decorations.

Huis van Arent toe Boecop: Dating from 1396, it was the town hall 1400–1953.

Stadhuis: The present town hall occupies the monastery of St.Agnes founded in 1418 and consisting of two tall wings at right angles to one another. The building also houses a *museum* of silver and old weapons and an *organ museum*.

Emmen, farmhouse

Vischpoort: The fishermen's gate (1592), a part of the old town wall,– survives in good condition. Today there is a *museum of fishery* in the building.

Emmen
Drente   p.287☐O 3

Emmen is the largest community in Drente. Since World War 2 it has developed into an important industrial centre and can boast of a number of interesting examples of modern architecture.

Megalithic tombs: The tomb on the *Schimmeresch*, the finest of the eleven megalithic tombs in the town, is quite long with two burial chambers inside an elliptical ring of stones. More megalithic tombs are to be found on the way to Odoorn, in the Emmerdennen by the railway line, in Angelslo, on the way to Erm, and in Westenesch.

Oudheidkamer 'De Hondrsrug'

(17 Marktplein): A farm dating from 1865 with exhibits of local historical interest, prehistoric finds, costumes, and pewter objects. Opening times: Apr., May and Sept. Wed.–Sat. 10 a.m.–12 noon and 1–5 p.m., Sun. 1–5 p.m.; June–Aug. Mon.–Sat. 10 a.m.–12 noon and 1–5 p.m., Sun. 1–5 p.m.

Also worth seeing: The *Dutch Reform church* (1856) has a 12C tower. A *neolithic bridge* for crossing the moor and consisting of a 10 ft. wide path built of logs, has been discovered in the SE of the town near *Nieuw-Dordrecht*. There is a *Bronze Age burial mound* near *Weerdinge*.

Environs: Aalden (12.5 km. W.): This well-preserved village has a village square surrounded by oaks and thirteen farmsteads. *Hol-An* a farmhouse (1668) in *Oud-Aalden is splendid*. In the *Aalder-es* there is an octagonal *corn mill* (1891).
Berger-Compascuum (12 km. E.): The *moorland museum village of "'t Aole Compas'* (4 Berkenrode) is an open-air museum with mud huts. An example of a village in the moor, it has a barn church, a graveyard and paved paths across the moor, etc. Opening times: the week before Easter–Oct. 9 a.m.–6 p.m. daily; Nov.–week before Easter: 9 a.m.–5 p.m. daily.
Exloo (14 km. N.): Furnishings and turf-cutting utensils are on display in the *'Bebinghehoes' farm museum* (8 Zuiderhoofdstraat), a farmhouse of 1722 set amid tall trees. Opening times: June–Aug. Mon.–Fri. 8.30 a.m.–12.15 p.m. and 1.30–5.30 p.m.; Sept.–May Mon.–Fri. 9.30 a.m.–12 noon and 1–4.30 p.m.; 15 May–31 Aug. open on Saturdays too from 1.30–5 p.m.
Oosterhesselen (14 km. W.): The unattached tower of the *Dutch Reform church* was built in the second half of the 15C. The *De Klencke farm* is an 18C country house with a Louis XIV. The best of the splendid *farmhouses* are those at 12, 29 and 42 Burgem. de Kockstraat. Some of them still

timber-framed decorations with infillings of wicker-work and clay.
Schoonoord (13 km. NW): *'De Papeloze Kerk'*, a megalithic grave on the way to Sleen has been restored to its original condition. The *'De Zeven Marken* open-air museum (73 Tramstraat) has reconstructed 17C moorworkers' huts. Opening times: Palm Sunday–Oct. 9 a.m.–5 p.m. daily.
Sleen (9 km. W.): *Two megalithic tombs* and the *'De Galgenberg' burial mound* from the Bronze Age. The *Dutch Reform church* (c. 1400) has a nave and two aisles with rib vaults, an unusual design for Drente. The choir was probably increased in height in c. 1500. The tower was given a new pointed spire in 1922–3. Prehistoric finds are on display in the *'De Deel' museum* in a farm (6 M.Altingstraat). Opening times: Easter–Oct. Mon.–Sun. 10 a.m.–12 noon and 2–4 p.m.
Zweeloo (11 km. W.): The attractive mid-13C *Dutch Reform church* has a ridge turret with oak shingles. Vincent van Gogh drew the church. Interesting *farmhouses* (18 Kruisstraat, 11 Hoofdstraat and 17–19 Klooster).

Enkhuizen
North Holland   p.286☐I 3

In 1355, Count Willem V united two villages to form the town of Enkhuizen. Once prosperous the town gradually fell into decline due to a combination of factors including the silting of the harbour, the growing dominance of Amsterdam and the destruction of the herring-fishing fleet in 1625. At its peak the town had over 25,000 inhabitants; after 1636 the figure had dwindled to 6,000, partly owing to an outbreak of plague.

Zuider- or St.-Pancraskerk: A two-aisled late Gothic hall church probably begun about 1423 when the S. choir was built. Work on the tower began in 1450; its exhuberant top

Enkhuizen, St.-Pancraskerk

Enkhuizen, gate of Dromedaris

dates from 1518–26 (the Hémony carillon originally had 35 bells, a further 10 were added later). The wooden vaults above the two aisles have remnants of paintwork dating from 1484; these had been painted over in the 17C and only came to light in 1903–14.

Westerkerk or **St.-Gommarus-kerk:** A spacious hall church (built in 3 phases during the 15C and early 16C) with a nave and two aisles, each of which has a striking apse. The belfry (1519), with its 19C neoclassical wooden facing, stands in the E, separated from the church by the sacristan's lodging which has a stepped gable (1600). Inside: splendid *choir screen* of 1542 with good carvings, *pulpit* (1567–8) with John the Baptist and the four Evangelists. The *library* has early-17C decorations and 400 theological works.

Stadhuis: The town hall (1686–8) has a sandstone façade by Steven Vennecool from Amsterdam. This unique example of 17C Dutch architecture has hardly been altered either internally or externally. Inside there are a large citizens' hall and a mayor's room with a fine door. Ceiling paintings by Dirk Ferreris, a local artist. A rather picturesque *prison building* (1612) stands behind the town hall.

Fortifications: The only part of the early-16C fortifications to have survived is the *Dromedaris* (1540), a round building with a gate. Its height was increased in 1649. Formerly used as a prison, cells are still visible. Two small water gates, *Boerenboom* and *Oude Gouwsboom*, survive from the town's new ramparts built in 1595–1600 under the supervision of Adriaan Anthonisz. The *Wester-* or *Koepoort* (1649) at the end of the

Enkhuizen, open-air museum

Nieuwe Westerstraat was given its present roof and domed turret in 1730.

Waag: An early Renaissance building of 1559. The figures on the eaves represent Justice, Belief, Hope, Love and Strength.

Museum van Historische en Moderne Wappens (Zwaanstraat): A former prison (1612), with exhibits ranging from stone mallets to modern weapons. Opening times: By arrangement with the VVV (tourist office).

Stedelijk Waagmuseum (Kaasmarkt): Features of this small museum in the weigh-house are the Chirurgijnskamer, the weighing-scales department, cheese presses, and cheese baskets. Opening times: Tues.–Sat. 10 a.m.–12 noon and 2–5 p.m., Sun. 2–5 p.m.

Rijks Zuiderzeemuseum (18 Wierdijk): A fine museum accommodated in the picturesque 'Peperhuis' storehouse (1616) of the East India Company, and also in other old houses. There are two departments: the Binnenmuseum and the Buitenmuseum. The Binnenmseum has old fishing boats, costumes, furniture, paintings, and models of ships. The Buitenmuseum (reached by steamer from the car park of the Lelystad-Enkhuizen dyke) consists of streets and alleys with 130 houses, including a house for smoking fish, a sailmaker's, a leather tannery and a lime kiln. The museum demonstrates village life over a period of some 100 years up until 1932, when the Zuiderzee was completed. The houses on display come from the mud flats, the Zuiderzee, the harbour of Marken, the church of Den Oever, an alleyway from Zoutkamp, houses from Urk and

Enschede, Dutch Reform church

Marken, and a cheese warehouse from Landsmeer.

Opening times: Binnenmuseum: Mid-Feb.–31 Dec. Mon.–Sat. 10 a.m.–5 p.m., Sun. and holidays 12 noon–5 p.m. Buitenmuseum: Mid-Apr.–mid-Oct. 10 a.m.–5 p.m. daily.

Enschede
Overijssel   p.287☐O 5

The town received a charter in 1325. The great fire of 1862 destroyed most of the old town. Enschede experienced an economic revival when textile manufacturing was industrialized.

Dutch Reform church: Rebuilt in the original style after the fire of 1862. The present design dates originally from 1480 when the Romanesque structure (*c.* 1200) was enlarged, and from 1842 when it was converted into a hall structure. The lowest storey of the tower is late Romanesque and dates from the early 13C; the three subsequent storeys are from the second half of the 13C.

St.-Jacobskerk: A stately building of 1933 with Romanesque and Gothic features.

Raadhuis: The town hall (1930–3) by G.Friedhoff shows the influence of Swedish architecture.

Natuurhistorisch Museum (2 De Ruyterlaan): Devoted to flora and fauna from Twente, the E. part of Overijssel. Opening times: Tues.–Sat. 10 a.m.–12.30 p.m. and 1.30–5 p.m., Sun. and holidays 2–5 p.m.

Pinetum 'De Horstlanden' (Tech-

nical College, Drienerloo): Conifers from Europe, America and Asia. Opening times: 9 a.m.–5 p.m. daily.

Rijksmuseum Twente (129 Lasondersingel): Medieval religious art and paintings by great painters like Memling, Lucas Cranach the Elder, Ruysdael and van Goyen. Collection of 19C animal paintings. Opening times: Tues.–Sat. 9 a.m.–1 p.m. and 2–5 p.m., Sun. and holidays 2–5 p.m.

Twents Textielindustriemuseum (Jannink complex on corner of Haaksbergenstraat and Industriestraat): Equipment ranging from old peasants' implements to the machines used in today's textile industry; also textiles and lace. Opening times: Tues.–Sat. 10 a.m.–12 noon and 2–5 p.m., Sun. 2–5 p.m.

Also worth seeing: The *Elderinkshuis* (1783), 35 De Klomp, was one of the few houses to survive the fire of 1862. The *Jewish synagogue* (16 Prinsestraat) is one of the finest in Europe. The bronze war memorial of 1953 can be seen in the people's park.

Environs: Losser: (8 km. E.): A village by the river Dinkel. The parish church (*c.* 1500) with its saddleback roof has been torn down, and only the *tower* survives. Nearby there are some old *houses* and *farmsteads*.

Ezinge

Groningen   p.287☐N 2

Ezinge occupies a terp 16 ft. high. Excavations in 1931–4 revealed the remains of foundations of houses dating from *c.* 700–600 BC– 1300.

Dutch Reform church: The single-aisled church and the free-standing saddleback tower are both 13C. The church walls are now back in their original state thanks to the radical restoration work completed in 1959.

Also worth seeing: The *Huize Allersma*, in a charming location surrounded by canals consists of a single-storeyed S. wing (15C) and a two-storeyed E. wing added in the E. (18C).

Environs: Niehove (4 km. S.): The simple early-13C *Dutch Reform church*, which is a long building, stands in the middle of the village.
Oldehove (3 km. S.): The N. façade is the best-preserved part of the originally 13C *Dutch Reform church*. The general appearance of the village is characterized by the stately 15C *church tower* and the two mills, the larger '*De Leeuw' mill* (1855) and the '*Aeolus' mill* (1846).
Saaksum (2 km. W.): A *Dutch Reform church* (1850) by D.H. Bos, the town architect from Groningen. The saddleback roof (1550) survives in a not entirely unaltered state.

Franeker, Stadhuis, portal

Franeker/Frjentsjer

Friesland p.286□K 2

History: There was a settlement in Franeker in *c.* 1085 and ramparts were built around it in *c.* 1200. Franeker, an influential centre in the Middle Ages, was granted a charter in 1417. As a university town in the 16&17C, Franeker was the cultural and scientific centre of Friesland, as well as being a stronghold of Friesian Calvinism. The university was founded in 1585. Its status was lowered by Napoleon, and it was finally closed in 1843.

Dutch Reform Martinikerk: A large basilican structure (probably *c.* 1420) with a nave, two aisles, an ambulatory and a tall tower. It has four Gothic choir benches from the late 15C and a large number of tombstones of university professors.

Stadhuis: A fine Renaissance building, and one of the best examples of the national style developing in the Netherlands around 1600. Built in 1591–4, it was restored in 1885 and has three stepped gables and an elegant turret. A rich façade with a traditional statue of the Goddess of

Franeker, gable stone,
Korendragershuisje ▷

Justice and shields with coats-of-arms. A fine staircase outside.
Opening times: Mon.–Fri. 9 a.m.–12 noon and 2–4 p.m.

Korendragershuisje (28 Eise Eisingastraat): This corn porters' house was built in 1634 for the guild of corn porters' founded in 1557. Above the door there is a fine relief with a corn measure.

Martenahuis (35 Voorstraat): Built in 1498, the house has a tall octagonal staircase tower and is the only dwelling-tower (stins) in the town to have survived in good condition. Until 1983 it was the administrative office for the urban disrict of Franekeradeel.

Museums
Planetarium (3 Eise Eisengastraat): The planetarium (a means of projecting the image of the night sky) stands opposite the town hall and is the town's great pride and its chief item of interest. It was built 1774–81 by Eise Eisenga, wool-comber and later astronomer, behind his house and is still fully operational. Opening times: 1 Jan.–1 May: and 1 Sept.–1 Jan.: Tues.–Sat. 10 a.m.–12.30 and 1.30–5 p.m.; 1 May–1 Sept.: Mon.–Sat. 10 a.m.–12.30 p.m. and 1.30–5 p.m.

't Coopmanshûs (49 Voorstraat): This former professor's house has many exhibits relating to the university along with documents concerning the town's history. There are also paper cuttings, embroideries and other items of craftwork by Anna Maria van Schuurman, one of the most famous learned women of the time. In the senate room there are numerous portraits of professors.
Opening times: 1 May–1 Oct.: Tues.–Sat. 10 a.m.–12 noon and 1.30–5 p.m.; 1 Oct.–1 May: Sat. 11 a.m.–4 p.m.

Fries Munten en Penningkabinet (12a Voorstraat): A collection in the

◁ *Tzum (Franeker), church tower*

late medieval *Camminghahuis*, showing the coins minted in Friesland from the 7C to the 18C.
Opening times: 1 May–30 Sept. Mon.–Fri. 1–5 p.m.

Also worth seeing: The beautiful medieval *Botniahuis* in the Breede Plaats was formerly a charitable foundation for orphans. The *Camminghahuis* in Voorstraat dates from the mid 15C/early 16C. 't *Coopmanshuis* (18C) is one of the many former university professors' houses. 'Bogt van Guné' is one of the oldest surviving students' inns.

Environs: Achlum (5 km. S.): The 17C decorations of the 12C *Dutch Reform church* survive almost in their entirety. The *Groot Deersum*, a farmstead surrounded by a canal, is some 2 km. outside the village (leaving the village via the Stinspoort which has stepped gables on both sides).
Firdgum/Furdgum (5 km. N.): A tall slender *saddleback tower* (probably 13C) stands solitary in the *churchyard*. The church was torn down in 1794.
Sexbierum/Seisbierum (5 km. W.): The rococo decorations in the 13C *Dutch Reform church* include a sumptuous carved pulpit by Johannes Goerg Hempel (1768). The pulpit and abat-voix have Biblical decorations and are supported by two branches which grow out of a stem. The Friesian admiral Tsjerk Hidde de Vries, killed in the two-day naval battle against the English in 1666 and buried in Harlingen, was born in the *house at 3 Alde Buorren*, which has a pretty relief in the façade. The *church* and the *Liauckama estate* were the only buildings spared when the village was pillaged by the Normans. The estate was torn down in 1824 and only a 17C entrance gate has survived.
Tzum (4 km. S.): This village has a sturdy late Gothic *tower* (*c.* 1548), which at some 236 ft. high is one of the tallest towers in Friesland.

Geertruidenberg
North Brabant   p.290☐H 6

Probably the oldest town in Holland, Geertruidenberg was granted a charter in 1213. The town has had a turbulent history including outbreaks

Geertruidenberg, St.Geertruidskerk

of fire, the flood of St.Elizabeth (which severed the town's connection with Dordrecht), and fighting with Spanish troops in the Eighty Years' War. The fortress was taken by Maurice of Orange in 1593 after a siege.

St.-Geertruidskerk: Standing near the market this church is the town's finest building. It became a collegiate church in 1310 and takes the form of a hall church with a nave and two aisles. The massive N. tower dates back to the 14C, although the upper storey was lost in the siege of 1593.

Stadhuis: The town hall near the market dates from the Middle Ages but was given a completely new façade in Louis XV style in 1768. Fine black fireplace (1624) in the mayor's room.

Gieten
Drente   p.287☐O 3

Dutch Reform church: Stands at the S. end of the village green. The tower dates from 1804, the nave from 1849. 17C pulpit and a beautifully carved memorial plaque to Nicolaas Harm Echten (d. 1742).

Also worth seeing: Exhibitions in *Klein Hilbingshof*, a farmhouse (No. 2 Bonne). The '*Hazewind*' mill (1883). '*Eendracht*' (1904).

Environs: Gasselte (3 km. S.): This pretty village with a village green is documented from the 14C along with its small *church*, which was altered in 1787 & 1851 and is now roughcast in white.

Giethoorn
Overijssel   p.287☐M 3

Founded in *c*. 1280 by a sect of flagel-

lants, the village is notable for an unusually large number of waterways (even for Holland) and innumerable bridges. Little lakes and ditches were formed by random digging for peat which was then transported along the waterways.

Dutch Reform church: A wooden bell tower (1633) stands beside the simple village church.

Museum De Oude Aarde (43 Binnenpad): Exhibits include minerals, semi-precious stones and crystals. There are also iguanas, tortoises and exotic birds. Opening times: 10 a.m.–5.30 p.m. daily. Closed on Wed. 1 Oct.–1 May.

Museum De Speelman (123 Binnenpad): Old instruments, particularly for street entertainment. Opening times: 21 Mar.–1 Nov. daily: 10 a.m.–6 p.m.; 1 Nov.–21 Mar.: 11 a.m.–5 p.m. during the school holidays only.

Events: Illuminated punts pass through the canals on the last Saturday evening in August.

Environs: Wanneperveen (4 km. SE): A moorland village. The *Schultenhuis*, an early-17C house, has a fine stepped gable. In the churchyard near the Dutch Reform church (1502) there is an oak bell tower. Many *Saxon farmhouses* in the surrounding area.

Goes
Zeeland   p.288☐E 7

The main town of Zuid Beveland which comprises the water sports centre of Wolphaartsdijk on Lake Veerse, the dyke village of Kattendijke on the Oosterschelde, Kloetinge with a picturesque village square and

Gieten, 'Hazewind' mill ▷

streets lined with linden trees, and 's Heer Arendskerke.

Grote or Maria Magdalenakerk: Dating from the second half of 15C/first half of 16C this cruciform basilica was built in Brabant-Gothic style; no tower. The organ dates from 1643.

Stadhuis: The Gothic town hall was originally built in 1463 and much altered 1771–5. The old tower has survived but with a new octagonal crown. Rich rococo decorations. The council chamber has fine panelling and a stuccoed ceiling.

Museum voor Zuid- en Noord-Beveland (13 Singelstraat): Housed in the former orphanage (16C); exhibits relate to the region's history. Opening times: Tues.–Sat. 10 a.m.–12 noon and 1.30–5 p.m.

Also worth seeing: The Gothic *Vleeshal* (meat hall) and *old houses*, (mainly in the *market square* and *Turfkade*).

Wanneperveen (Giethorn), Schultenhuis

Environs: Baarland (10 km. S.): The foundations of *Kasteel Hellenburg* were excavated and made safe in 1958 and the castle is now open to the public. It would seem that the castle developed from a residential tower built probably by Jan van Renesse in the early 14C. In the 15C the castle had eight towers, three of which are the round towers on the E. side. The storm flood of 1477 led to the castle's decline.

Colijnsplaat (12 km. N.): A town in the Oosterschelde very near the Seeland bridge. The district includes the village of Kortgene on Lake Veerse which has a small 17C church. The *main street* of Colijnsplaat is lined with linden trees and is typical of the Seeland islands. The village ends at the ferry house on the dyke side and on the land side at the church.

The old *mill* is still regularly in operation.

Chapel (8 km. SE): The *church of the Virgin Mary* (Onze-Lieve-Vrouwekerk) has an early 14C choir; the rest was built in the 2nd half of the 14C and in the 15C.

Goor, Kasteel Weldam

Kruiningen (12 km. SE): This town on the S. coast of Zuid-Beveland is the departure point for the ferry across the Westerschelde to Perkpolder in Zeeuws-Vlaanderen. Nearby is the Den Inkel nature reserve.

Interesting buildings include the medieval *church* and the mills '*De Hoed*' and '*De Oude Molen*'.

Wemeldinge (10 km. NE): This village with a beautiful wide main street and linden trees has one of the few surviving early medieval *terpen* in Zuid-Beveland. (A terp is a manmade hill for refuge in storm floods.) The *Dutch Reform church*, restored in 1898, has a late-14C tower and choir.

Wolphaartsdijk (6 km. NW): The *Dutch Reform church* (1861) by H.Hana and J.Smits has a tower on the façade; fine example of the 'Waterstaatsstijl' style.

church was built here in *c*. 800 and demolished in 1581 after a devastating fire. The present late Gothic building (*c*. 1600) is single aisled and was rebuilt and enlarged in the 19C. The 15C tower survives.

Kasteel Weldam: This castle developed from a farmstead (1568) in around 1645, when it was acquired by Johan Ripperda and his wife Sophia Margaretha van Raesfelt. The two small projecting wings and the main building have beautiful chimneys. Two late-19C towers at the rear. The fine garden is by Hugo Poortman (1886).

Also worth seeing: Many *country houses* nearby, most of which were formerly farms. The white 16C *Huize Heeckeren* was once a stronghold of the Bishop of Utrecht and the bailiffs of Twente.

Goor
Overijssel   p.287□N 5

Dutch Reform church: A parish

Gorinchem
South Holland   p.290□H 6

Gorinchem (abbreviated to Gorkum),

an old fortified town on the border between South Holland on the one side and Gelderland and North Brabant on the other, was one of the first towns to be liberated from Spanish rule (1572). The old inner town is surrounded by ramparts and bastions, most of which are still intact.

Dutch Reform church: The tower of St.Jans, built in 1517 and 197 ft. tall, is all that survives of the old parish church. The enormous church itself dates from 1845.

Bethlehemshuis (25 Gasthuisstraat): The '*Dit is in Bethlehem*' *museum* is housed in this Renaissance building with an ornate gable (1566). Opening times: Wed.–Sun. 2–5 p.m.. Closed on 25 Dec. and 1 Jan.

Dalempoort: The only gate to have survived in the 16C town walls.

Gorinchem, corn mill

De Doelen (Molenstraat): 16C house with two wings with saddle roofs and stepped gables. At the back of the house there is a slender hexagonal turret with onion dome.

Matthijs-Marijke house (Molenstraat): Above the entrance there is a striking Renaissance frieze of Christ among orphans; coats-of-arms.

Also worth seeing: Two 18C *corn mills* on the ramparts. The *town pump* of 1607 in Pompstraat.

Gouda
South Holland   p.289□H 5

This town, situated where the Gouwe flows into the Hollandse IJssel, has always been an important centre for trade. It was granted a charter in

1272. The town is famous for its cheese.

St.-Janskerk: A late Gothic cruciform basilica with chapels, it is the longest church in the Netherlands with a nave 405 ft. long. The original 13C building was damaged several times in town fires; only the choir was left undamaged in the fire of 1552. Reconstruction was supervised by Cornelis Frederiksz. Of the church's 70 *stained glass windows,* 13 are the work of the brothers Dirk and Wouter Crabeth (1555–71). The windows were donated by wealthy parishioners as their contribution to the church's reconstruction. Various Dutch towns also presented the church with windows in the Protestant period after 1572. The most recent window is by Charles Eyck (1947). The choir screen (1778–82), in marble and brass, has an ornate gable. The organ

Gouda, Stadhuis, detail ▷

(1733–6) is one of the richest-sounding in Holland. The church is open to the public Mon.–Sat. 9 a.m.–5 p.m. (1 Nov.–1 Mar.: 10 a.m.–4 p.m.).

St.-Barbarakapel: The tower of this small former chapel (16C) in Kuiperstraat has interesting patterns in brick and stone. The chapel was rebuilt in 1635.

Jeruzalemkapel: A twelve-sided chapel behind the choir of St.-Janskerk; stone stellar vault (*c.* 1496).

Stadhuis: Today's town hall is a free-standing building in the market place. Built 1448–59 on the site of a previous 13C building, it has a fine gabled façade; the side gables are 19C reconstructions. The 15C architect was Jan III Keldermans who was one of a famous family of architects and sculptors active in the Netherlands from the 14C to the early 16C. On the left side of the building there is a set of mechanical figures surrounding the town coat-of-arms (Count Floris of Gouda is shown conferring the town's charter every half hour—an event which actually occurred in 1772); above this is a clock. A stone scaffold survives at the back of the town hall (the former wooden scaffolds in other towns have all disappeared). Opening times: Mon.–Fri. 9 a.m.–12 noon and 2–4 p.m.

Waaghuis: The weigh-house (1668) in the large triangular market-place behind the town hall is a delightful little building by Pieter Post. An interesting relief above the front entrance shows goods being weighed.

Weeshuis (Spieringstraat): This orphanage has a lovely curved gable (1643); above the entrance there is a coat-of-arms with figures of a man and woman.

Stedelijk Museum 'Het Catharina Gasthuis' (32 Achter de Kerk): The museum is housed in the restored hospice of St.Catherine (1665) and the adjoining chapel (*c.* 1400). Exhibits include paintings of huntsmen and civic officials, a collection of 19C paintings, paintings by Paul Citroen (a Bauhaus artist) and a

Gouda, Waaghuis, relief

reproduction of the town dispensary as it was *c.* 1669. Opening times: Mon.–Sat. 10 a.m.–5 p.m., Sun. and holidays 12 noon–5 p.m.

Also worth seeing: The Fundatie van Christina Ghysberts (1625) and the Fundatie van Cornelis Cing (1700) are two *foundations for old people* in Nieuwe Haven. The *tower of the Virgin Mary* (Onze-Lieve-Vrouwetoren) dates back to *c.* 1490. The *Vismarkt* consists of two 17C wooden colonnaded halls.

Environs: Bodegraven (8 km. N.): This little town on the Oude Rijn, documented as *Bodelo* in 1018, is a centre of trade in cheese (there is a cheese market every Tuesday). The late Gothic *church* was burned down in 1672 when the French invaded but has since been rebuilt. *Paardenburgh,* a fine old farm can be seen on the way to the village of Zwammerdam.

Haastrecht (9 km. E.): This pretty town situated where the Vlist flows into the Hollandse IJssel was dominated by the Bisdom van Vliet family for many years. The family's elegant house at 166 Hoogstraat is now a *museum* with 19C decorations and a porcelain collection. Opening hours: Tues.–Thur. and Sat. 10 a.m.–4 p.m., Sun. 2–5 p.m. The lower part of the 15C *Dutch Reform church* is early Gothic. The delicate wooden church spire was rebuilt in 1964 after a fire. The ruins of *te Vliet castle*, on the way to Oudewater, include medieval walls.

Ouderkerk aan de IJssel (8 km. SW): The single-aisled *Dutch Reform church* is one of the oldest in the province of South Holland, parts of it dating from 12C. The stone portal has a coat-of-arms on the gable.

Woerden (20 km. NE): Situated on the Oude Rijn in an area devoted to crop growing. The town was granted a charter by Albrecht van Beiren in 1372; the *former Kasteel*, founded by Jan van Beieren in 1407, is now a military store. The ground floor of the former *town hall* dates from 1501, while the upper storeys were built in Renaissance style in 1614. There is a stone pillory on the right corner of the main façade. The '*De Windhond*' *mill* can be turned to catch the wind.

Haastrecht (Gouda), museum

Woerden (Gouda), windmill

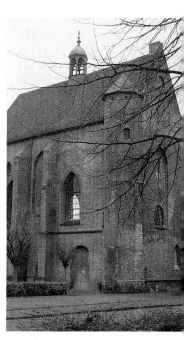

Grave, Dutch Reform church

Grave

North Brabant   p.291 □ L 6

This old fortified town on the river Maas stands in the middle of countryside typical of South Holland. Today it is known for the dam built when the river was canalized. The settlement, of strategic importance in the Roman period, developed into a village in the 13C.

St.-Elisabethkerk: This *Roman Catholic church*, parts of which are late Gothic, has splendid carved wooden figures and a marble sarcophagus.

Dutch Reform church: Formerly a chapel belonging to the Franciscan convent, this small 15C building has a staircase tower on the W. façade.

Also worth seeing: The 16/17C *town hall* and *museum* are now part of the modern civic centre. The market place has a late-18C stone *pump* with Louis XVI motifs. The *Hampoort* (1688) is all that remains of the old fortification.

Environs: Beers (8 km. SE): Since 1940, this town has been notorious for flooding frequently by the Beerse overflow, a lower section of the Maas. A memorial commemorating the floods can be seen on the road from Beers to Cuijk. The tower is the only 15C part of the *Roman Catholic church* (many niches) to have survived. The top storey of the tower has been rebuilt.

Ravenstein (8 km. NW): This little town grew up around the Kasteel van Walraven van Valkenburg. Until the French period it was an independent territory subordinated to the Electors

Grave, St.Elisabethskerk

The Hague, St.-Jacobskerk, tower

of Palatinate-Neuburg. The *Roman Catholic St.-Luciakerk* (1735) has an octagonal tower. The *oldest tower in Brabant* dating from the 10C can be seen in the hamlet of *Neerlangel*.

's-Gravenhage/Den Haag/ The Hague

South Holland   p.288☐F 5

The Hague is the capital of the province of South Holland, the seat of the government and the residence of the Royal Family.

History: The first important building in The Hague was called 's-Gravenhage (the count's hedge), a hunting lodge belonging to the counts of Holland. In 1248 Wilhelm II built a castle which his successors expanded into the present building.

The town then developed around the castle. The town's economic upswing began in the late 14C when the judiciary moved from Holland and Zeeland to The Hague. Maurice of Orange (1567–1625) chose The Hague as his residence and from this time on it was the seat of the stadholders and the government. The States General, the assembly of delegates from the provinces, met here 1584–1795. The Hague was granted a civic charter by Louis Bonaparte, brother of Napoleon, who moved the seat of government to Amsterdam (and back to The Hague in 1813). At around the turn of the century, the town became important as a conference centre and the headquarters of many institutions (among them the Academy of International Law and the International Court of Justice of the United Nations). Today it is a beautiful city, liberally provided with parks and numerous cultural institutions, and a centre of political life. Scheveningen, Voorburg and Rijswijk are now suburbs of the Hague.

Religious buildings
Grote or St.-Jacobskerk (Kerkplein): Originally 14C, this hall church assumed its present appearance after the fire of 1539. The hexagonal tower, almost 330 ft. tall, and the large carillon of bells (some 51) all date from 1959. The carved wooden pulpit dates from 1550. Many monuments.

Kloosterkerk (2 Lange Vorhout): An early-15C church.

Nieuwe Kerk (173a Spui): Built 1649–65 by Pieter Noorwits in harmony with the architectural ideas of Hendrick de Keyser, whose skilful construction of rafters (where there are no supports inside the building) turned the original nave into a completely centralized spatial formation.

Schuilkerk (13 Juffr. Idastraat and 38 Molenstraat): A Catholic church of

1722 with fine baroque interior decoration.

Evang. Lutherse Kerk (8 Lutherse Burgwal), 18C church.

Secular buildings
Oude Stadhuis: Dating from 1564/5 the old town hall on the corner of Kerkplein/Groenmarkt was one of the first Renaissance buildings in North Holland to have been built under the influence of Antwerp town hall. The upper of the two main storeys, which are of equal value architecturally, is articulated by decorative fluted pilasters. In the middle of the roof there is a tall oriel window, crowned by a gable. The *former court room* on the ground floor has the original bench for the jury and three allegorical depictions (1671). A large wing in Louis XIV style was added on the side overlooking the church square in 1733.

Binnenhof (Stadhouderslaan): Composed of the *Ridderzaal*, dating from 1230, the *Rolzaal*, with late-Romanesque windows and dating from

Den Haag, Hoge Raad building

1511 and the *Lairessezaal*, so-called because of the seven linen paintings (1688) by Gerard de Lairesse (author of 'Het groot Schilderboek': 'The great book of painters'). The Ridderzaal, the Gothic knights' hall, is flanked by two round towers and was built under Count Floris V (1256–96). When restoration was carried out during the last century, side façades were given battlements and turrets, probably in accordance with the original building. Today the hall with its impressive wooden ceiling is used for ceremonies such as the proclamation of the States General on the third Tuesday in September (Prinsjesdag), when the Queen makes a speech from the throne.

Around the knights' hall there are many government buildings which in times past served other functions, e.g. the former Goud- en Zilversmidsgildehuis which has a narrow 17C gable. The *Grenadierspoort* on the E. side (giving access to the Mauritshuis), a fine brick building (1634) with massive sandstone ashlars around gateway, is just one of the innumerable doors and gates in the inner courtyard. In the W., the Buitenhof precedes the inner courtyard, linked by a Renaissance gate known as the Stadhouderspoort. Opening times: Mon.–Sat. 10 a.m.–4 p.m., closed on Sun.; July and Aug., Mon.–Sat. 9 a.m.–4 p.m.

Gevangenpoort (Buitenhof): In the 15C a prison was built on to this 14C gatehouse which has a vaulted passage. The resulting simple building has a plate stepped gable and now houses a *historical museum*, whose exhibits include old instruments of torture (see Museums).

Huis ten Bosch (Haagse Bos, Bezuidenhoutseweg): In 1645 Pieter Post built this castle (in the middle of a forested area in the town) for Amalia of Solms, who turned it into a monument to the stadholder Friedrich Heinrich, her dead husband. The main façade is articulated by pilasters. In 1734–7, the palace was altered by Daniel Marot. The addition of the two side wings in 1751 considerably altered the orignal character. The *Hall of Orange* was decorated with

Paleis Noordeinde with statue of William I of Orange

paintings glorifying her husband based on sketches by Jaob van Campen. The largest picture, showing the Triumph of the Prince, is by Jacob Jordaens. In all ten painters worked on the room.

Former Koninklijke Bibliotheek (34 Lange Voorhout): Built in 1734 by Daniel Marot for Adrienne Marguérite de Huguéton, who married Karel of Nassau-Beverweerd five years later. The rich baroque gable façade is dominated by a central section built to a design by J.Baurscheit the younger.

Mauritshuis (29 Plein): The second finest building in the city after the Binnenhof. Begun by Jacob van Campen and Pieter Post in 1633, the front has a large pilaster order uniting the two main storeys above the ground floor. The central part of the ground floor has pilasters and window frames in ashlars which contrast effectively with the dark brick of the main body of the building.

Paleis Noordeinde (Lange Voorhout): The royal palace dates back to 1533; rebuilt in 1640 by Jacob van Campen and Pieter Post, it was enlarged to its present form by King Wilhelm I in 1814. Rebuilt in the old style after a fire in 1948.

Pagehuis (6 Lange Voorhout): One of the many fine patricians' houses in Lange Voorhout, it has a splendid stepped gable. The pages of Wilhelm III, king and stadholder, lived here in the 18C.

Vredespaleis (Carnegieplein): This neo-Gothic palace (1907–13) by L.M. Cordonnier was built to house the Permanent Court of Arbitration whose function was to try to promote peace and suppress war. Today, the *International Court of Justice* (founded in 1920) and the *Academy of International Law* are housed here.

Schilderijenzaal Prins Willem V. (35 Buitenhof): This hall of paintings, decorated as it was in 1774–95, was the first museum in the Netherlands. The walls are entirely covered in paintings, which include the work of

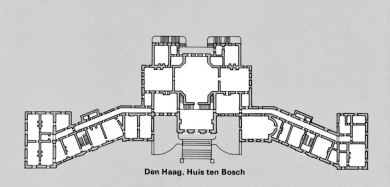

Den Haag, Huis ten Bosch

Rubens, Steen, Potter, Wouwerman, Jordaens, de Vos and many others. Opening times: 11 a.m.–2 p.m. daily. Admission free.

Museums

Museum Bredius (6 Prinsengracht): 17C Dutch paintings, items of decorative art and old porcelain. Opening times: Mon.–Sat. 10 a.m.–5 p.m., Sun. and holidays 1–5 p.m., Wed. 8–10 p.m. also.

Letterkundig Museum (11 Juffr. Idastraat): Documentation and curiosities concerned with Dutch literature.

Koniklijk Kabinet van Schilderijen 'Mauritshuis' (29 Plein): An important collection including works by Vermeer ('View of Delft'), Rembrandt ('Anatomy of Doctor Tulp'), Rubens (portraits of Isabella Brant and Helene Fourment), Holbein the younger, Cranach, Memling, Jordaens and others. Opening times: Mon.–Sat. 10 a.m.–5 p.m., Sun. and holidays 11 a.m.–5 p.m., closed on 1 Jan.

Museum Meermanno Westreenianum (30 Prinsessegracht): This museum is devoted to books, including modern bindings, illustrations and manuscripts, first editions, as well as Egyptian, Greek and Roman finds. Opening times: Mon.–Sat. 1–5 p.m.

Museum Mesdag (Laan van Meerdevoort, No. 7 and following houses): Paintings from the Hague school and the school of Barbizon and works by Corot, Courbet and Israels. Opening times: Mon.–Sat. 10 a.m.–5 p.m., Sun. and holidays 1–5 p.m., closed on 1 Jan.

Museum voor het Onderwijs (2E Hesterhuis): A museum of education with a collection of educational aids for science, technology, biology, ethnology etc.

Oudheidkndig en Visserijmuseum (92 Neptunusstraat): Museum of 19&20C fishing.

Panorama Mesdag (65b Zeestraat): The largest panoramic view in the world, it measures some 18,300 sq.ft.

Schilderijenzaal Prins Willem V.

and, depicts Scheveningen as it was in c. 1880.

Koninklijk Penning-Kabinet (71b Zeestraat): This coin museum has Dutch coins and medals from the Middle Ages to the present; also Greek and Roman coins. Opening times: Mon.–Thur. 10 a.m.–1 p.m. and 2–4 p.m., Sat. 10 a.m.–1 p.m.

Politiemuseum (20 Burg. de Monchyplein): A police museum.

Museum voor het Poppenspel (Nassau Dillenburgstraat): Puppet museum, with historical dolls and puppets. Opening times: Sun. 12 noon–2 p.m.

Also worth seeing: *Hofvijver* (Hofteich): From here there is a wonderful view of the Binnenhof and the Mauritshuis. *Groenmarkt square* and *Plein 1813* (a fine 19C Tudor quarter). *Congrespalast* (1964–8) has a mosaic by Karel Appel. *Grote Marktstraat* with the fantastic 'De Volharding' building (1828) and the *'De Bijenkorf'* (bee-

Gevangenpoort, coat-of-arms at entrance

hive) department store by Piet Kramer (1926).

Districts and suburbs of the town Rijswijk: The expansion of 's-Gravenhage turned the village of Rijswijk into a suburb. Work by artists from Rijswijk can be seen in the *Museum Rijswijk* (67 Herenstraat). *Huis Hoflust* (the former town hall), and *Huis Hornwijk* are typical of the *country houses* formerly outside the town. *Huis Cromvliet* is a very fine 17C example.

Scheveningen: The *miniature town of Madurodam* (175 Haringkade) can be seen on the way to Scheveningen. Some of the most interesting buildings in the Netherlands are reproduced here, one-twentyfifth of the original size. Scheveningen, once a fishing village (fish auction in the nearby harbour) is today an important bathing resort and holiday centre. The sanatorium, a lavish palace on the beach, was built by the German architects Henkenhof and Ebert in 1884. The 15C *Visserkerk* is at 8 Keizerstraat.

Voorburg: Possibly the site of the Roman naval base Forum Hadriani. The late Gothic *Dutch Reform church*, a brick building stands on Herenstraat. 14C tower; in its present form the choir probably dates from 1511. In the same street, *Huis Swaensteyn* (1632) has a relief of swans above the entrance; next door the *''t Swaentje'* inn has a pretty sign. The originally 14C *Kasteel de Binkhorst* was given its present form in the 16&17C. *Huis Hofwijck* (2 Westeinde) was built in 1641–3 by Pieter Post as a country seat for Constantyn Huygens, poet and statesman (today the *Huygensmuseum*). The garden, at one time a model 17C geometric design, has been partly restored to its former splendour. Opening times: Tues.–Sun. 1–4 p.m.

Environs: Leidschendam (5 km. NE): This town, which dates from 1938 when the villages of Veur and

Stompwijk were united, took its name from the dam built at the same time as the Rijn-Schie canal. The small *lock-gate* was built in 1887, the pretty *lock-gatehouse* in 1888. The octagonal *Dutch Reform church* (1654) was fundamentally redesigned in 1865 (the domed roof was replaced by a conical structure). 17C pulpit.

Groesbeek
Geldern   p.291 □ L 6

The villages of De Horst, Bredeweg, Heilig Landstichting and Berg en Dal, set in splendid hilly wooded countryside, are part of the district of Groesbeek.
Groesbeek has a 15C Gothic *church* and the *Zuidmolen* (1857), a round stone mill, which is open to visitors on Saturdays. *Berg en Dal Afrikamuseum* has a reconstructed African village and a small zoo. The *Bijbels Open-luchtmuseum* in *Heilig Landstichting* is an open-air museum with reconstructions of Biblical scenes.

Environs: Gennep (14 km. S.): This town on the E. shore of the Maas is in the province of Limburg. The *Dutch Reform church* is Renaissance in style. The *town hall*, built 1641–59, has an octagonal tower with a clock and bells. The two gable façades show a combination of a stepped gable with concave and convex curves.

Groningen
Groningen   p.287 □ N 2

History: In 1040, the German king (later Emperor) Heinrich III granted the country estate of *Gruoninga* the right to mint coins and levy taxes for St.-Maartenskerk in Utrecht. The bishops' authority had waned by the mid 13C, by which time the town, now fortified, was actively engaged in commerce. In the course of its history, the town held its own in conflicts with the surrounding Ommelanden. Groningen also survived Spanish sieges and a siege by the troops of the Bishop of Münster. The 20C has seen Groningen develop into a provincial capital and a centre of administration and industry.

Martinikerk: The Dutch Reform church, originally a Romanesque-Gothic cruciform basilica (*c.* 1230), was altered in late Gothic style during major rebuilding in the 15C. The old choir was replaced before 1425 by a very tall Gothic choir with an ambulatory. A net-vaulted chapel and rib-vaulted sacristy were later added to the N. side of the choir. Magnificent *Renaissance wall paintings* of New Testament scenes (late 16C) came to light in 1924. The splendid organ dates originally from 1480, although it has been much altered (e.g. by A.A.-Hinsch and F.C. Schnitger in 1729–30). The church has numerous memorials and fine stained-glass windows (1770) in the ambulatory. The tower (at 315 ft, the second highest in the Netherlands) was built

Den Haag, Binnenhof, knights' hall

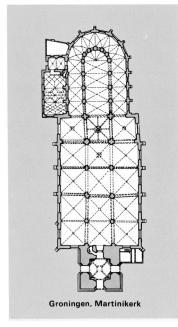

Groningen, Martinikerk

in 1469–82 and given its present spire in 1627.

A-Kerk: The Dutch Reform church was built in 1247 in Romanesque style, although later alterations and the tall choir (1452) give it a mainly Gothic appearance today. The tall crown of the tower was built by the town architect Albert Meyer in 1710–12. The carved pulpit dates from 1700. The organ of 1702 by Arp Schnitger was altered in 1814.

Noorder- or Nieuwe Kerk: This cruciform church (1665) by Coenrat Roelofs was modelled on the Noorderkerk in Amsterdam. The four arms of the cruciform building are of equal length and have office buildings in between. The fine decorations date from the time the church was built.

Gerechtsgebouw (36–38 Oude Boteringestraat): The complex consists of three parts. That on the right, probably originally medieval was altered in 1612. The lower part on the left dates from 1626 and has a gable of a later date. The wing between these has a beautiful sandstone portal (1626). A second portal dates from 1754 and has a figure of the Goddess of Justice.

Goudkantoor (Grote Markt): A splendid Renaissance building (1635) built to house the tax office. It takes its name from the Gold Office, where gold was assayed and stamped, which later occupied the building.

Hofjes: The many fine *residential courtyards* include *the Aduarder Gasthuis* (3 Munnekeholm) built in 1604, *Anna Varvergasthuis* (Nieuwe Kijk in 't Jatstraat) dating from 1635, the *Armshuiszittend Convent* (22 A-Kerkstraat) from 1437, the 13C *Heilige Geest-* or *Pelstergasthuis* (Pelsterstraat), the *Jacob en Annengasthuis* (Gasthuisstraatje) of 1494 and the *Juffer Tette Alberda Gasthuis* (22 Nieuwe Kerkhof) dating from 1658. *Geertruits-* or *Pepergasthuis* (2–22 Peperstraat) from 1405 has courtyards and fine porches. *St-Anthony Gasthuis* (19 Rademarkt) dates from 1517 with many alterations. *Zeyls Gasthuis* (50 Visserstraat) dates from 1646 and has a richly decorated gable façade.

Korenbeurs (Vismarkt): This corn exchange altered in neo-classical style in 1865 is the finest in the Netherlands and one of the largest in West Europe. The roof is crowned by a statue of Mercury; Neptune and Ceres are seen on the other side of the main door.

Prinsenhof (23 Martinikerhof): This 15C building, originally a monastery, was converted into the Stadholder's Residence in 1594. The Zonnewijzerpoort (1730) which leads to the 17C garden has a fine sundial above the entrance.

Groningen, Provinciehuis

Provinciehuis (Martinikerkhof): The former main building of the St.-Maartenschool (*c.* 1550), it was thoroughly restored in *c.* 1900. There are late-17C portraits of the house of Orange in the *Statenzaal;* the delegates' hall was decorated with oak panelling and wooden barrel vaults in 1697. A tall Renaissance style tower stands between the two wings.

Stadhuis (Grote Markt): This monumental neo-classical building (1802–10) was built to the designs of Jacob Otten Jusly. It is connected to the contrasting modern building (1962) by a glazed footbridge.

Archaeological Museum (6 Poststraat). Opening times: Wed. 2–5 p.m.

Groninger Museum (59 Praediniussingel): Exhibits relate to the history of the town and the province of Groningen. Also Japanese and Chinese ceramics and silver. Opening times: Tues.–Sat. 10 a.m.–5 p.m., Sun. 1–5 p.m.

Natural History Museum (9 St.-Walburgstraat): Birds, mammals, fossils, minerals, etc. Opening times: Tues.–Fri. 10 a.m.–5 p.m., Sat. and Sun. 2–5 p.m.

Niemeyer Nederlands Tabacologisch Museum (24 Brugstraat): The Tobacco Museum documents the history of tobacco smoking and includes examples of Red Indian pipes. Opening times: Tues.–Sat. 10 a.m.–5 p.m., Sun. and holidays 1–5 p.m.

Volkenkundig Museum Gerardus van de Leeuw (104 Nieuwe Kijk in 't Jatstraat). The folk museum opens:

Tues.–Fri. 10 a.m.–4 p.m., Sat. and Sun. 1–5 p.m.

Also worth seeing: The *Rode-* or *Burgerweeshuis* (orphanage) was set up in 1599 in the former Monastery of St.Agnes, of which the refectory and chapterhouse survive. The ornate gate depicts two orphans among the decorations. The most distinguished *residential houses* in Groningen occupy the central squares and the streets leading off them, i.e. *Grote Markt* with *Martinikerkhof, Poelestraat, Oude Ebbinge-* and *Boteringestraat, Ooster-* and *Gelkingestraat,* and also in *Guyotplein* and *Ossenmarkt.*

Environs: Haren (4 km. S.): The 13C *Dutch Reform church* has a tower (restored to its original form in 1914) with an attractive octagonal spire. The carved pulpit dates from 1725. The *'De Hoop' oil mill* was built in 1843.
Leegkerk (1 km. W.): The W. and N. wall still survive from the 13C Romanesque-Gothic *Dutch Reform church.* The choir and S. wall are late Gothic, and the ridge turret is 18C. Pulpit

Groningen, Martinikerk, tower

(1647) and Ten Commandments panel (1653).
Noordlaren (11 km. S.): There are the remains of a *megalithic tomb* near the village. The lower half of the brick *Dutch Reform church* is early 13C. The choir has a late Gothic rib vault above.

Groot-Schermer
North Holland   p.286☐H 4

Groot-Schermer, at the centre of the Schermerpolder, lies 13 ft. below sea level. Over 50 windmills were used to drain it in 1631–5 and some of these still stand.

Raadhuis: The fine town hall has three gables and dates from 1639. It was enlarged in 1938–9 during restoration work, at which time the old court building from Noord-Schermer was reconstructed alongside.

Environs: De Rijp (3 km. S.): Part of Graft, De Rijp is the birthplace of Jan Adriaansz Leeghwater, who was responsible for much of the draining of the land locally. The late Gothic *Dutch Reform church* is single-aisled (1529) with a transept and choir of 1635 built to the designs of J.A.-Leeghwater. The church was given a tall tower in 1661 after a fire in 1654. The 23 windows date from just after the fire. The *town hall* (1630), also designed by Leeghwater, has gable stones commemorating shipping and herring fishing which made the town prosperous in the 16&17C before the area was drained.
Graft (3 km. S.): This delicate and richly designed *town hall* (1613) has three stepped gables in bright red stone.
Schermerhorn (3 km. N.): The late Gothic *Dutch Reform church* (1634–6) has fine decorations from the time of construction. In *Hollands Schaats- en Wintermuseum Hans Brinker* there are sledges, ice skates, and other such

things. Opening times: 15 June–15 Sept. Tues.–Sun. 12 noon–4 p.m. A mill, formerly part of a complex of three 17C mills has been made into a *museum* in which utensils and the 19C miller's lodging can be seen. Opening times: 1 May–1 Oct. Tues.–Sun. 10 a.m.–5 p.m.; 1 Oct.–1 May, Sun. 10 a.m.–4.30 p.m.

Grouw/Grau
Friesland   p.287 □ L 2

Dutch Reform Pieterskerk: 12C church with a 15C saddleback roof; oak furniture and brass candlesticks inside the building. Above the portal there is a coat-of-arms on a shield (1673).

Gemeindemuseum in Gemeentehuis (15 Stationsweg): Collection of utensils, paintings of the town, model ships, and costumes. Opening times: July and Aug. Sat. 10 a.m.–12 noon or by arrangement.

Also worth seeing: The *town hall* (1940), with its carved Frisian sayings and symbols, designed by A.Kropholler. The pretty *gate* (1665) S. of the church was formerly part of a castle keep. The *spinning-head mill* is probably 18C. There is a relief of the Goddess of Justice on the gable of the *former courthouse,* now a hotel. The *Blauwe Steen,* a large stone behind the parish church has notches on it said to have been caused by the sabres of the Bishop of Münster's soldiers in 1672.

Environs: Eernewoude/Earnewâld (10 km. NE): An old fishing and peat village alongside a lake which resulted from peat removal. Formerly a hunting-ground belonging to the stadholders (hence the name 'Princehof'), it is today a water sports centre, with the 'De oude venen' nature reserve nearby. The *Dutch Reform church* has a fine pulpit (1699). Turf and bone carvings, as well as wicker-

work are on display in the *Museum 't Kokelhus van Jan en Sjut'* (16 Flietstech). Opening times: June–Aug. Mon.–Sat. 10 a.m.–5 p.m.

Oldeboorn/Boarn (9 km. SE): This very old village has retained its original character. St.Boniface is said to have lived here and performed baptisms at a fountain over which the present church was built. Today's *Dutch Reform church* dates from 1753 and has a slender tower, 98 ft. tall. The Louis XIV entrance portal has coats-of-arms and bears the names of the village mayors.

Oudega/Aldega (14 km. NE): This pretty village is situated in the 'Friese Wouden', an area of forest and water. The 12C *Dutch Reform church* is a Romanesque building in tufa with a Gothic choir. A wooden block and chain on the free-standing tower once restrained petty offenders. Inside the church there are eleven richly decorated memorial slabs commemorating members of the Haersma family (1707–92), a 17C pulpit and five windows with stained-glass coats-of-arms (1717).

Wartena/Warten (7 km. N.): The

Groningen, Goudkantoor, entrance

'*It Earmhûs*' *museum* in the former deacon's house by the bridge has exhibits related to shipping, angling and reed-cutting. Opening times: July and Aug. Sat. 10 a.m.–12 noon and by agreement.

Gulpen
Limburg   p.291□L 9

Kasteel Neubourg: This stately home in the valley of the river Gulp has three courtyards and three bridges over two small islands surrounded by ditches. The lowest part of the walls is all that survives of the 13C castle. A large square tower with a baroque roof dates from the early 17C. The rest is mainly 18C. The influence of the Westphalian architect J.C.Schlaun (1695–1773) is easily apparent. The barbican was altered in the late 18C. The early-19C entrance gate was designed by Matthias Soiron. Today the castle, which was modernized inside in the early 20C, is a hotel.

Environs: Eijsden (15 km. SW): The *Eijsden castle* in Maas-Renaissance style was built in *c.* 1636 and rebuilt in 1650 after a fire; restored in 1881–6. A large and splendid building, it has delicate towers has two wings at right angles to one another on a square piece of ground surrounded by a ditch.
Gronsveld (12 km. W.): Renaissance *Kasteel Gronsveld* (1833), an elegant white building with pointed turrets was built on the foundations of a medieval castle. In the 15C it was owned by the nobles of Bronckhorst-Batenburg. Their coats-of-arms decorate the organ and the altars in the little church nearby. The monumental *corn mill* is the only tower mill still surviving in the Netherlands. It is in operation on Saturdays.

◁ *Gulpen, Kasteel Neubourg*

Haaksbergen
Overijssel   p.287□O 5

St.-Pancratiuskerk: Roman Catholic hall church with nave and two aisles. The slender tower and S. aisle are mid 16C; the rest dates from 1887 and was designed by A.Tepe. Open to visitors: Tues. & Thur. 3–5 p.m. in summer.

Dutch Reform church: A small church built in 1811 with financial help from Louis Bonaparte.

Richtershuis (Nos. 6–8–10 Jhr. von Heijdenstraat): Above the Louis XIV entrance (1720) there is a frieze with inscriptions and the coat-of-arms of Joan van der Sluys, the founder.

Mills: The *Oostendorper water mill* (1548) on the Buurser is a double mill for both corn and oil. Visits can be made to the '*De Korenbloem*' corn mill (1798) in Fazantstraat by prior arrangement.

Haamstede
Zeeland   p.288□E 6

Slot Haamstede: A residential tower dating from the 13C and enlarged and rebuilt after a fire in 1525. The left wing was further extended in *c.* 1609, when the bridge and little gate were also built. The building was further altered in the 18C. The tower is open to visitors in summer.

Also worth seeing: The *Haus Het Anker* (2 Sluispad) is a former hunting lodge with a stepped gable. The 16C *cruciform church* has good decorations.

Environs: Renesse (5 km. NE): *Slot Moermond*, founded in the 13C by a member of the van Renesse family, was devastated in the late 15C and today the only parts of the fortified 14C structure can be seen in the gatehouse. The present castle developed in the 16C from the 14C gatehouse. During 17C rebuilding it received the octagonal tower which gives the castle a feudal appearance. The building was excavated and restored in 1957. There are guided tours through the garden in summer.

Haarlem
North Holland　　　　　　　　p.286□G 4

History: In the 12C, Haarlem was one of the residences of the counts of Holland and a market centre for the Kennemerland. The town grew rapidly and prospered from shipping, weaving, bleaching and the brewing of beer.
In 1573, during the War of Independence, Haarlem was besieged by the Spaniards for seven months before surrendering. Numerous stories recall this time. Since the 17C the town has experienced an economic upswing, which was given an added impetus by the opening of the first Amsterdam-Haarlem railway line in 1839 and the subsequent industrialization.

Grote Kerk or **St.-Bavokerk:** This late-Gothic Dutch Reform basilica has a cruciform ground plan and a slender tower over the crossing.

Building began in the last years of the 14C with the building of the choir. The transept (1445–*c.* 1465) was built under the supervision of Evert Spoorwater, Antwerp's town architect. The present nave was erected after the first had been torn down in 1473; the wooden vaults of the choir and aisle date from 1530–8. The tower over the crossing was given its present form in 1519–20. The outside of the baptismal chapel S. of the nave is by Lieven de Key (1593), while the Gothic consistory (1658) SE of the choir is by Salomon de Bray. Many of the *decorations* of this splendid church are pre-Reformation. The choir screen (1509–17) and the copper choir desk (1499) are by Jan Fierens from Mechelen. The choir stalls (1512) have early Renaissance carved ends (1535). In the S. ambulatory there is a painting (*c.* 1515) of the church of St.Bavo (the tower shown over the crossing probably accords with a design which was never carried out). The pulpit dates from 1679 and the small organ N. of the choir is *c.* 1600. The monumental and richly designed large organ (1738) by Christian Müller was designed by Daniel Marot. Mozart played this organ in 1766 when he was ten years old. The large marble relief (1738–41) below the organ gallery is by J.B.Xavery. The tower has a carillon by the Hémony brothers.

Nieuwe Kerk: Dutch Reform church, the original building of which was replaced in 1645–9 by a structure designed by Jacob van Campen (the delicate tower of 1613 by Lieven de Key was retained). The painters Philips Wouwerman and Jacob van Ruysdael are buried near the church.

Other churches: The nave and lower part of the tower of the *Dutch Reform Bakenesserkerk* are late 15C, while the rich sandstone crown of the fine tower dates from *c.* 1530. *St.-Janskerk* was originally the monastery

Haarlem, Amsterdamse Poort ▷

church of the Knights of St.John. This single-aisled building with nave (probably 14C), a 15C choir, and a delicate tower of 1595 is a local archive today and is not open to visitors. The 14C *Waalse Kerk,* formerly the church of the Beguine convent, has a 16C sacristy with a wooden vault. The Roman Catholic churches, *St.-Anthonius van Padua* (Nieuwe Groenmarkt) and *St.-Jozef* (Jansstraat), were built in the 'Waterstaatsstijl' in 1843. The *Roman Catholic St.-Bavokathedraal* (1895–1930) by J.T.Cuypers and J.Stuyt combines neo-Gothic, Byzantine and other styles.

Hofjes: Haarlem has many almshouses (hofjes) mostly concealed in out-of-the-way streets and behind porches. The *Hofje van Staats* (39 Jansweg), with a tall central section and an elegant exterior, dates from 1730. *Hofje van Noblet* (2 Nieuwe Gracht), built in 1758–60, has a warden's room with gold leather wall decorations, portraits and 18C furniture. *Hofje de Bakenesserkamer* (11 Wijde Appelaarsteg), the oldest hofje

in the town, was founded by Dirk van Bakenes in 1395, rebuilt in the 17C and further altered in 1756. The *Hofje In De Groene Tuyn* (23 Warmoesstraat) was founded in 1616 for Roman Catholic women over the age of 50. The *Brouwershofje* (8 Tuchthuisstraat), founded in 1472, was rebuilt in 1586 after a fire in 1576. The *Frans Loenenhofje* (1607) at 24 Witte Heerenstraat, with a fine entrance gate, has a beautiful regent's room with a portait of the young Frans Loenen by Jan van Scorel. One of the most picturesque of the hofje is the *Hofje van Guurtje de Waal* (40 Lange Annastraat) built in 1616, whose courtyard of little white houses is full of flowers. The monumental *Teylershofje* (1787, 64 Koudenhorn) on the river Spaarne, has 24 Louis XIV dwellings. The pretty *Hofje van Heythuysen* (135 Kleine Houtweg) outside the centre of the town was founded in 1651.

Hoofdwacht: This very old building in the market place, with a façade dating from 1650, was formerly the main guard building. It is reputed to

Grote Markt with Grote Kerk

have housed the town's first town hall.

Nieuwe- or **St.-Jorisdoelen** (144 Grote Houtstraat): House of the archers of St.George, also known as Proveniershuis, it was probably built by Willem the abbot in 1591.

Stads- or **Kloveniersdoelen** (32 Gasthuisstraat): Former archers' house with a gate dating from 1612 and two wings which probably date from 1562. Franz Hals' paintings of archers once hung in the hall; today the pictures are in the Frans-Hals-Museum.

Paviljoen Welgelegen (Frederikspark): This elegant pavilion (1785–8) built for Hope, the banker from Amsterdam, lies outside the centre of town. Today it is the Provinciehuis, with statues by Godecharle, a sculptor from Brussels.

Spaarnwouder- or Amsterdamse Poort: This late-14C fortified gate is the only surviving old gate in Haar-lem. The main building is flanked by two octagonal turrets, and the low outside gate in the canal has two round towers.

Stadhuis: The town hall is situated in the Grote Markt dominated by St.-Bavokerk. The oldest part is mid 14C; the entrance, balcony and some windows date from 1630. The slender tower in the corner on the right was pulled down in 1772 but rebuilt from old drawings in 1914. The two projecting wings are originally 15C, although they were altered in 1633, probably by Salomon de Bray. The fine building (1620) along the Zijl-straat was designed by Lieven de Key. Inside, the oldest part is the large mid-16C hall, the Gravenzaal, with a heavy timber ceiling; numerous other rooms have paintings and beautiful fireplaces. Two tapestries dating from 1629 depict the conquest of Damiate and the granting of Haarlem's coat-of-arms.

Statue of Laurens Janszoon Coster (Grote Markt): The statue to Cos-

Grote Kerk, interior

Santpoort (Haarlem), Brederode castle

ter was set up in 1856. Coster was born at 25 Grote Markt and invented printing at almost the same time as Gutenberg.

Vleeshal (Grote Markt): This splendid Renaissance market for meat was built 1602–03 to a design by Lieven de Key.

Waag (corner of Damstraat and Spaarne): This weigh-house (1597–8) was probably designed by Lieven de Key, Haarlem's first town architect, active from 1593 onwards.

Museums
Frans-Hals-Museum (62 Groot Heiligland): The former hofje, an almshouse for old men, was built in 1608 under the supervision of Lieven de Key, town architect. It performed its original function until 1810, after which it was used as an orphanage. The building was purchased by the town in 1906, and since 1913 it has been open to the public as a museum. Clever design ensured that the delightful appearance of the original courtyard has been preserved and the old garden was also restored. The result is one of the finest and most intimate museums in the world. The central feature of the collections is the magnificent cycle of portraits by Frans Hals (b. later than 1580, d. 1666) dating from 1616–64. Opening times: Mon.–Sat. 11 a.m.–5 p.m., Sun. and holidays 1–5 p.m.

Teylers Museum (16 Spaarne): The oldest museum in the Netherlands, it was set up in 1778 based on the collections of Pieter Teyler van der Hulst. In 1780 it was housed in the building designed by Leendert Viervant. Exhibits include fossils, skeletons and minerals, instruments used by natural scientists from the 17&18C, including an electrostatic machine built by M.van Marum in 1784, along with a large collection of 19C and early 20C drawings and oil paintings. Opening times: Tues.–Sat. 10 a.m.–5 p.m. (Oct.–Feb.) 10 a.m.–4 p.m.), Sun. 1–5 p.m.

Museum Enschede (5 Klokhuisplein): A collection devoted to the history of Dutch printing. Opening

Haarlem, Stadhuis Gravenzaal

times: Mon.–Fri, by prior arrangement only.

Treasure chamber of St.-Bavo-kerk (146 Leidsevaart): Gold and silver religious objects. Opening times: 1 Apr.–1 Oct. Mon.–Sat. 10 a.m.–12 noon and 2–4.30 p.m., Sun. 2–4.30 p.m.

Environs: Bloemendaal (3 km. W.): In the De Kennemerduinen National Park. The *Dutch Reform church* dates from 1635–36. Nearby the *garden pavilion* dates from 1791 and is in Louis XVI style. 18C *country houses* e.g. *Sparrenheuvel*.
Heemstede (4 km. S.): This Gothic *Dutch Reform church* (1623–5) by Hendrick Staets and Cornelis Dankertz was built on the foundation walls of a previous church which burned down in 1573. The marble tomb to Adriaan Pauw, a councillor (d. 1653), is in the choir. The late medieval *castle of Heemstede* was pulled down in 1810. Parts of the building have survived, along with the ornate bridge leading to the Friedensburg (named after the peace of

Münster) built for Adriaan Pauw in 1648. There are some elegant 18C *country houses*, including *Bosbeek, Huis te Manpad* and *Hartekamp*, where Carl von Linné (or Linnaeus, the Swedish naturalist) resided from 1735–7 and drew up an inventory of the botanical and zoological collections belonging to Clifford, an Amsterdam businessman. In Manpadslaan there is an *obelisk* commemorating the expulsion of the Flems in 1304 and the failed attempt to rescue Haarlem in 1573. The *Museum de Cruquius* (27–32 Cruquiusdijk) not far from Haarlem occupies the 'De Cruquius' steam-pump mill which was taken out of operation in 1933. Along with two other mills, this one was used to drain the Haarlemmer lake from 1849–52. Museum opening times: Apr.–Sept. Mon.–Sat. 10 a.m.–5 p.m., Sun. and holidays 12 noon–5 p.m.; Oct. and Nov.: Mon.–Sat. 10 a.m.–4 p.m., Sun. and holidays 12 noon–4 p.m.
Santpoort (5 km. N.): *Brederode castle* probably dates from the early 13C and was partly destroyed in 1426; later rebuilding was not complete. In

Haarlem, Spaarne with weigh-house

recent years there has been extensive conservation work and today it appears as a fine example of a medieval castle. Opening times: 1 Mar.–1 Dec. Sun.–Fri. 10 a.m.–5 p.m. Along the road to Velsen there are a number of *country houses* belonging to Amsterdam businessmen. They include the 18C *Beekkestein* with fine decorations and splendid gardens. Opening times: June–Sept. Wed.–Fri. 10 a.m.–12 noon and 2–5 p.m., Sat. and Sun. 12 noon–5 p.m.; Oct.–May Wed.–Sun. 2–5 p.m. Gardens open to the public.

Spaarndam (6 km. N.): The *Dutch Reform church* (1627) was enlarged in 1664. The interior is barrel vaulted and has decorations dating from *c.* 1665. Nearby stands the *monument to Hans Brinker,* who is said to have closed a hole in the dyke with his thumb.

Velsen (10 km. N.): Most of the N. wall and W. façade survive from the single-aisled 10C or 11C Romanesque *church*. St.Willibrord is said to have built a church on the same site in *c.* 690. The tower (*c.* 1200) was probably increased in height in the 14C; the relief above the tower entrance may be 13C. 18C E. section.

Harderwijk

Geldern   p.286☐K 4

Harderwijk, granted a charter in 1231, was once an important Zuiderzee port and a member of the Hanseatic League. From 1647–1811 it was a university town. Carl von Linné, or Linnaeus, the Swedish naturalist (1707–78) and the Dutch chemist and physician Hermannus Boerhaave (1668–1738) both studied here. The Linnaeus turret in the former botanical garden commemorates this.

Dutch Reform church: The collapse of the tower in 1797 led to the decline of the church. The 14C choir has survived; splendid *ceiling paintings* came to light in the most recent restoration.

St.-Catharinakerk: Dating from 1502 today this church is used to stage cultural events.

Heemstede (Haarlem), Hartekamp

Veluws Museum van Oudheden: Local history museum with documents, costumes and model ships.

Dolfinarium (Strandboulevard): Killer whales and dolphins, underwater panorama and seal house. Opening times: 25 Feb.–29 Oct. Mon.–Sun. 9 a.m.–5.30 p.m.

Also worth seeing: Parts of the *town wall*, the *Vispoort* and the *Smeeport* survive from the former fortifications.

Environs: Ermelo The 11C *Dutch Reform church* has a Romanesque tower. In the choir there are corbels decorated with symbols of the human virtues. A small *museum* has exhibits from the Stone Age (prehistoric tombs have been discovered nearby) to the present.

Harlingen/Harns
Friesland   p.286□K 2

Harlingen, a charming old fortress town, is the only Frisian port still connected to the open sea.

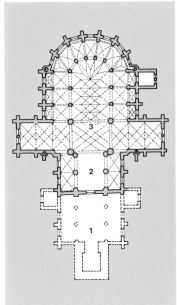

Hardewijk, Dutch Reform church 1 Tower (collapsed in 1797) and W. section **2** Surviving 14C sections **3** Transept, choir and crypt from c. 1400/1420

Harderwijk, Dutch Reform church

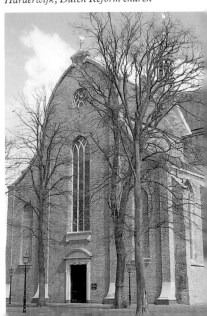

History: The town probably received a charter in 1234. A centre for trade, maintaining relations with Hamburg, Denmark and the Baltic countries, it never became a member of the Hanseatic League. The town was at its zenith around 1664 when the admiralty of Friesland moved here from Dokkum. Trade was subsequently expanded to include Portugal, Spain, France and other countries. Whaling and associated industries were carried out from 1634 to 1865.

Stadhuis: An elegant building (1730) on the Noorderhaven. The tower has a figure of St.Michael, the town's patron Saint. There is another figure of St.Michael above the charming entrance. Most of the decorations date from the time of building.

Dutch Reform church: A church with a cruciform ground plan built in 1771–6 on the site of a previous church of which only the tower (c. 1200 and increased in height in the 15C) has survived.

Museum Hannemahuis (56 Vor-

straat): Model ships and seascapes. Opening times: (in the tourist season) Tues.–Sat. 10 a.m.–5 p.m.; (before and after the season) 2–5 p.m.

Also worth seeing: The town resembles an open-air museum having 500 *gabled houses* from the late Gothic and Renaissance periods and the 17–19C. Voorstraat, Vijverbuurt, Zoutslot, and Kleine and Groote Bredeplaats, are all witness to Harlingen's former heyday. Many more fine *houses* are to be seen in the *Noorderhaven*, where there are also four statues of lions of a menacing appearance. On the dyke outside the town the '*De Stenen Man' monument*, commemorates Caspar de Robles, who began the work of repairing the dyke after the All Saints' flood of 1570. The statue, erected in 1774 on the site of an earlier statue of 1576, shows a Janus head guarding the dyke.

Hasselt

Overijssel   p.287□M 4

This old member of the Hanseatic League was granted a charter in 1252. The town became well known for being the place from which Bentheim stone was shipped and also for the printing of the incunabula of the Italian book-printer Peregrinus Barmantlo in 1480–90.

St.Stefanuskerk: This Dutch Reform church, a late Gothic hall church with a massive tower, was built 1380–*c.* 1500 on the site of an older building. The present crown of the tower was replaced by another which was destroyed by fire in 1725. Inside, the large pillars, wide arches and wide roof vaults create a feeling of space.

Stadhuis: Delicate late Gothic town hall with a W. section dating from *c.* 1500, and a richer E. section with a stepped gable which dates from 1550.

Hasselt, Stadhuis, stepped gable

Today it is a *museum*, with fine old weapons. The museum also houses the only painting (1657) known for certain to be the work of Nicolaas van Galen, the painter from Hasselt. Opening times: Mon.–Fri. 9 a.m.–12 noon and 1–5 p.m.

Also worth seeing: Remains of the old *town wall* are to be found near the 14C Vispoort. Fine 17C *houses* in *Herengracht* and *Hoogstraat*.

Environs: Genemuiden (5 km. NW): The Bishop of Utrecht granted Genemuiden a charter in 1275. The town is also known for its reed-mat industry. Trade in hay was also important, which explains why smoking in public was banned by a police regulation.

Staphorst (7 km. NE): An old town first mentioned in 1150, it is predominantly a community of very strict orthodox Protestants. There are a number of reed-covered 18&19C farmhouses. The town should be visited only on weekdays and the tourist should not take any photographs without permission. Many of the inhabitants are still to be seen in their traditional local costumes at the market held from 8 a.m.–1 p.m. on Thursdays in the church square.

Zwartsluis (5 km. N.): The 17C *Dutch Reform church* (with its fine pulpit) and some pretty *houses* are witness to the town's former prosperity from merchant shipping. The *Natuurhistorisch Museum Schoonewelle* (133 Zomerdijk) exhibits fauna from the Overijssel. Opening times: Mon.–Sat. 9 a.m.–12 noon and 2–5.30 p.m.

Hattem

Geldern   p.287☐M 4

Dutch Reform church: A small church of the Order of St.John stood here in 1307. The present church is mainly 14C with 13C rib vault and good wall paintings.

Stadhuis: The town hall was rebuilt in Renaissance style from 1619 onwards; altered in 1770, it was restored in 1871.

Also worth seeing: The *Dijkpoort*, a town gate belonging to the former fortifications and now used as an exhibition room for the museum of bakery (where bread and cakes are still baked in traditional manner). The originally 15&16C *Kasteel Molencaten* stands surrounded by water a little way outside the town. It took on its present appearance in the 17C and 19C.

Havelte

Drente   p.287☐M 3

In contrast to the other villages in Drente, this delightful village does does not have a green. This area was probably inhabited 15,000 years ago as flint tools have been found here.

Megalithic tombs: Two megalithic tombs lie in open country. One of

Hattem, 'De Fortuin' mill

them is 62 ft. long and has 24 upright stones and 10 horizontal stones.

Dutch Reform church: Unusually this church lies outside the village. The main tower has an inscription stating that it dates from 1410; on its S. side there is a staircase. The Romanesque building was extended in the 15C when the nave and choir were built. Rib vaults rest on carved corbels. The carved pulpit dates from 1663. The organ dating back to 1819 came from Assen in 1897.

Overcinge: Originally a 17C castle, this was converted into a country house in 1870. There are three wings around a courtyard with a gatehouse on the fourth side.

Also worth seeing: Marking stones, which formerly indicated the extent of someone's land, are to be found in Piet Soerplein. Of the many interesting *farms,* most of which typically bear the date on a projecting anchor on the façade, the best are those in the *Dorpsstraat* and in the *Helomaweg* and

in the main date from the mid 18C to the mid 19C.

Environs: Uffelte (3 km. N.): This village, mentioned in an Utrecht document of 1040, has preserved its former character well.

Wapserveen (10 km. NW): The *Dutch Reform church* (1803) was rebuilt in Gothic style on another site, using the old material. The only wooden *bell tower* in Drente stands beside the graveyard. The village has some large *farms* and many trees.

Heerenveen/It Hearrenfean
Friesland   p.287☐L 3

History: Heerenveen is the oldest high-moor village in the Netherlands. In 1551 peat-cutters began to settle near the ditches they had dug. The town is also known as 'the Frisian Hague', because the Frisian stadholders built themselves a summer residence near Oranjewoud. The presence of the court meant that many

Havelte, megalithic tomb

distinguished families took up residence here.

Crack-State: An impressive building of 1606, now the *town hall*. Its broad classical front (1647) is topped by a belfry.

Grovestins State: The façade of today's inland revenue office was rebuilt in 1876 to a 17C model.

Museum Willem van Haren (50–52 Van Harenspad): This 17C mansion has an exhibition of 'Friese Nassau's' and 'Friese Haagje'. Opening times: Mon.–Fri. 10 a.m.–5 p.m., Sat. 11 a.m.–4 p.m.

Environs: Katlijk/Ketlik (5 km. E.): A little village whose small late Gothic church has an interesting double *bell tower*—one of the finest to have survived in Friesland.
Oranjewoud/'t Oranjewâld (5 km. E.): Today this town has coalesced with Heerenveen. Albertine Agnes, the daughter of Frederik Hendrik and Amalia van Solms, built herself a *country seat* here in *c*. 1665. It was destroyed in the early 19C, but rebuilt in 1830 above the vaulted cellars of part of the old building.

Heerlen
Limburg   p.291☐M 9

St.-Pancratiuskerk: The lower part of this Romanesque church is 12C, the upper part 14C. Near the choir is the square joker's tower, a remnant of the former fortress of Herle.

Museums: Museum of the *Rijksgeologische Dienst* (numerous fossils) and ,the *Thermen Museum* (remnants of the Roman thermal baths from the fortress of Coriovallum, AD 50). Opening times: Tues.–Fri. 10 a.m.–5 p.m., Sat., Sun. and holidays 2–5 p.m.

Environs: Schaesberg (3 km E.):

Kasteel Schaesberg was among the finest castles in Limburg, but it suffered neglect and damage from subsidence, and has survived only as a ruin. *Kasteel Strijthagen,* in the middle of a park with ponds, is a large country house dating from *c*. 1700.
Voerendaal (3 km. W.): Formerly an area rich in castles and country houses. Among those still surviving is the 15C *Kasteel Cortenbach* built by a member of the van Cortenbach family. The two massive corner towers in the courtyard are original. The house itself was built in 1776 as a large mansion with two wings and a gable above the rear entrance. Medieval ditches still surround the entire complex.
Wijnandsrade (5 km. NW): 18C *Kasteel Wijnandsrade* is surrounded by water.

Heeswijk-Dinther
North Brabant   p.290☐K 7

Kasteel Heeswijk: This castle with its irregular silhouette was founded in

Heerenveen, Crack-State

1196. While the barbican has retained its 16C Renaissance style, the main building received neo-Gothic additions and decorations in the 19C. The best features are the neo-Gothic *Iron Tower* and the *colonnaded passage* with the coats-of-arms of the family of Baron van den Bogaerde van Terbruggen, ruler of Heeswijk at that time. The building is a good example of the 19C romantic concept of a knightly castle.

Norbertijnerabdij van Berne: A Premonstratensian abbey—the Premonstratensians were founded by St.Norbert of Xanten (1082–1134)—it is today a 19C classical building. Organ concerts held in the abbey church are famous.

Huis Zwanenburg in Dinther: Originally 17C with later alterations. The house is picturesquely located on the Aa.

Meierijsche Museumboerderij (20 Meerstraat): This farmhouse, some 250 years old, was opened to the public as a *museum* of farm life. Fur-

Voerendaal (Heerlen), entrance gate

nishings and fittings date from *c.* 1900. Opening times: Whitsun–Sept. Wed., Sat. and Sun. 2–5 p.m.

Den Helder
North Holland   p.286□H 3

This former fishing village dates back to *c.* 1500 and later became known as a Dutch Royal Navy base. Michiel de Ruyter, Witte de With and Jacob van Heemskerck, all famous naval heroes, set off from Den Helder to fight their sea battles. During the Napoleonic period it was one of the most powerful fortresses in Europe. Hardly anything of the old town survived World War 2.

Helders Marine Museum 'Het Torentje' (Hoofdgracht): This museum documents the history of the Dutch Royal Navy since 1813 and has models of many ships. There are also uniforms, paintings, and old maps and sea charts. Opening times: Tues.–Fri. 10 a.m.–5 p.m., Sat. and Sun. 1–4.30 p.m.; in summer it is also open on Mon. 1–4.30 p.m.

Reddingmuseum Dorus Rijkers (1a Keizerstraat): Museum of sea rescue, dedicated to Dorus Rijkers, well-known for his rescues at sea. Opening times: Mon.–Sat. 10 a.m.–5 p.m., Sun. 1–5 p.m.

Hellendoorn
Overijssel   p.287□N 4

Dutch Reform church: Single-aisled Romanesque nave (12C), late Gothic choir with small side chapels and a sacristy from 1485, and a squat mid-15C tower. The choir has remnants of a wall painting of the Last Judgement.

Oudheimkamer 'Oald Heldern' (1 Reggeweg): An old Saxon farmhouse with examples of tools used in agriculture and handicrafts. Opening times: 15 May–15Sept. Mon.–Fri. 10–11 a.m. and 2–4 p.m.

Helmond
North Brabant   p.291 □ L 7

The town was first mentioned in 1178. Today, Helmond is the centre of the Peelland and an industrial town of growing importance. (The Peelland derives its name from the Latin palus meaning 'marsh').

Kasteel Helmond: Built in *c*. 1400 at the time the town was being fortified. Emperior Maximilian I of Austria visited the town on 2 August 1494. The castle was rebuilt after a fire in 1549; late Gothic towers in the forecourt date from this time. The *district museum,* documenting the history of the Peelland, is housed in a section of the town hall. 'La Danseuse',a statue by Giacomo Manzù, the Italian sculptor (b. 1908), stands in the park along with some other modern sculptures.

Huis met de Luts: ('House with the protective roof'; 1594). Standing in the market this is one of the town's oldest houses and provided a shelter for merchants selling their goods.

Arts centre: By the Dutch architect Pieter Blom (b. 1933) the building consists of 18 cubes. A theatre auditorium within is covered by a tent-like concrete roof, which was painted inside by Har Sanders.

Environs: Beek en Donk (6 km. N.): A district consisting of two villages on the southern Wilhelm canal. The Eyckenlust country estate has a *gatehouse* from *c*. 1500. The massive tower is all that survives of the *church* which was demolished in the 19C.

Deurne (8 km. E.): The *Groot* or *Nieuw Kasteel* (second half of 15C) was enlarged in the late 17C. The building was devastated in 1944, and today the ruins are part of the Deurne public park. Opposite this is the *Oud* or *Klein Kasteel* (also known as Slot van Peelland), consisting of a 14C medieval tower flanked by a white

Gemert (Helmond), Kasteel Gemert

19C house with a saddle-back roof and some 18C outbuildings. '*De Wieger*' a local museum has paintings from 1920–40.

Gemert (11 km. N.): *Kasteel Gemert* was the headquarters of the Teutonic Knights from 1366 until the late 18C. The 15C castle keep has stepped gables and delicate corner turrets. The main building dates from *c.* 1740 and resembles a palace. In 1881 the castle was sold to French Jesuits who, in 1907–09, erected a new wing with round corner towers to replace some ruined outbuildings. Today this extensive complex with its two 16C gatehouses and a drawbridge is owned by the Dutch Congregation of the Holy Spirit.

Helvoirt
North Brabant   p.290☐I 7

Dutch Reform church: 15C building with nave and two aisles, saddle-back roof and a sturdy tower with a spire. Inside there is a 17C pulpit and an early-19C organ. Vincent van Gogh's father preached here 1870–4 and the artist lived and painted in the priest's house.

Huis Zwijnsbergen: Still partly surrounded by a ditch, the building has stepped gables and a hexagonal tower with an interesting spire (both late 16C). Alterations were carried out in later centuries.

Also worth seeing: The farmhouse known as '*De Putakker*' (1 Loonse Baan), which probably dates from the mid 16C; reed roof and cistern. The classical *town hall* (1792) has a colossal order on the main façade.

Hengelo
Overijssel   p.287☐O 5

The old centre of Hengelo, a town with textile and metalworking industries, was destroyed in World War 2 and today the town has many modern buildings.

Stadhuis: The town hall was built in

Helmond, arts centre

1963 to the designs of Berghoef who was inspired by the Palazzo Vecchio in Florence. With 46 bells, the tower has one of the largest carillons in the Netherlands. The large assembly room is often used for concerts.

Oudheidkamer 'Oald Hengel' (51 Beekstraat): This museum occupies a mid-19C house and has interesting exhibits of the tools and products associated with weaving. Opening times: Tues.–Fri. 10 a.m.–12 noon and 2–5 p.m., Thur. also 6–9 p.m., Sat. 2–5 p.m.

Also worth seeing: The neo-Gothic *Roman Catholic St.Lambertus* (1889–90), a hall church. There are some early-18C *houses* in *Pastoriestraat*. The *stilt houses* in the so-called *Kasbah* are part of a housing experiment. '*De Olde Meul*' a water-mill in the village of *Oele* dates originally from 1334, although it was rebuilt after a fire in 1690.

Environs: Borne (2 km. NW): The late Gothic *Dutch Reform church* has a sturdy tower, an early-15C choir and two aisles (*c.* 1480) of equal height. The paintings (*c.* 1500) on the walls and vaults depict the Apostles, Christ between the Virgin Mary and St.John, and the Saints Christopher, Roch, and Antony Abbot and the Tree of Jesse. In the choir there is a late-Gothic tombstone with relief figures of J.van Weleveld (d. 1526) and Wilhelmina van Rutenborch (d. 1525). The priests' unmarried housekeepers lived in the *Klopjes* lodgings which are 18C. A *house* of 1779, occupied by Bussemaker, a linen manufacturer, still has the original decorations.

's-Hertogenbosch/ Herzogenbusch

North Brabant   p.289☐I 6

The capital of the province of North Brabant (also known as Den Bosch), it has been an important trading town since ancient times owing to its favourable location on the Dieze and the S. Willems Canal. The town's importance, however, decreased in the early 19C. Ramparts, town walls, bastions and round towers on the S. side remain from the medieval fortified town.

St.-Janskathedraal (Parade): A late-Gothic cruciform basilica, probably begun in *c.* 1280 as a Romanesque parish church or collegiate church, it is the largest church in the Netherlands, being 377 ft. long and 203 ft. wide. The nave is 92 ft. high, while under the dome it is 135 ft. The church was rebuilt and enlarged between 1330 and 1530, from which time the richly carved decorations also date. Architects include Alard Duhamel, Jan Heyns and Jan Darkennis. The exterior combines a diversity of flying buttresses and a contrastingly plainer tower. There are remains of the Romanesque church in the lower section. Outer walls, portals and buttresses have an abundance of carvings, many of which depict

's-Hertogenbosch, St.Janskathedraal

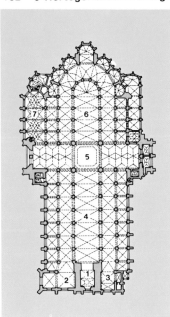

's-Hertogenbosch, St.-Janskathedraal 1
Late-Romanesque (13C) tower with late-15C
upper **part 2** Chapel of the Virgin Mary (1268) **3**
14C baptismal chapel **4** Early-16 nave **5** 15C
transept **6** Choir, probably completed before
1415 **7** Chapel of the Sacrament (1480-96)

popular figures of medieval life. The
interior is light and airy with 150
sturdy bundles of pillars supporting
the vaults of the nave and four aisles.
Seven chapels surround the magnificent choir. The chapel of the Virgin
Mary (1268) contains the late-13C
miraculous image known as 'Zoete
Lieve Vrouw van Den Bosch' ('Sweet
Virgin Mary of Den Bosch'). Outstanding carved choir stalls date from
1480. The copper font (1492) is by
Aert van Tricht. Further, there is a
winged altar (*c.* 1500) from the
Antwerp school, a 16C pulpit, and a
large 17C organ. The 20C carillon of
50 bells can be heard on Wed. from
11.30 a.m.–12.30 p.m. The church is
open to tourists every day.

Kruithuis (Citadellaan): The hexagonal powder magazine (1618–21) by
Jan van der Weeghen has walls some 3
ft. thick and a gable crowned by a
coat-of-arms over the portal.

Huis De Moriaan (77 Markt):
Dating from *c.* 1220, this was the first
house in 's-Hertogenbosch to be built
of brick. Today it houses the tourist
office.

Provinciehuis (1 Brabantlaan): Built
1968–71 to the plans of the architect
H.Maaskant, it stands some is 340 ft.
high at the edge of the town, and has
sculptures by Arthur Spronken,
Pieter d'Hont and Karel Appel; wall
tapestries by Abakanowicz, Prassinos
and Tourlière.

Stadhuis (Markt): The originally
Gothic town hall, redesigned in
classical style in 1670, is on the S. side
of the triangular market place. The
façade with a gable and colossal order
was designed by Pieter Minne from
The Hague. Under the gable, which
bears the town's coat-of-arms, there is
a mechanical device with little horses
(carved by Jacob Roman), which
spring into action on the hour and
half-hour. The entrance hall has wall
paintings dating from 1892 and 1897
by Antoon Derkinderen, a fin-de-siè-
cle artist. In the council chamber
there is a pretty series of 17C tapestries (1679). The vaulted cellar of the
Gothic town hall, today a restaurant,
was omitted from the classical conversion. The *statue* of Hieronymus Bosch
(*c.* 1450–1516), who came from 's-
Hertogenbosch, stands outside the
town hall.

Zwanenbroederhuis (94 Hinthamerstraat): The 'Illustre Lieve
Vrouwe Broesderschap', one of the
oldest religious associations, was
founded in 1318 and called 'Zwanen-
broeders' after the swans served at the

*'s-Hertogenbosch,
St.Janskathedraal* ▷

annual banquets since the 14C. The peculiar neo-Gothic building (1846) is by J.H. Laffertée; the four figures (1962) on the gable above the façade are by Marius van Beek. Today the building houses a *museum* with sumptuously decorated 15&16C psalters and hymn books. It is open to the public every Fri. from 11 a.m.–3 p.m. (closed in Aug.).

Noordbrabants Museum (4 Bethaniestraat): Devoted to the history, art and folklore of Brabant, the museum includes Roman tomb finds from Esch, paintings, drawings, coins, glass and pewter. Opening times: Mon.–Fr. 10 a.m.–5 p.m., Sat., Sun. and holidays 1–5 p.m., closed on Easter Sunday and Christmas Day.

Museum Slager (16 Choorstraat): Works by the Slager family of painters from P.M. Slager (1841–1912) to Tom Slager (b. 1918). Opening times: Tues.–Fri. and every first Sat. and Sun. in the month, 2–5 p.m.

Also worth seeing: The *church of St.Catherine* (also known as *church of the Cross*) in the Kruisbroedershof. The choir, which goes back to 1533, is not overwhelmed by the rest of the church, which dates from 1917. The early-16C *Refugiehuis* (on the corner of Spinhuiswal and St.-Jorisstraat) was built as a refuge in times of siege. Opposite, on the Bastion Oranje, there stands the De Boze Griet cannon dating from 1511 and 21 ft. long. Old houses include the *Gouvernementshuis* (41 Verwersstraat), altered by Pieter de Swart in 1765–9, the late Gothic *De Dry Hamerkens* (57 Hinthamerstraat), and the 17C *De Gulden Hopsack* (3 Orthenstraat).

Environs: Berlicum (8 km. E.): Little has survived of the *Dutch Reform church* after World War 2, when the 15C nave in particular was destroyed. The choir was restored and enlarged and the 13C tower rebuilt. The *Huize De Wamberg* NW of the village is partly 16C, another part dates from 1769; the gatehouse is particularly impressive. *Veebeek* a stately country house has a porch flanked by two heraldic stone animals.

Bokhoven (8 km. NW): From the

's-Hertogenbosch, St.Janskathedraal, winged altar

13C to the late 18C this village was independent and Roman Catholics could freely profess their faith here. The *Roman Catholic church of St.Anthony Abbot* has an early-15C tower and a nave built in 1498 after a fire. Inside there is a monument (1561) to Engelbert van Immerzeel, first Count of Bokhofen, and his wife Hélène de Montmorency, a work by Artus Quellinus the elder, the Flemish sculptor.

Vught (4 km. S.): The massive 16C *tower of St. Lambert* tapers towards the top. A remnant of the former church, it is built of layers of brick and tufa. The white *town hall* (1890) was originally the neo-Gothic Villa Leeuwenstein. In 1937 H.W. Valk converted it into a community hall. The council chamber has stained-glass windows by Charles Eyck, and in the hall there is a charming pair of Brabant peasants carved in oak by Jacob Maris. *Kasteel Maurick* near Vught was probably built in 1504–09 by Jan Heyns, one of the builders of the St.-Janskathedraal in 's-Hertogenbosch.

Hilversum
North Holland   p.289☐I 5

Hilversum has been an independent community since 1424. For a long time a poor village, today it is the largest town in Gooiland and the centre for both radio and television broadcasting in the Netherlands.

Stadhuis: The town hall (1928–31), a Functionalist structure by the architect W.M.Dudok and has a window (1931) by Joep Nicolas in the hall.

Museum de Vaart (163 Vaartweg): Prehistoric finds, geological objects and porcelain. Opening times: Mon.–Fri. 10 a.m.–12 noon and 2–5 p.m., Sat. and Sun. 1–5 p.m.

Environs: 's-Graveland (4 km. W.): The *Dutch Reform church* (1657–

8) was designed by Daniel Stalpaert. Trompenburgh, a 17C country house resembling a ship rising from the water, was built for Admiral Cornelius Tromp.

Kortenhoef (7 km. W.): The little village has a picturesque situation; the *Dutch Reform church* is probably late 15C with a nave rebuilt in 1640).

Nederhorst den Berg (15 km. NW): The *Dutch Reform church* with a Romanesque tower, 12C nave, and a choir probably from the 14C, stands on a natural hill in the middle of this little village.

The present appearance of the 13C *Kasteel Nederhorst*, which was restored after a fire in 1971, hardly differs from its appearance in *c.* 1635.

Hindeloopen/Hynlijppen
Friesland   p.286☐K 3

Hindeloopen is a picturesque little town on a headland in the IJsselmeer.

History: Only a small settlement in

Nederhorst den Berg (Hilversum), church

the 8C, Hindeloopen became an important Hanseatic town in the 14C and flourished economically in the 17&18C thanks to its position on the shipping route to Scandinavia. The Swedish king gave the town certain privileges (there is a street called Hindeloopen near Spitzbergen). Many wooden bridges and houses belonging to ships' officers typify the town's appearance.

Dutch Reform church: Originally 17C with 19C alterations. In 1724 a three-storeyed wooden crown was added to the typically Frisian medieval tower. Of interest inside the church are two lists which give the names of all the priests from 1580 to the present day.

'Likhuzen': Small houses in which sailors' wives spent the summer while their husbands were away at sea.

Sluishuis: This lock house of 1619 was given its wooden bell turret in the 19C. The so-called 'Leugenbank' ('bench of lies') behind the house

dates from 1785 and has a relief of the miraculous draught of fishes.

Hidde Nijland Museum (1 Dijkweg): The former town hall dating from 1682 has documents relating to the town's past, as well as objects of decorative interest. Opening times: 15 Mar.–30 Oct.: Tues.–Sat. 10 a.m.–5 p.m., Sun. and holidays 1.30–5 p.m.

Fries Schaatsmuseum: Collection of ice skates, etc. and documentation of the ice skating race held by the eleven towns, the last one of which took place this year (before this, the last was in 1963). Opening times: May–Sept. Mon.–Sat. 11 a.m.–5 p.m.

Also worth seeing: Fine houses all over the town. The *houses at 12 Buren*, in the *Nieuwstad* and in *Nieuwe Weide* are especially good. Hindeloopen is still known today for its painted furniture (particularly flowers and creepers in pastel shades) which show both Oriental and Scandinavian influences. Various workshops can be visited.

's-Graveland (Hilversum), country house, Trompenburgh

Hoensbroek

Limburg   p.291 □ L 9

Kasteel Hoensbroek: The many towers, various courtyards and the canal system make this castle one of the most imposing in Limburg, which more closely resembles German or French models than Dutch ones. Only the round tower is medieval (14C); most of the castle was built in *c.* 1640 in Maas Renaissance style to the plans of Mathieu Dousin (or Dosin) from Visé. The part to the right of the entrance stands on medieval foundations and was built in the first half of the 18C on the orders of Arnold Adriaan van Hoensbroek. The entrance is flanked by two tower-shaped pavilions with delicate baroque helm roofs. The castle was thoroughly restored in 1928–43. Opening times: 10 a.m.–12 noon and 1.30–5.30 p.m. daily, 1 May–1 Sept.: 10 a.m.–5.30 p.m.

Environs: Amstenrade (4 km. N.): *Huis Amstenrade* was begun in 1781 to the plans of Barthélémy Digneffe (including the sturdy 17C corner tower) but not entirely completed. The neo-Gothic *Roman Catholic church* (1853), an early work by C.Weber, takes the form of a hall church and has stuccoed vaults and two towers.

Brunssum (4 km. NE): The *Brikke Aove district museum* has a fine collection of medieval earthenware, Roman archaeological finds, fossils and rocks.

Nuth (3 km. W.): The nobles of Reimersbeek near Nuth were mentioned in 1356, and the existing rectangular *house* with its octagonal corner turret may have been built in the 16C and rebuilt in the 18C. Alternate layers of brick and natural stone were used. The courtyard is formed by three wings and a taller gatehouse.

Hoogebeintum/Hegebeintum

Friesland   p.287 □ L 2

This village is romantically situated on the highest terpen in Friesland,

Nuth (Hoensbroek), Kasteel Reimersbeek

Hindeloopen, Dutch Reform church

some 30 ft. above sea level. From the village many of Friesland's towers can be seen.

Dutch Reform church: This small 12C tufa church was extended in brick at the W. end. The tower dates from 1717. Inside the building, there are 15 memorial panels dating from 1689–1906 and decorated with various escutcheons and symbols of death. 17C noblemen's pew.

Environs: Janum/Jannum (8 km. SE): Early-14C *Romanesque-Gothic church* on a terp surrounded by scattered farms. The oldest part of church is the choir which is round. The present nave replaced an older one. There is a simple belfry. The church may formerly have been part of the Cistercian monastery in Rinsumageest. Today it is a *branch of the Leeuwardener Fries Museum* and has exhibits of statues, sarcophagi, altar stones, fonts, holy-water stoups and other works of medieval church art. Opening times: 9 a.m.–5 p.m. daily.

Hoogeveen

Drente   p.287☐N 3

The village of Hoogeveen, dating from sometime after 1625 when the surrounding moor was cultivated, has now developed into a town. Pretty gabled houses in Alteveerstraat and Schutstraat remain from the old village. The removal of peat was organized by the 'Compagnie van de Vijdduizend Morgen'.
Every Sunday morning the inhabitants were called to worship by a town crier; a drummer keeps up this old Calvinist tradition to this day.

Dutch Reform church: Founded in 1652. The late-17C cruciform church was converted in 1766–1804 to form the present hall church with a nave and two aisles. 19C pulpit and organ.

Museum Venendal (9 Hoofdstraat): A museum occupying a mansion dating from 1653 exhibiting peat-cutting utensils. Opening times: Mon.–

Amstenrade (Hoensbroek), Huis Amstenrade

Fri. 10 a.m.–12 noon and 2–4.30 p.m., Sat. 2–4.30 p.m.

Environs: Echten (4 km. W.): *Huis te Echten*, is an elegant 18C country house surrounded by water. Remains of older buildings survive.

Ruinen (10 km. W.): The lower tufa sections of the nave and tower of the *Dutch Reform church* probably date from the time the chapel of a Benedictine monastery chapel occupied the site. The tower dates from 1423; the spire is probably from 1663. The monastery cellar beneath the priest's house can still be seen. The former *Posthuis te Anholt*, a gabled building with a taproom, old tiles and an 18C fireplace, is E. of the village. Post coaches formerly changed horses here. The *Oudheidkamer* (12 Smeestraat) has a room in rustic Drente style. Visits can be arranged with the VVV (tourist office). The *Bezoekerscentrum De Schaapskooi* (38 Benderse) is a sheepfold and shepherd's lodging. Information on moorland sheep, beekeeping, and moorland flora and fauna, is available here. Opening times: 10 a.m.–12 noon and 2–6 p.m. daily.

Ruinerwold (17 km. W.): The originally Romanesque *Dutch Reform church* in Blijdenstein was altered in the 15C. Many richly decorated 18C and early-19C *farmhouses* along Dr.Larijweg, the so-called Bovenboer. The *Museum Oude Boerderij* (21 Dr.Larijweg) occupies a farmhouse dating from 1860 and contains old decorative objects and implements. Opening times: May–Aug.: Mon.–Sat. 9 a.m.–6 p.m.; Sep.–Apr.: Mon.–Sat. 10 a.m.–5 p.m. The tile museum, 53 Dr.Larijweg, has old tiles, tiled ovens and open stoves. Opening times: May–Sept. Mon.–Sat. 10 a.m.–5 p.m.

Hoorn
North Holland   p.286☐I 4

History: Built in *c.* 1300 as a settlement for North German and Danish merchants. Granted a charter in 1357. Hoorn was an important port on the Zuiderzee in the 16&17C, and the East and West India Companies and the Noordse Compagnie had branches here. Hoorn joined with William of Orange at the beginning of the Eighty Years' War and in the sea battle of 1573 Admiral Bossu, who was aligned with the Spanish, was defeated by the Sea Beggars. With the rise of Amsterdam in the 18C Hoorn lost much of its importance as a port, and in the Napoleonic period it also relinquished its role as an administrative centre.

Noorderkerk: A pretty late Gothic church founded in 1426. The nave dates from 1441, the transept and choir are from 1450, and the aisle was completed in 1519. Also interesting are a late Gothic spiral oak staircase (1497), pulpit (1635) and choir screen (1642).

Oosterkerk: A late Gothic church founded in 1450. Choir and transept date from 1518–19; 1615–16 the old

Ruinen (Hoogeveen), Dutch Reform church

nave was replaced by the present single-aisled structure with a splendid Renaissance façade. The charming turret above the crossing is said to date from *c*. 1600. The naval battle of Gibraltar (1607) is depicted in a window dating from 1620.

Stadhuis: In 1796, the town hall was moved to the Gecommiteerde Raden inn, a site formerly occupied by the St.-Ceciliaklooster (founded 1402; only the chapel survives). The façade of the present building has an ornate double stepped gable (1613). The council chamber (*c*. 1787) with beautiful panelling was originally a dining hall for the Gecommitteerde Raden of the monastery chapel.

Fortifications: The *Maria-* or *Kruittoren* tower on the N. side is part of the new town wall begun in 1508. In the same style, but much larger, is the *Hoodtoren,* a massive fortified tower (1532) with a delicate turret (1651). When the town was enlarged, the Renaissance *Nieuwe Oosterpoort* (1578) was built in the E., with a

Hoorn, Hoofdtoren, town fortifications

guard house (1602) of charming appearance above.

Waag: The weigh-house (1609) was designed by Hendrick de Keyser. Outside is the statue of Jan Pietersz. Coen, the town's most famous son, who founded Batavia the capital of Indonesia, now called Jakarta.

Westfries Museum: (1 Rode Steen): This is housed in the headquarters of the Gecommitteerde Raden van het Noorderkwartier which was built in 1631–2 and is one of the finest buildings in Hoorn. The apex and curving sides of the gable of the lavish stone façade (with an order of pilasters) are decorated with seven lions with the coats-of-arms of the towns of Noorderkwartier, West Friesland and Orange. The museum has collections of pictures of hunters, 17&18C decorative objects, and documents relating to the town's history. Opening times: Mon.–Fri. 11 a.m.–5 p.m., Sat. and Sun. 2–5 p.m.

Also worth seeing: The middle part of the façade of the *former house of the guild of St.Sebastian* (Achterstraat) dates from 1615; the left wing with a colossdal order of pilasters dates from 1648, while the right part is late 18C. The splendid gable façade of the *St.-Jansgasthuis* (39 Kerkplein) dates from 1563 and is one of the most beautiful early Renaissance façades in the Netherlands. The many small *portals* include that of the *former admiralty* (1607) behind the Grote Kerk (1881–3) and, to the left of this, the gate of the *former Oude Vrouwenhuis* (1610). Other examples include *2 Doelenpoortjes* behind the Maria- or Kruittoren (1638), and the gate of the *orphanage* in the Korte Achterstraat. There are many old 17&18C *gable façades* on houses and warehouses in the *Grote Oost, Bierkade, Grote Noord, Veermanskade* and in the *Munnikenveld.* The three so-called *Bossuhuizen* near the Oosterpoort are decorated with friezes depicting the battle of 1573.

Environs: Spanbroek (12 km. NW): The small *town hall* (1598) has two stepped gables. The late Gothic *Dutch Reform church* has a splendid memorial stone to Johannes van Gheel, a Spanbroek nobleman (d. 1668) by Rombout Verhulst,
Sybekarspel (11 km. NW): The small *Dutch Reform church* (1547) has a pretty pulpit and a bell dating from 1682. The village has some fine *Stolphoeven*, or farms in which the farmhouses, stables and barns are all gathered under a pyramidal roof.
Wognum (5 km. NW): A 15&16C late Gothic, single-aisled *Dutch Reform church* with a fine large tower and a tall choir.

Hulst
Zeeland   p.288□F 8

Hulst, the shopping centre for eastern Zeeuws-Vlaanderen, is a fortified town full of character with gates and ramparts still in good condition. The original medieval fortifications were reinforced in the 17C by Menno van Coehoorn the fortress architect. Three city gates still lead into the town; the water and land gate has been modernized for modern traffic.

St.-Willibrordusbasiliek: The oldest part of this building is the Romanesque tower (*c.* 1400) over the crossing; the Gothic tower dates from 1462. In 1469 the nave burned down and reconstruction work lasted until 1562. The church was redesigned for the Dutch Reform church in 1645, and in 1806 it was divided in two: Reform worshippers were given the nave, while the choir and crossing went to the Roman Catholics. The dividing wall was dismantled in 1929 when Reform worshippers gave up their section of the church to the Roman Catholics. The tower, which had in the meantime been rebuilt by Petrus Josephus Hubertus Cuypers, was damaged in 1944 and now has a concrete crown.

Hoorn, Westfries Museum, painting of swordsmen

Stadhuis: The town hall (1528–34) in white ashlars is by Laurijs Keldermans. The Gothic exterior disappeared almost entirely during rebuilding work in 1844. Stone lions are by Michiel van Rijselen, the sculptor from Antwerp. Opening times: Mon.–Fri. 8.30 a.m.–12 noon and 1–4.30 p.m.

Environs: Axel: (9 km. W.): The *local museum of Het Land van Axel* has a reconstruction of a room from a 19C farmhouse, local costumes, agricultural implements, as well as archaeological finds from nearby. Opening times: 1 Apr.–30 Sept. Wed.–Sat. 1.30–5 p.m., July and Aug. also Fri. 7–9 p.m.

Kloosterzande (14 km. N.): The town derives its name from the monastery in Zande. Its former chapel is now the *village church*. 13C choir; 17C nave.

IJlst/Drylts
Friesland   See p.267

IJsselstein
Utrecht   See p.267

IJendijke
Zeeland   See p.268

◁ *Hulst, St.Willibrordusbasiliek*

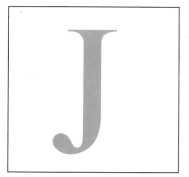

Joure De Jouwer

Friesland   p.287☐L 3

Joure, originally only a suburb of Mestermeer, developed faster than its parent town in the 17C. Parts of the harbour (1614) survive.

Dutch Reform church (Midstraat): This church (1644) has a tower (1628) with an open lantern. In 1939 the roof was destroyed by a fire which also damaged the interior decorations. This damage has now been repaired. The pulpit comes from a church in Leeuwarden. The carillon of 37 bells was donated in 1955.

Heremastate: The site of this former mansion is now occupied by the modern town hall building.

Museums: *Johannes Hessel Huis* (1 Geelgieterstraat) has a natural history department, an exhibition devoted to coffee and tea, and a collection of tobacco pipes. Opening times: Mon.–Fri. 10 a.m.–12 noon and 2–5 p.m., Sun. 2–5 p.m. In the house where *Egbert Douwes* was born one can see an 18C Frisian one-room dwelling. Same opening times as above.

Also worth seeing: *De Witte Os*, a tea- and sweetshop in 19C style; there

Joure, Dutch Reform church ▷

144 Kampen

is also a clockmaker's workshop which is open to the public. The town has two splendid *mills,* the 'Penninga's Molen' in the Molenweg (grinding is done here on Sat. mornings) and the 'Groene Molen' (1800) in the Groenendijk, a spinning-head mill.

Events: The *Jouster Merke,* a large fair and horse market on the fourth Thur. in Sept., has been held since 1466.

Environs: Goingarijp/Goajingaryp (8 km. NW): An attractive *small church* dating from 1770 has survived in good condition in its picturesque location by the village pond.

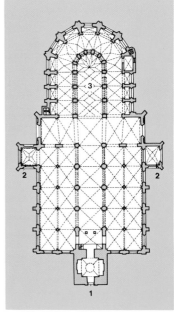

Kampen, Boven- or St.-Nicolaaskerk **1** Tower on 13C foundations **2** Portals from c. 1500 **3** 14C choir and ambulatory

Kampen
Overijssel   p.287☐L 4

History: Kampen was situated where the IJssel flows into the Zuiderzee, which is now the IJsselmeer. First buildings date from *c.* 1170 and it was granted a charter between 1236 and 1248. An important trading centre due to its favourable location, Kampen joined the Hanseatic League in 1441; in 1495 Emperor Maximilian I of Austria granted it the right to call itself a 'Free Imperial Town'. An economic decline began when the IJssel silted up in the 16C. Only when the Zuiderzee was drained did Kampen again become important as a centre of communications.

Bovenkerk or **St.-Nicolaaskerk:** A large Gothic cruciform basilica (probably begun *c.* 1325) with a slender tower, nave and four aisles, choir, ambulatory and a ring of chapels. Herman de Steenbicker and his brother worked on the church in *c.* 1345, and Rüdiger of Cologne, son of Michael, the architect of the Cologne cathedral, is said to have been at work here in 1369. Building work on the church was still in progress in 1456. The portals on the N. and S. sides of the nave date from *c.* 1500; the tall spire seen on the tower today was erected in 1808. The spacious interior

Kampen, Broederpoort ▷

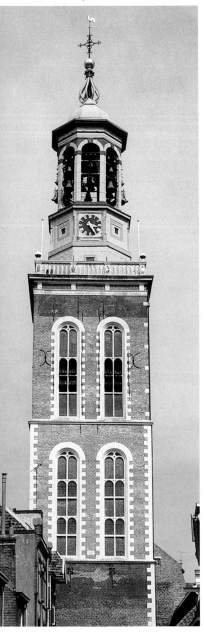

is more impressive than the exterior would lead one to believe, especially fine is the monumental *choir*, which represents a high point of Northern Dutch Gothic.

Broederkerk: This Dutch Reform church, which was mainly built 1473–90, was formerly the church of the Minderbroedersklooster (Franciscan). In the W. part of the building, the two aisles are divided by slender columns with foliate capitals. There is an attractive stepped turret over the choir.

Onze-Lieve-Vrouwekerk or **Buitenkerk:** This Roman Catholic hall church was originally a 14C cruciform church. Rüdiger of Cologne is again thought to have been the original architect. The tower was probably built in 1453–4.

Doopsgezinde Kerk (Broederweg): This single-aisled Mennonite church (late 15C) was originally the chapel of the Cellezustersconvent.

Lutherse Kerk (Burgwal): A small single-aisled neoclassical church (1843) by Nicolaas Plomp.

Stadhuis: The oldest part of the town hall dating from the late 14C is a small but very richly decorated late Gothic building with a tower on the side facing the river. Projecting balustrades along the roof date from rebuilding after a fire in 1543. The *statues* on the *façade* were made in 1933–8 by Johan Polet to replace their weather-worn late Gothic predecessors; they depict Charlemagne, Alexander the Great, Temperance, Faith, Justice and Mercy. The splendid *Schepenzaal* or council chamber has a richly decorated Renaissance fireplace (1543–5), splendid oak panelling and doors and the fine burgomaster's seat by Master Frederik the town's master carpenter.

◁ *Kampen, Nieuwe Toren*

Broederpoort: The gate's four corner towers, which in their original form date from 1465, were attractively redesigned in Renaissance style by Thomas Berendsz in 1615.

Cellebroederspoort: This square gatehouse (1465) flanked by two massive round towers was, like the previous gate, redesigned in Renaissance style by Thomas Berendsz in 1617, again more for effect than for defence. Beyond the two gates there are mid-19C ramparts with gardens designed by Zocher.

Koornmarktpoort: This square gatehouse on the IJssel probably goes back to the 14C and round corner towers were added in the 15C. The roughcasting dates from 1848.

Nieuwe Toren: The 'New Tower' is a free-standing building (1648–64) with a passageway beneath. The octagonal wooden crown was designed by Philips Vingboons, and the carillon of 1660 is by François Hémony.

Stedelijk Museum (158 Oudestraat): This museum occupies the town's only surviving late Gothic house (*c.* 1500). Stone façade with very large windows.

Frans Walkate Archief (41 Burgwal): Exhibits concerned with the topography of the town and province; 19&20C views of the town.

Also worth seeing: *Residential houses* including *119 Oudestraat* with a Renaissance façade from 1596 and *100 Boven Nieuwstraat* (*c.* 1630) with a façade in the style of Hendrick de Keyser.

Katwijk
South Holland   p.289☐G 5

The town of Katwijk is composed of two districts, Katwijk aan Zee and

Katwijk aan de Rijn (also known as Katwijk-Binnen) which gradually coalesced to become one.

Katwijk aan de Rijn: The tower and main choir of the *Dutch Reform church* date from *c.* 1300; the nave is mostly mid 15C. The sumptuous marble tomb (1663) of Willem van Lyere (d. 1654) and Maria van Reygersberg (d. 1673), is one of the best works by Romhout Verhulst the sculptor, and can be seen on the N. side of the choir. The upright '*De Gerechtigheid*' *corn mill* dates from 1740.

Katwijk aan Zee: The *old Dutch Reform church*, which was probably built shortly after 1461, had a nave, two aisles and a slender tower. After the village was pillaged by the Spanish, the church was rebuilt on a smaller scale in 1572 and enlarged in 1709. The neo-Renaissance *new Dutch Reform church* (1887) is by H.J. Jesse. S. of the village there is a firebeacon (1605), a forerunner of lighthouses.

Kerkrade
Limburg   p.291☐M 9

Until a few years ago Kerkrade was a typical coal-mining town, but recently efforts have been made to introduce other industries. The first coal mine (1742) was set up by monks from Rolduc abbey.

Rolduc abbey: This former Augustinian abbey, today a Roman Catholic junior seminary belonging to the diocese of Roermond, was founded in 1104 by the Belgian monk Ailbert. The 'Annales Rodenses', the original manuscript of the monastery chronicle, gives the architectural history of the abbey church, a 12C Romanesque basilica which has suffered frequent damage but today once again has an impressive Romanesque interior. (Today the manuscript is in the

imperial archive in Maastricht.) Repair work was supervised by the neo-Gothic Dutch architect Petrus Josephus Hubertus Cuypers from 1853 onwards. The fine trefoil *crypt*, whose E. section is 12C, has capitals richly decorated with human and animal forms amid leafy tendrils. The nave has the tomb of Walram III, Duke of Limburg (d. 1226), with a relief of the dead man in armour (a 17C copy). In 1189, Walram III took part in the Third Crusade under Richard Lionheart. He is regarded as a forefather of the House of Orange. The 17&18 monastery buildings have broad gable façades.
Opening times: 1 May–15 Sept.: Tues.–Sat. 9 a.m.–5 p.m.; 15 July–15 Aug.: also Sun. 1.30–5 p.m.; 15 Sept.–1 May: Tues.–Fri. 1–4.30 p.m., and 1–4.30 p.m. on the second Saturday of every month.

Also worth seeing: The *Roman Catholic church* (1843), with a nave and two aisles. Enlarged in 1956; the 18C tower was increased in height in 1959–60. The early-19C *Nieuw-Ehrenstein* has a mansard roof.

Kollum
Friesland   p.287☐M 2

Dutch Reform church: This brick church from the first half of the 15C has two aisles and a tower (*c.* 1200; partly built of tufa). The tower was increased in height in the 15C, and its spire dates from 1661. Inside there are fragments of vault paintings, 17C pews decorated with coats-of-arms, a pulpit of 1692 and interesting tombstones.

Also worth seeing: The *town hall* is in an early-19C mansion in the Empire style. Remains of stucco decorations survive inside the building.
Fine *houses* in *Oostenburgstraat* and *Westerdiepswal*.

Environs: Burum/Bûrum (8 km. E.): A satellite ground station with dishes 94 and 105 ft. tall stands in the open country outside the village. The *Dutch Reform church* is a simple structure with a tower (1784). The *corn mill* dates from 1694.
Veenklooster/Feankleaster (5 km. SW): *'Fogelsangh State'* (a country house) was built on the site of an old Premonstratensian monastery in the 17C. The gable façade dates from *c.* 1730. In 1873 it was increased in height and given a roughcast finish. Today it is a *regional museum* and a branch of the Fries Museum in Leeuwarden. Large collection of toys.
Opening times: 1 May–30 Sept.: Mon.–Sat. 10 a.m.–5 p.m.; 1 July–30 Sept.: also Sun. 1–5 p.m.

Leek
Groningen   p.287☐N 2

Huize Nienoord: Two small portals (late 17C) and a rich stone gate (1708) survive from this former 16C castle. The present building was erected in *c.* 1880 on older foundations. In 1958 the *Nationale Rijtuigmuseum* came to occupy the building and its grounds. The museum has a large collection of coaches, carriages, covered wagons and old wheeled vehicles of all kinds. The fine park has various statues and a pretty 18C *summerhouse*, the inside of which is a shell grotto. Opening times: Good Friday–1 Oct.: 9 a.m.–5 p.m. daily.

Also worth seeing: The *Dutch Reform church* (1660), a small single-aisled church with pointed-arched windows and a fine pulpit (1752).

Environs: Lutjegast (12 km. NW): A panel on the wall of the *Dutch Reform church* (1877) commemorates the birth here of Albert Tasman, the famous explorer (1604–59) who discovered Tasmania in 1642 and the Tonga and Fiji islands in 1643.
Midwolde (2 km. N.): The 12C *brick church* in this village in Westerkwartier is the oldest in origin of any church in the province. The marble tomb (1665–9) of Carel Hieronymus v. Innen Knyphuizen is an important work by Rombout Verhulst. In 1714 his wife, Anna van Ewsum, commissioned Bartholomeus Eggers to add to it the figure of Georg Wilhelm v. Innen Knyphuizen, her second husband.
Tolbert (0.5 km. NW): The *Dutch Reform church* (13/14C) has an enor-mous tower (probably 13C) with an upper storey dating from *c.* 1600.

Leens
Groningen   p.287□N 2

Dutch Reform church of St.Peter: Tufa nave from *c.* 1100, transept and choir from *c.* 1200; the tower was built in 1863. Decorations from the Protestant period include a pulpit and a large organ (1733) by A.A. Hinsch.

Borg Verhildershum: The original 14C castle surrounded by moats was formerly inhabited by the Tjarda van Starkenborgh family. It was con-verted into a country house in the 17/18C. The interior, decorated in 19C style, is open to the public as a *museum* with porcelain, portraits of former residents, and an exhibition on the history of the province. Opening times: Good Friday–Nov.: Tues.–Sat. 10.30 a.m.–5.30 p.m.

Environs: Baflo (11 km. E.): The

Leek, Huize Nienoord

Dutch Reform church has been considerably altered both outside and inside. The W. section is probably still 12C; the free-standing tower with saddleback roof would seem to be no earlier than 1300.

Eenrum (6 km. E.): This village in the middle of the marshland of North Groningen has a *Dutch Reform church* which is probably late-13C. The dominant W. tower (1646–52) has an octagonal lower section. Early-19C decorations survive almost in their entirety.

Mensingeweer (6 km. E.): The core of the *Dutch Reform church* is medieval, although the rest is much altered. 18C turret. The '*Hollands Welvaart*' *corn mill* was built in 1855.

Pieterburen (8 km. N.): The picturesquely located Gothic *Dutch Reform church* dates from the first half of the 15C; the N. transept is much later and the tower dates from 1805. Inside there is an ornate Louis Seize pulpit, a fine baptismal railing, shields bearing coats-of-arms and a late-18C noblemen's pew.

Wehe-den Hoorn (2.5 km. E.): The *Roman Catholic church* has a sand-

Leerdam, Hofje van Aerden

stone Virgin from the first half of 16C which may be from the Aduard monastery.

Leerdam
South Holland   p.290□I 6

Today this little town on the Linge is the centre of the glass-making industry which was set up in the 18C. Remains of the old fortifications have survived; three square tower dwellings on the ramparts are of interest.

Dutch Reform church: Late Gothic church with a partly Romanesque tower and a choir built in the second half of 15C with a stone net vault.

Hofje van Aerden: A religious institution of 1770 for women. It occupies the site of the former castle of the van Arkel family. The rococo warden's room houses a collection of paintings (mostly portraits) by Frans Hals, Gerard Terborch, Philips Koninck and Hendrik Jakobsz. Dubbels. Opening times: Tues. and Thur. 2–4 p.m.

Nationaal Glasmuseum (28 Lingedijk): Fine ancient and modern glass from Holland and abroad, including work by Berlage and Frank Lloyd Wright. Opening times: Tues.–Fri. 10 a.m.–1 p.m. and 2–5 p.m., Sat., Sun. and holidays 1–5 p.m. (Nov.–Mar.: closed Sat. and Sun.).

Leeuwarden/Ljouwert
Friesland   p.287□L 2

History: Leeuwarden, the capital of the province, was mentioned in the 11C. Built on three terpen at the point where the Ee flows into the sea, Leeuwarden was an important port before its approaches were silted up. The town received a charter in the late 13C. Albrecht of Saxony con-

quered Leeuwarden for Emperor Maximilian I in 1498. It then became the administrative centre of the stadholders and later their place of residence (1584–1748).

Grote or Jacobijnekerk: This Dutch Reform church originally belonged to the church of the Dominican monastery founded in the mid 13C. The large 14C *choir* has survived and since 1588 it has been the burial site of the Frisian members of the Nassau family, whose names and coats-of-arms can be seen on the walls, along with a stone commemorating the peace of Münster. The S. side of the choir stands beyond the Oranjepoortje, a gate dating from *c.* 1660. There is a small gate (1663) on the E. side of the Broodkapel chapel which was added in the early 16C. The church was enlarged and increased in height in the 15C, and the interior was redesigned in classical style in 1842.

Westerkerk (Bagijnestraat): The former church of the Beguine monastery (*c.* 1510) was enlarged in *c.* 1680 and redesigned inside in 1845.

Oldehove Toren: The main body of this large late-Gothic tower on the top of a terp was begun in 1529 to a design by Jakob v. Aachen based on the tower of Utrecht cathedral; it was left incomplete in 1532 probably because the ground had subsided.

Kanselarij (Turfmarkt): What is today the imperial archive was built as a courthouse in 1566–71. The extended façade is crowned by balusters; above the entrance there is a delicate gable decorated with statues. Ornaments, partly late Gothic and partly early Renaissance, contribute to the building's singular appearance.

Paleis van Justitie (Wilhelminaplein): A stately classical government building of 1846–52 by T.Romein, the town architect.

Provinciehuis (52 Tweebaksmarkt): An existing house was converted in 1580, enlarged in 1710 and given a new façade in 1784. The windows of the neo-Gothic *Statenzaal* (1893) are decorated with the coats-of-arms of Frisian towns, provinces and districts; coats-of-arms belonging to the ruling Frisian families are set in the vaulted ceiling.

Stadhouderlijk Hof (Hofplein): Acquired in 1587 for use as the stadholders' residence. The building was enlarged in 1603 and decorated under Willem Frederik and Albertina Anna. The dining hall has 18C panelling and portraits of the family of Orange.

Stadhuis: The town hall (1713) by Claes Bockes Balk stands on the foundations of a residential tower which was demolished. Statues of Justice and Peace stand atop the entrance and above the triangular gable there is a domed turret with a carillon of bells from 1688. The interior has fine decorations including a room for weddings (1845) in classical style.

Leeuwarden, Princessehof

Waag (Nieuwstad): The weigh-house is a Renaissance building dating from 1596–98). Between the two storeys there is a stone frieze with triglyphs and metopes.

Fries Museum (24 Turfmarkt): A museum of Frisian cultural history in an 18C mansion. Opening times: Tues.–Sat. 10 a.m.–5 p.m., Sun. 1–5 p.m.

Gemeentelijk Museum Het Prinsessehof (9–15 Grote Kerkstraat): This museum has a good collection of porcelain from China, Japan and Indonesia covering the period from *c*. 300 BC until *c*. 1900. Opening times: Mon.–Sat. 10 a.m.–5 p.m., Sun. 2–5 p.m. The *Pier Pandermuseum* exhibits his sculptures. Opening times: Tues.–Sat. 9 a.m.–1 p.m. and 2–5 p.m.

Fries Letterkundig Museum en Documentatiecentrum (28 Grote Kerkstraat): This museum devoted to literature occupies the house where Mata Hari (Margaretha Geertruida Zelle), legendary dancer and spy, lived from 1883–90. Opening times:

Mon.–Fri. 9 a.m.–12 noon and 2–5 p.m.

Fries Natuurhistorisch Museum (13–15 Heerestraat): Flora and fauna from Friesland. Opening times: Tues.–Sat. 10 a.m.–12 noon and 2–5 p.m., Mon. 2–5 p.m.

Verzetsmuseum Friesland (13 Turfmarkt): Documents and photographs from World War 2 and the 1940–5 occupation. Opening times: Tues.–Sat. 10 a.m.–5 p.m., Sun. 1–5 p.m.

Also worth seeing: The *Roman-Catholic Bonifatiuskerk church* (1882) is a neo-Gothic cruciform basilica by Petrus Josephus Hubertus Cuypers. The *main guardhouse* (1688) was redesigned by T.Romein in classical style in 1845. The *Stadhouderlijke Rijschool* (stadholder's riding school, 17 Grote Kerkstraat), rebuilt in 1680, has an ornate portal. The town has many attractive *gates: 1 Jacobijnerkerkhof* (1675); the *rear entrance of post office in Galileerkerkstraat* (mid 17C); *Schoenmakersperk*, a classical gate of

Leeuwarden, weigh-house, detail

the former Anthoniusspital hospital; *54 Noordersingel* (1658); the *Poptapoortje* (South Nieuwstad, near to No. 54) dating from 1696.

Environs: Beers/Bears (7 km. S.): The 13&14C *Dutch Reform church* has a tower and W. façade (1858), a fine Renaissance railing (*c.* 1540), and decorations mainly from the 18C. Today the church houses the *'De Poarte fan Bears' museum*. Opening times: Beginning of May–30 Sept.: Mon.–Sat. 10 a.m.–12 noon and 2–5 p.m.

Boksum or **Boxum** (3 km. SW): The nave of the *Dutch Reform church* is partly 12C, the choir 13C. The tower dates from 1843. Inside there is a memorial panel to those who fell in the battle against the Spanish at Boksum in 1586.

Britsum (4 km. N.): A 13C Romanesque-Gothic building with tower is concealed beneath the roughcast finish (1875) of the *little church*. Inside there are a pulpit and two 17C noblemen's pews. Menno van Coehoorn, the famous fortress architect, was born in Britsum.

Kornjum/Koarnjum (3 km. N.): This gate, dating from 1620 and coming from a Leeuwarden building demolished in 1849, was erected here in 1955. Today it leads to the recently built *Martena estate*. The gate is flanked by two pilasters and a gable on which the Frisian coat-of-arms stands between two lions.

Oenkerk/Oentsjerk (10 km. NE): The *Dutch Reform church* has a late Romanesque nave and a tower of somewhat later date; in the portal there are tombstones and sculptures of *c.* 1550 by Vincent Lucas. The elegant *Stania State country house* (1843) is set in a large landscaped park with 18C statues.

Stiens (8 km. N.): The *Dutch Reform church* (11–13C) with a 16C saddleback roof stands in the middle of a round graveyard with four entrances.

Leiden

South Holland · p.289□G 5

A settlement called *Leythen* was mentioned in the 10C. It rapidly devel-

Oenkerk (Leeuwarden), Stania State's garden

oped into the main town in the Rhine district and in 1266 Count Floris V granted the town a charter. In the 14&15C it was a flourishing centre of the cloth industry. After the town had successfully withstood a siege by Spanish troops, the university founded by Wilhelm of Orange in 1575 led to the town's revival, this time as a stronghold of learning. The French philosopher Descartes and the theologians Arminius and Gomarus all studied here, and Hermannus Boerhaave, the medical scholar, was a teacher here. After the golden age of the 17C, Leiden fortunes declined and did not recover until about the mid 19C. Today the town is once again a centre of industrial and scientific life.

Religious buildings

Pieterskerk: This late Gothic cruciform basilica was begun in the late 14C under the supervision of Rutger van Kampen, and continued from 1409 onwards under Aernt Bruun, who built the cathedral in Utrecht. The sacristy was completed in 1399, and the choir was consecrated in

Leiden, Pieterskerk, interior

1412. The present nave and four aisles were completed by the late 15C on the site of a ruined 12C nave. The tower which was still standing at that time collapsed in 1512, and the nave with its wooden tunnel vault was built in its place. The two broad transepts with two aisled were added at a later date (*c.* 1500). The broad, light interior has a richly carved late Gothic *pulpit* (*c.* 1525) and an *organ* (1639–41). The white marble tomb monument (1663) to J.A. Kerchove in the N. transept is the work of Rombout Verhulst.

Hartebrugkerk (Lange Mare): A Roman Catholic church (1835–6) built by R.Molkenboer in the Waterstaatsstijl style. The façade has an unusual portal with Ionic columns on a rusticated plinth. The tower dates from 1892; the choir from 1896–7.

Lodewijkskerk   (Steenschuur): Originally, in 1538, this was the chapel of the St.-Jacobsgasthuis hospital. It became a Roman Catholic church in 1808 by order of Louis (Lodewijk) Bonaparte, king of Holland from 1806–10. Restored and enlarged in 1956–7. The wooden top (1588) of the tower was actually built for one of the towers in the town, but was installed here in 1593.

Marekerk (Oude Vest): This Renaissance Dutch Reform church (1639–49) built to plans by Arent van 's-Gravesande, is a centrally planned octagonal structure. Jacob van Campen added the monumental standstone portal a short time later. The pulpit dates from 1649; the organ (1629) was brought here from the Pieterskerk in 1733.

St.-Pancras- or Hooglandse Kerk (Hooigracht): Today a Dutch Reform church. The 14C tower is the oldest part of this former collegiate church. The choir was begun in the second half of the 15C, and the transept dates from *c.* 1500. Work on the nave seems to have been stopped in the first half of the 16C after proceeding as far as the old tower. The Gothic W. portal dates from 1665. The plan was probably that the whole church should have stone vaults, but they were only built in the ambulatory and aisles. There are 19C wooden stellar vaults in choir and transept. A memorial slab (1661) by Rombout Verhulst is dedicated to Mayor van der Werff (d. 1604), who defended the town in the siege of 1574.

Waalse Kerk (64 Breestrat): Originally the late Gothic chapel of the St.-Catharinagasthuis hospital, it was enlarged in 1634–5. The present façade and baroque turret date from 1737–9. Parts of the hospital, which formerly adjoined the church on both sides, have survived.

Secular buildings
Academie (73 Rapenburg): This rectangular building, formerly the church of the Dominican convent, was consecrated in 1516. In 1581 it became the main building of the university. The wooden turret (1670) is by Willem van der Helm. An ornate Renaissance monument (1556) to Vincent Lucas reminds the visitor of the building's original function. The Senaatskamer, with its many portraits of university professors, was redesigned by Hieronymus van der Mij in 1733–7. The *Academisch Historisch Museum* is open from 2–5 p.m. on Tue. and Fri.

Bibliotheca Thysiana (25 Rapenburg): Founded in 1655 and built to the plans of Arent van 's-Gravesande. The façade with Ionic pilasters on the upper storey survives in good condition, as do the original decorations.

Burcht: This castle at the confluence of the Oude and Nieuwe Rijn was probably built in *c.* 1200 on a man-made hill 39 ft. high formerly used as a refuge in storm tides. The almost round wall surrounding the castle courtyard is about 115 ft. in diameter. On the inside of it there are large arched niches, with a wall passage above. Many sections have been rebuilt and repaired over the years.

Doelenpoort (Groenhazengracht): The present entrance gate (1645) of the Doelen barracks is by Arent van 's-Gravesande; crowning figure is St.George on horseback.

St.-Elisabethsgasthuis (Ceciliastraat): A former hospital founded in 1428 and converted into an old people's home in 1970–1.

Gemeenlandshuis van Rijnland (59 Breestraat): The late-16C house of the dyke association has been rebuilt several times. Inside there is a courtroom (second half of 17C) by Pieter Post, with a painted wooden barrel vault.

Gravensteen: This building (probably originally 13C) near the Pieterskerk was formerly the county

Leiden, Academie

prison and later became the town prison. Enlarged in the 17C. Wall paintings from 1566 have been discovered in the cells (Christ on the Cross, and the Mocking of Christ).

Hofjes: Leiden is well-known for its many picturesque Hofjes or *almshouses* which often bear the founder's name. Despite the Reformation, *St.-Annahofje* (9 Hooigracht) founded in 1492 has retained the chapel with its original decorations. The sandstone gate dates from 1685. The *Hofje van Broekhoven* (1640) at 16 Papengracht is probably by Arent van 's-Gravesande. *Meermansburg* (159 Oude Vest), founded in 1681, is the largest Hofje in the town and has portraits by Jacob Cuyp and Jan de Baen. *Tevelingshof* (1666) at 7 Vierde Binnenvestgracht is attributed to Willem van der Helm, the town architect.

Korenbrug and **Korenbeurs:** This bridge across the Rhine dates from 1642. The cereal market, which consists of two open colonnaded structures, was added to it by Salomon van der Paauw, town architect in 1825.

Leiden, Bibliotheca Thysiana

Lakenhal (29 Oude Singel): The former cloth hall (1639–40) by Arent van 's-Gravesande. The sculptures are the work of Bartholomeus Drijffhout and Pieter A.'t Hooft (see Museums).

Stadhuis (Breestraat): The town hall is medieval in origin. The fine *Renaissance gable façade* (1594–7) is by Lieven de Key. After the fire of 1929 it proved possible to restore the façade, but the rest of the town hall had to be rebuilt.

Waag (corner of Aalmarkt and Mandmakerssteeg): The weigh-house and the butter hall (Boterhal) behind it are both by Pieter Post (1657–9). The gable façade of the weigh-house is entirely of sandstone, and has reliefs by Rombout Verhulst.

Museums

Museum Boerhaave (1a Steenstraat): Collections covering mathematics, natural science and medicine. Opening times: 1 Oct.–1 June: Mon.–Sat. 10 a.m.–4 p.m., Sun. 1–4 p.m.; 1 June–1 Oct.: Mon.–Sat. 10 a.m.–5 p.m., Sun. 1–5 p.m.; closed on 1 Jan., 3 Oct. and general holidays.

Koninklijk Nederlands Leger- en Wapenmuseum 'General Hoefer' (7 Pesthuislaan): This army museum in the former plague building (1658–61) has an entrance relief by Rombout Verhulst. The items on display include films about World War 2. Opening times: Mon.–Fri. 9 a.m.–5 p.m., Sun. 1–5 p.m.; closed on 25 Dec., 1 Jan., 30 Apr. and 3 Oct.

Molenmuseum 'De Valk' (1 Binnenvestgracht 2de): The miller's lodging, workshop and smithy are on display in the windmill (1743) along with models of mills and other exhibits. Opening times: Tue.–Sat. 10 a.m.–5 p.m., Sun. and holidays 1–5 p.m.

Pilgrim Fathers Documentatie

Centrum (2a Boisotkade): The items in the Pilgrim Fathers information centre include town views from the first few decades of the 17C. Opening times: Mon.–Fri. 9 a.m.–12 noon and 2–4.30 p.m.; closed on 3 Oct. and holidays.

Prentenkabinett of the Rijksuniversiteit (65 Rapenburg): History of photography, collection of copper etchings, drawings and photographs. Opening times: Mon.–Fri. 2–5 p.m.

Rijksmuseum van Geologie en Mineralogie (17 Hooglandse Kerkgracht): Devoted to the geology of the Netherlands, history of life on Earth, minerals, meteorites, tektites and precious stones. Opening times: Mon.–Fri. 10 a.m.–12 noon and 2–5 p.m.; closed on 3 Oct. and general holidays.

Rijksmuseum van Oudheden (28 Rapenburg): Archaeology of the Netherlands, finds from Egypt, Mesopotamia, the Middle East, Greece and Italy. Opening times: Mon.–Sat. 10 a.m.–5 p.m., Sun. and holidays 1–5 p.m.; closed on 1 Jan. and 3 Oct.

Rijksmuseum voor Volkenkunde (1 Steenstraat): Objects of both use and beauty from all non-European countries. Opening times: Mon.–Sat. 10 a.m.–5 p.m.; Sun. and holidays 1–5 p.m; closed on 1 Jan. and 3 Oct.

Stedelijk Museum 'De Lakenhal' (28–32 Oude Singel): This world-famous museum has a paintings by Lucas van Leyden, Jan van Goyen, Jan Steen, Gerard Dou and an early work by Rembrandt, who was born in Leiden. There are also sculptures, works of decorative art and archaeological finds. Opening times: Mon.–Sat. 10 a.m.–5 p.m., Sun. and holidays 1–5 p.m.; 3 Oct.: 10 a.m.–12 noon; closed on 1 Jan.

Also worth seeing: The *fountain* (1692–3) in the Vismarkt was probably designed by Jacob Roman, town architect at the time. Two gates by Willem van der Helm, the *Zijlpoort* (1667) and the decorative *Morschpoort* (1668–9), survive from the 17C fortifications. The *orphanage* (Weeshuis, 17 Hooglandse Kerkgracht) is a picturesque group of 17C buildings. The following fine *gable façades* should be mentioned: *72 Oude Singel* (c. 1615), *9 Pieterskerkgracht* (1620), and *56 Breestraat* (c. 1629). The *Rapenburg*, the 'most beautiful canal in Europe' is overlooked by many more gables (somewhat later than those mentioned before). The house where Rembrandt was born used to stand opposite the Stadstimmerwerf (the town carpenter's house; 1612) beside the Golgewater; this house now stands on the Weddesteeg and has a stone commemorating Rembrandt.

Environs: Oegstgeest (2 km. NW): Originally one of the oldest churches in Holland. The present *Dutch Reform church*, standing on the site of a 15C building, was built in 1600 (nave) and 1662 (transept). Inside:

Leiden, Stadhuis

wooden vault and 17C decorations. *Oud-Poelgeest*, a mansion from the mid 17C was the residence of Herman Boerhaave from 1724 onwards; much altered since.

Voorschoten (4 km. SW): The *Dutch Reform church* (1868) stands on the site of an older church of which only the massive tower (1539) survives. The *town hall* (1925) by W.Verschoor is a modern building in the style of the Amsterdam School, in whose work much importance is attached to careful design of the façade. The 13C dungeon and some 15C masonry were used in the construction of the *Huis Duivenvoorde* in 1631. This fine building on a U-shaped ground plan has a remarkably large number of windows. There are guided tours of the inside which is richly decorated (1 Apr.–1 Oct.: Tue., Thur. and Sat. 10 a.m., 11.30 a.m., 2 p.m. and 3.30 p.m.).

Loenen
Utrecht   p.289 □ I 5

Dutch Reform church: The oldest section of this late Gothic church is the mid-15C choir. Nave and transept (gutted by fire in 1945, but since rebuilt) are 16C. The tower with its two galleries (the original balustrades were replaced in *c.* 1700) was probably built by Jan Poyt in *c.* 1500.

Environs: Abcoude (12 km. NW): A peaceful village by the water, at the confluence of the rivers Gein and Angstel. Inside the splendid 14&15C *Dutch Reform church* there is a carved Renaissance pulpit. The neo-Gothic *Roman Catholic church* (1888) has a 16C Renaissance organ.

Baambrugge (8 km. NW): A *Dutch Reform church* with a pretty spire. The octagonal *Hoog en Groenland'* mill (1753) stands by the river Angstel.

Loenersloot (4 km. NW): The former medieval *castle* surrounded by a moat was largely rebuilt in the 19C but still looks imposing, mainly due to the round fortified tower (probably 13C).

Nieuwersluis (3 km. SW): There are some charming *country houses* along the left bank of the Vecht. *Over-Hol-*

Loenersloot (Loenen), Kasteel

land (1676) was converted and enlarged in c. 1755. *Rupelmonde* is late 17C, *Sterreschans* is 18C. The *Vreedehof* (1749) has a splendid rococo grille (c. 1760). *Nieuwerhoek* is an 18C country house with roughcast façades and annexes.

Vreeland (4 km. N.): The old *bascule bridge* over the Vecht is the most striking feature here. One of the country houses on the Vecht has Moorish features and makes a somewhat alien impression in this landscape.

Loppersum
Groningen   p.287☐N 2

Dutch Reform church: This church in the village in the Groningen Hogeland resembles a cathedral. In spite of a late Gothic conversion, some medieval features have survived. Massive 14C saddleback tower and early-13C nave which, on its N. wall has remains of a Romanesque tufa wall. A side aisle was added in the S. in 1529, and a little later net vaults were installed in the nave (which had been incresed in height) and the crossing. The transept is c. 1250, and the polygonal choir with side chapels and rib vaults is probably early-15C. The choir and the N. chapel of the Virgin Mary have late-15C and early-16C *paintings* on their vaults and walls. They show scenes from the life of Christ and the Virgin Mary, various Saints, and angels making music. The richly carved pulpit is late 17C, while the baroque noblemen's pew is later. The large organ (second half of 16C) was rebuilt in 1665 and 1735. There are many tombstones include one dating from 1540 to Bawe van Heemstra in the N. chapel. The S. part of the nave has a Renaissance tombstone (1576) with numerous coats-of-arms commemorating Maria van Selbach.

Vreeland (Loenen), bascule bridge

Maarssen
Utrecht   p.289□I 5

Maarssen was a popular residential town for rich merchants from Amsterdam in the 17&18C. Fine houses on the right bank of the Vecht are witness to this prosperity.

Dutch Reform church: On the W. side of the late-Gothic cruciform church (*c.* 1500) there is a Romanesque tower in tufa with pilaster strips, round-arched friezes and abats-voix.

Huis ten Bosch: A country house (1629) possibly by Jacob van Campen. The central section of the façade is two storeyed and decorated with Ionic pilasters and a triangular gable.

Also worth seeing: The 17C *Huis Doornburgh* was rebuilt in 1721. *Huis Goudestein* (1754) has attractive wrought-iron grilles. The originally medieval *Huis Bolestein* was given its present appearance in the early 19C.

Environs: Kasteel De Haar (5 km. SW): A modest fortress stood here in the Middle Ages. In the 15C it came to the family of Zuylen through marriage. Later devastated it was rebuilt in the 16C as a result of which it consisted of three round and two square towers rising on a pentagonal ground

plan. This was later rather freely rebuilt by P.J.H. Cuyper, in *c.* 1900, at which time the castle was ruined. The work was commissioned by Baron Étienne van Zuylen van Nijevelt and his wife Hélène van Zuylen-Nijevelt-de Rothschild who also had the park rebuilt by Henri Copijn and installed an *art collection* in the castle. Opening times: 1 Mar.–15 Aug. and 15 Oct.–15 Nov. Tue.–Sat. 9–11.30 a.m. and 1.30–4.30 p.m., Sun. 1.30–5 p.m.

Oud-Zuilen (3 km. S.): *Zuylen castle* on the Vecht, built in *c.* 1200 as a fortified house belonging to the Van Zuylen family, was given its present form (with four octagonal corner towers) in the late Middle Ages. It was 'modernized' under the supervision of Daniel Marot in *c.* 1753. The authoress Belle van Zuylen (Madame de Charrière; born 1740) spent part of her youth here. The castle, today open as a *museum,* has rooms devoted to her. A fine *hall* has early-18C tapestries by Maximilliaan van der Gucht. Opening times: 1 Apr.–30 Sept. Tues.–Sat. 10 a.m.–12 noon and 2–5 p.m., Sun. 2–5 p.m. Groups by arrangement up until 15 Nov.

St.-Maartensdijkl
Zeeland   p.288□F 7

Dutch Reform church: The main choir is *c.* 1400. The N. choir was built in the second half of the 15C out of a small tomb chapel (*c.* 1420). The nave is also second half of 15C. Barrel and semi-barrel vaults in the aisles are supported on columns with simple foliate capitals. The small vaulted portal on the W. bay of the N. aisle is early 16C. The originally simple 14C brick tower was given buttresses when the nave was built, and inside there are corbel stones for a vault rebuilt in restoration work in 1955. There are parts of the tomb of Floris van Borssele (d. 1422) and Oda van Bautersem (d. 1420) in the N. choir.

Raadhuis: The gable façade of the Renaissance town hall (1628) was restored to its original appearance during restoration work in 1962–4.

The town hall has a number of portraits (mostly members of the house of Orange-Nassau) from the castle which was demolished in 1820. A late Gothic residence joined on to the left of the town hall was included in the restoration. Opening times: May–Sept.: Tue. and Thur. 2–4 p.m.

Environs: Scherpenisse (5 km. E.): The choir and transept of the *Dutch Reform church* were demolished, leaving only the aisle and tower in elegant Brabant Gothic style (*c.* 1520). The pulpit dates from 1616 and the fine brass (two candlesticks in particular) are mainly 17C.

Stavenisse (7 km. NW): The old *Dutch Reform church* was replaced by a new building in 1910 and only the simple brick tower (1672) remained. Behind the pulpit is the white marble tomb of Hieronimus van Tuyll van Serooskerken (d. 1669) with a recumbent figure, an outstanding work by Rombout Verhulst.

Maastricht
Limburg   p.291 □ L 9

History: This town, among the oldest in the Netherlands, is at least Roman in origin. The crossing point over the river Maas, known as *Trajectam ad Mosam*, rapidly developed into a very important crossing point for many different routes. In 382 St. Servatius transferred the episcopal seat here from the Belgian city of Tongeren and in 721 the bishopric was moved to Liège. From 1204 onwards the town was jointly owned by the Dukes of Brabant and the Prince Bishops of Liège. Maastricht flourished in the 13–15C, mainly due to the expanding cloth industry. The States General of the United Netherlands took over the rights of Brabant in 1621. Maastricht was later enlarged into one of the strongest European fortresses in order to defend it against attacks from the South. The town had to endure 19 sieges (by Austria, Spain and France) with differing outcomes. The most recent siege was that of 1794. In 1815 Maastricht fell to the

St.-Maartensdijk, Dutch Reform church, tomb

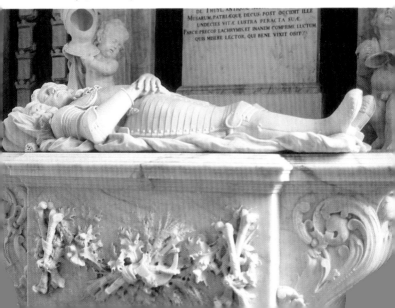

United Kingdom of the Netherlands.

Religious buildings
Former Augustinian church (Kesselskade): This small single-aisled hall church (1661) had a choir added to during restoration (1900).

Begijnhof (today the Roman Catholic Armenhuis de Nieuwenhof): Begun in 1489 as a small late-Gothic monastery with a chapel. Two tombstones, dating from 1286 and 1294 have relief figures. The monastery buildings are mainly 17/18C.

Bonnefantenklooster: This monastery was founded in 1626 and restored after a fire in 1672. The small single-aisled church was completed by Gilles Doyen in 1710. The three monastery buildings surrounding the courtyard are partly late 17C.

Chapel of Cellebroedersklooster (38 Brusselsestraat): This small late-Gothic building has net vaults and rich architectural features inside.

Former Dominicanerkerk and

Maastricht, Servatius Fontein

-klooster (1 Dominicanerkerkstraat): Since the time of its restoration (1912–17), the Dominican church, which is mainly 13C, has been used for secular purposes. Nave and choir were consecrated in 1294, and N. chapel (c. 1350) and a S. chapel of the Virgin Mary (mid 15C) have stellar vaults. The rib vaults in the rest of the church have remnants of paintings by Jan Vassens (1619).

Former Franciscanenkerk and -klooster (5 St.-Pieterstraat): Only fragments of the monastery have survived. The church, which since 1880 has been used as an imperial archive, has a basilican nave, which is possibly 13C and a 15C choir.

Former Grauwzustersklooster: 17&18C buildings are picturesquely and irregularly grouped together and are now used to house a *museum*. In 1673 the monastery occupied the house called Stad to the left of the entrance. The simple chapel dates from 1705.

St.-Janskerk (Hendrik van Veldekeplein): The Gothic parish church has a late-14C basilican nave, a choir with a chapel and mid-15C sacristy, and an elegant tower (two new upper storeys date from 1373 while the octagonal top storey is 15C; the spire is an unsuccessful result of restoration work in 1877–85). The church has been used by the Dutch Reform church since 1632.

Former Jesuit church and monastery: (1 Achter de Comedie): The church, built 1606–1614, has been a theatre since 1786; the remains of the monastery buildings have been converted into dwellings. The original structure by Petrus Huyssens, a Jesuit father, is only slightly discernible amid alterations.

Kruisherenkerk und -kloster (21 Kruisherengang): A monastery founded in 1483. The church choir was built by Petrus Toom and Johannes van Haren 1440–59. The nave was begun in 1501, but the net vaults are probably post 1579. The cloister, adjoining the S. side of the church, is formed by three wings of the monastery buildings which have housed an agricultural research institute since 1897.

St.-Mathiaskerk (Boschstraat): This small town church in Maas Gothic style is partly 14C (W. bays) and partly 16C (E. aisles). The whole building except the lower part of the tower built of marl. The church has an attractive late-15C Pietà and the figure of a Saint (*c.* 1520) in the organ gallery.

St. Martinuskerk: This church was completed by Petrus Josephus Hubertus Cuypers in 1858 in the Wijk district of town; fine font by Johannes van Venlo (1482; font cover 1717) and crucifix (possibly 14C German).

St.-Servaaskerk (Vrijthof): This cruciform basilica with its impressive

W. section was built in several distinct phases. The first building period began in *c.* 1000 with the nave and two aisles; transept, choir and crypt were probably added a little later; side walls survive from the second choir. The present E. choir and the choir towers are later than 1171; the old crypt under the choir was replaced by a new crypt under the crossing. After the church had been elevated to the status of an imperial church in 1087 and became the seat of the imperial chancellery, a second choir (for the emperor's chair) with two subsidiary choirs (built 1165–77 and then again after 1232) was planned for the W. side but not entirely completed. The storey above the choir has the splendid *imperial hall*. The outstanding S. door, the *Bergportal* with reliefs of the Virgin Mary in the tympanum is mid 13C. The chapels along the aisles are 14&15C, as are the vaults of the nave and transept, and the cloister on the N. side which has a fine *portal*. Extensive restoration carried out after 1869 was supervised by Petrus Josephus Hubertus Cuypers; the baroque tower above the imperial hall was rep-

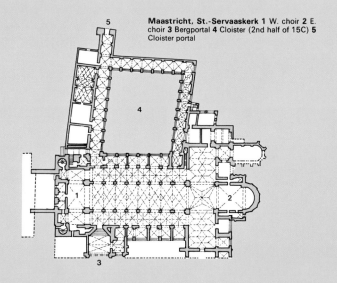

Maastricht, St.-Servaaskerk 1 W. choir **2** E. choir **3** Bergportal **4** Cloister (2nd half of 15C) **5** Cloister portal

laced by a neo-Gothic tower, and the two crypts were given new columns, pillars and vaults. The E. choir with its dwarf gallery and the choir towers, were rebuilt in the course of the various restorations.

Inside the building, the *capitals* in the W. part have rich decorations including figures. Behind the 19C statue of Charlemagne there is a Romanesque *relief* (now used as an altar retable) with depictions of the Virgin Mary and above them Christ between St.Peter and St.Servatius. The *crypt* has a shrine to St.Servatius, known as the Noodkist, a wooden Romanesque reliquary (*c.* 1160), gilded and richly adorned. *Church treasures* include a splendid bust of the saint, a late-16C gift from the Duke of Parma, pectoral cross, key, drinking goblet and the pilgrim's staff of St.Servatius as well as fragments of Oriental fabrics (6C and later) and a Brabant altar retable with scenes of the Passion (*c.* 1500). Opening times of treasure chamber: 1 May–31 Oct.: Mon.–Sat. 10 a.m.–5 p.m., Sun. and holidays 2–5 p.m.

Onze-Lieve-Vrouwekerk   (O.L.

Vrouweplein): This, the second large Romanesque church in the town, is a cruciform basilica vaulted entirely in stone. Like St.Servaaskerk, it was begun in *c.* 1000, and the lower W. section (upper parts *c.* 1200) is also from this period. The Romanesque nave and the transept were built in the mid-12C. The present E. choir is late 12C, while the gallery above the ambulatory is probably somewhat later. The early-13C NW portal was much rebuilt in the 15C. The 15C chapel to O.L. Vrouwe Sterre der Zee is situated in the W. wing of the late Gothic (early-16C) rib-vaulted cloister. In the early 18C the aisles' stellar vaults were added (copies of the 15C vault over the crossing, but noticeably less detailed). The *W. façade* which has a tower and two staircase turrets, is quite unique, as is the *E. choir* with its richly decorated capitals. Opening times of the church *treasury:* 1 June–15 Sept.: Mon.–Sat. 10.30 a.m.–5.30 p.m., Sun. 12.30–5.30 p.m.

Secular buildings
Fortification: The *Helpoort* with its

H.van Veldeke outside St.Servaas (left), Onze-Lieve-Vrouwekerk (right)

two slender turrets dates from the first fortifications (13C). To the W. of the gate, along Langgrachtje and Kleine Grachtje, there are extensive parts of the first *town wall*. The second fortification is late 14C; the almost round *Pater Vinktoren* and the lower part of the *De Reek water gate* both survive. This second wall which can be followed for a long stretch along the Jeker and the Aldenhofs-park, had a sentry walk. The third fortification from the early 16C includes two bastions, *Haat en Nijd* and *Vijf Koppen*, with part of the join-ing wall. Finally, remains of the fourth fortification (18C) including five bastions survive on the NW side of the town near the Statensingel.

Dinghuis (corner of Kleine Straat and Jodenstraat): This late Gothic building, which was the old town hall (*c.* 1470), has a splendid stone gable.

Former Hoofdwacht: (on the Vrij-thof near the choir of St.Servaas) Built inf 1736; outside altered in 1773.

Old Maas bridge: Also known as the Servatius bridge, it dates from the late 13C and links the town with the suburb of Wijk. Often rebuilt, seven semicircular arches of grey limestone survive today.

Stadhuis (Markt): A free-standing monumental stone building by Pieter Post (1659–64) in the square; the tower was completed in 1684. The entire main façade is subdivided by pilasters. Two staircases with balus-ters lead up to the entrance which consists of three projecting arches. The rooms in the building are grouped around a vaulted courtyard, one side of which has galleries and Ionic columns, while the massive rear with its Romanesque style round arches forms the lower part of the tower. Inside, the rooms have stucco ceilings, wall hangings and 18C paintings.

Houses: Most of the old 17&18C houses in Holland are in Maastricht and Amsterdam, but those in the Amsterdam were built under South-ern Dutch influence. The stones are also of different colours from those in

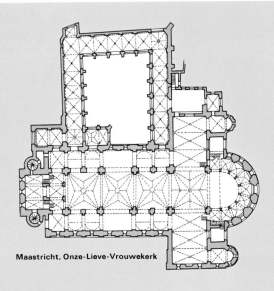

Maastricht, Onze-Lieve-Vrouwekerk

Amsterdam. Whole streets of houses, as well as many individual houses, survive including many in: the market, Boschstraat, Grote and Kleine Gracht, Brusselsestraat, the quays along the Maas, Grote Straat, Muntstraat, Vrijthof, Bredestraat, Wolfstraat, Stokstraat, Koestraat, Grote Looierstraat, Kapoenstraat, Lenculenstraat and Tongerse Straat, and in Wijk Rechtstraat and Hogebrugstraat.

Museums
Bonnefantenmuseum, Limburgs Museum voor Kunst en Oudhoden (5 Dominikanerplein): Archaeology, history, art including modern art. The museum derives its name from the former Bonnefanten Klooster, which housed it 1951–79. Opening times: Mon.–Fri. 10 a.m.–12 noon and 1–5 p.m., Sat., Sun. and holidays 2–5 p.m.; closed on 1 Jan., carnival days, Good Friday and 25 Dec.

Natural history museum (7 Bosquetplein): Geological, palaeontological and biological collections, herbarium, collection of grasshoppers

Maastricht, Renaissance bridge-house

and ants. Opening times: Mon.–Fri. 10 a.m.–12.30 p.m. and 1.30–5 p.m., Sun. and holidays 2–5 p.m.

Environs: Bemelen (4 km. E.): The marl tower of the *Roman Catholic church* is probably 14C, while the church dates from 1845.
Borgharen (5 km. N.): The W. section of *Slot Borgharen* forms a semicircle some 27 m. in diameter flanked at the sides by two square towers with two long wings. The building probably originated from a large tower-house with a surrounding wall (13C). The two side towers are post-1483. There were extensive alterations in 1555; the long side wings and the topmost storeys of the side towers were built in 1648–69. In 1776 the forecourt was completed with the addition of railings by Mathias Soiron. The new façade dates from 1785.
Cadier en Keer (2 km. SE): The lower part of the tower of the *Roman Catholic church* is 12C; the marl upper storeys are from the late 16C. W. African exhibits can be seen in the *Africa centre*. Opening times: Mon.–Sat. 9 a.m.–12 noon and 2–5 p.m., Sun. and holidays 2–5 p.m. (the Africa centre is closed on 1 Jan.).
St.-Geertruid (8 km. S.): The picturesquely located *Roman Catholic church* has a tower (probably early 14C), a nave and two aisles, a 15C choir, and a 16C funerary chapel at the E. end of the S. aisle.
Itteren (5 km. N.): The core of the *Huis Meersenhoven* is medieval. Today's building dates from 1743–4 and has a simple, severe form of French influence.
Kanne (4 km. SW): The town's *castle* is the only one with terraces in the Netherlands. Built in 1698 by order of Daniel v. Dopff, governor of Maastricht, the terraces have two octagonal and one square corner towers.
Limmel (4 km. NE): All that survives of the *Kasteel Bethlehem* (partly late medieval, partly 16C), is the round corner tower on the N. side of

the large modern house. The early-16C *Huis Jeruzalem* is late Gothic in form. The octagonal staircase turret survived 18C alterations.

Margraten (11 km. SE): The old nave of the *Roman Catholic church* was replaced in 1921–2 by a larger nave, transverse to the old axis. Items surviving from the old structure are the tower (probably 15C) and, by way of a side chapel, the old choir with its fine stellar and net vaulting (*c.* 1500).

Mheer (12 km. SE): The mid-17C *Kasteel* stands on the stone foundations of a medieval castle. The powerful round tower on the SE corner is among the oldest parts in the complex which consists of buildings around four sides of a courtyard.

Noorbeek (14 km. SE): The tower of the *Roman Catholic church* may be 13C, while the nave with its early-Maas capitals has probably survived from the early-14C basilica. The church was enlarged in *c.* 1500 and given a new choir and late Gothic rib- and net-vaults. The fine Renaissance pulpit (1641) has reliefs of the Evangelists. The chapel (*c.* 1740) of St.Brigida stands beside the choir.

Slenaken (18 km. SE): The *Roman Catholic church* (1793) was built to the plans of Wincqs, an architect from Brussels. Nave and two aisles have Tuscan columns supporting the barrel vaults of the nave and the flat ceilings of the aisles.

Makkum
Friesland   p.286☐K 2

The double village of Makkum-Statum is known for its faience which has been manufactured since 1660; two factories are open to the public.

Dutch Reform church: This church (1660) in Gothic style stands a little way outside the village. The tower (1652) has a wooden top storey. Inside there are 18C painted panels commemorating members of guilds and a 17C pulpit with fluted pilasters.

Waag: This tower-like building (1698) contains the weigh-master's lodging. Tiled throughout, it has an interesting *collection* of flags and Frisian faience.

Mheer (Maastricht), Kasteel

Also worth seeing: 18&19C *houses* in *Kerkstraat, Bleekstraat* and along the *canal*. Beside the harbour there is a 'Leugenbank' ('bench of false-hoods') and an old cannon.

Environs: Allingawier (4 km. E.): The village is situated on a terp. The small *Dutch Reform church* (1635) was altered in 1783 and has a saddleback tower. The *'De Izeren Kou'* farm museum occupies a former farmhouse (*c.* 1700) in which old decorations and folk art are displayed.

Marssum
Friesland   p.287☐L 2

Popta-State: This castle survives in splendid condition. Originally called Heringa State, it stands on a terp surrounded by trees in a beautiful location. The building was probably begun in 1524. In the 17C it was converted from a fortified structure into a pleasure seat. In 1687 it was acquired by Dr.H.Popta the lawyer who bequeathed it in his will to the Popta-

Marssum, gatehouse, Popta-State

gasthuis, a charitable foundation for elderly women which he set up in 1711. When the original building was converted, towers with onion domes were added. The gatehouse (1631) still has the coats-of-arms of the owners, Heringa, Eisinga and Popta. The fine entrance is flanked by pilasters with carvings in the architrave. The inside, with its wooden panelling, fine fireplaces, old furniture and bed niches, reveals how the landed gentry lived in the 17C.
Opening times: 1 Apr.–30 Sept.: Mon.–Fri. 9 a.m.–12 noon, 2–5 p.m., closed on Sat., Sun. and holidays.

Poptagasthuis: This armshouse right next to the castle has a Louis XIV portal crowned by the coat-of-arms of Popta the founder and two allegorical female figures. Buildings surround a courtyard on four sides.

Dutch Reform church: This 12&13C church occupies the highest point of the terp and has fine decorations from the second half of the 17C. Original wooden panelling.

Also worth seeing: A polder mill (1903) and a spinning-head mill (1888) contribute to the village's charm.

Environs: Dronryp The tower (1544) of the late Gothic *Dutch Reform church* is crowned by an octagonal lantern and a small Renaissance dome (unusual for Friesland). The *Vredehof* was founded in 1744 as an almshouse for women. The astronomer Eise Eisinga was born here (the house has a memorial stone) and buried here (his tombstone has an arithmetical puzzle). Laurens Alma Tadema the painter was born in Dronryp (1836). He died famous as Sir Lawrence Alma Tadema and was interred in St.Paul's Cathedral in London. The elegant 18C house at 447 Dubbelstraat bears the memorial plaque: 'A great painter. A brave worker. A strong friend.'

Marsum

Groningen   p.287☐O 2

Dutch Reform church: A small church from the second half of the 12C. It is one of the oldest Romanesque brick buildings. The semiround apse still has the old roof tiles. The two lower rooms of the saddleback tower have round arches opening towards the nave. The church has a 16C choir screen and a pulpit (1791–2). The beamed ceiling was rebuilt in restoration work (1949–51).

Medemblik

North Holland   p.286☐I 3

Medemblik, the oldest town in West Friesland, was mentioned in 960 and acquired the status of town in 1289. After a brief heyday in the early 17C, the town was overtaken by Hoorn and Enkhuizen. In the course of its history, Medemblik has suffered numerous sieges, conquests, lootings and devastations.

Dutch Reform Bonifaciuskerk: A late-Gothic 15&16C hall church with a strong early-15C tower. E. section altered in 1895. Inside there are a pulpit (*c.* 1550), a delicate rococo organ, and six stained-glass windows (*c.* 1800).

Slot Radboud: The castle was founded by Count Floris V in *c.* 1288 in order to keep in check the West Frisians who had just been subjected. The castle was partly torn down in the early 17C and later became much dilapidated. In the late 19C it was partly rebuilt with the assistance of Petrus Josephus Hubertus Cuypers, but probably not in accordance with the original. Inside there are two late Gothic fireplaces (mid-15C), an early Renaissance portal (*c.* 1550), and wooden ceilings in the cellars. Today the castle is a cultural centre. Opening times: Sun. 2–5 p.m., 1 June–1 Sept.: 10 a.m.–5 p.m. daily. Son et lumière entertainments are held here in summer.

Waag (Kaasmarkt): The weighhouse has a 17C stepped gable façade.

Oudheidkamer Medemblik (Torenstraat): This *museum* with etchings, paintings and archaeological finds occupies a house from 1787. Opening times: 1 July–1 Sept.: Sat. 2–5 p.m.

Also worth seeing: Early-17C *staircase gables* in *Nieuwstraat, Oosterhaven, Westerhaven* and *Vooreiland*. The new *town hall* (1940) by A.J.Kropholler accords well with the town's character.

Environs: Twisk (5 km. SW): Here and in the surrounding villages there are many typical *West Frisian farms*, some of which are 17&18C, when this type of building was at its zenith. The late Gothic *Dutch Reform church* has a fine slender tower with an octagonal spire, a nave (probably originally 14C), and a tall early-16C choir.

Twisk (Medemblik), church

Megen
North Brabant   p.289☐K 6

This little town is a single parish uniting the church villages of Haren and
Macharen. Megen received a charter
in 1359. Earlier there may have been a
castle, the remains of which probably
lie beneath St.-Josephsberg, a convent of the Poor Clares built in 1721.

Franciscan monastery: The
monastery complex (1648–53) is
modest but perfectly preserved. A
number of stained-glass windows
have the founders' names and their
coats-of-arms. The church (1670)
with stone vaulting has an ornate high
altar (*c.* 1680) and a fine pulpit (1696).

Gevangentoren: This gatehouse
tower with mid-14C stepped gables is
all that survives of the fortifications.

Also worth seeing: On the way to
Macharen there is a small *chapel*
(1733) dedicated to Onze Lieve
Vrouw der Zeven Weeen (Our Lady
of Sorrows), with a 16C Virgin Mary.

Environs: Haren (3 km. S.): The
Penitentenklooster Bethlehem has been
extended in recent times. An early-
17C wing and a small chapel dating
from 1520 (much restored) has
survived.
Macharen (3 km. SW): The 15C
tower (whose height was increased in
1862) is all that survived when the old
church was demolished.

Meppel
Drente   p.287☐M 3

Dutch Reform church: Founded in
1422 the church consists of two aisles;
the S. aisle dates from the second half
of the 15C and the N. aisle from 1517.
The monumental 15C tower is
crowned by a dome (1827). Fine
decorations include a pulpit (1696), a

Medemblik, Slot Radboud

baptismal grille (1782), and an organ
completed by F.C. Schnitger from
Hamburg in 1722.

Also worth seeing: The *former
Schultenhuis* (7 Kruisstraat), formerly
also the town hall, is a monumental
classical building (*c.* 1830). The
houses at *12* and *15 Kruisstraat*, and
also *50 Hoofdstraat*, have 17C *stepped
gables*.

Environs: Kolderveen (3 km. NW):
This village dates back to the 13C.
The *Dutch Reform church* (1471) has
survived in good condition with a
tower (probably 14C) and good
decorations including a pulpit from
1703. *No 24, a farmhouse* is an elegant
18C building with a fine front door
and decorations.
Nijeveen (4 km. NW): The *Dutch
Reform church*, founded 1477 and
altered in 1627, was built in the style

of Drent farmhouses; wooden pillars separate the aisles.

De Wijk (5 km. E.): There are fine *country houses* in the area around the little river De Reest. *Havixhorst* (1753) has a central baroque section. *Dikninge*, on the site of a fomer abbey of the same name, is in late Empire style with a colonnaded portal. *Voorwijk* (1783) is in traditional style. The village also has good 18&19C *farmhouses*. The *upright mill* with an unusual lower section dates from 1829.

Middelburg

Zeeland   p.288☐D 7

History: The main town of the province of Zeeland, it was probably built in the Carolingian period. First mention of a settlement around a castle dates from 1103. The status of a town was conferred in 1217 and renewed in 1254, whereupon the town was expanded. Further expansions occurred in 1549–91 and 1595–8. In the Middle Ages, Middelburg was the centre of the English trade in cloth and wool. This prosperous period, which was at its zenith in *c.* 1600 was followed by a long period of comparative insignificance. Serious damage by bombs dropped on 17 May 1940 has now been repaired.

Religious buildings
Abdij: Hardly anything of the original Romanesque and early Gothic monastery complex has survived. All that was left of the 15&16C late Gothic monastery after the bombing of 17 May 1940 was an expanse of ruins. However, most of the monastery has been rebuilt. The monastery, dissolved in 1574 and

used for secular purposes thereafter, consists of a cloister and surrounding buildings, a courtyard on the E. side, the Nederhof courtyard on the N. side surrounded by various office buildings and the Balanspoort, and two churches with a tower on the S. side. The churches are known as Koorkerk (*c*. 1300) and Nieuwe Kerk (enlarged after 1568). Because of the fine stone net vaulting added in the 16C, the tall single-aisled Koorkerk ('choir church') was damaged less seriously than the Nieuwe Kerk ('new church'). Of the latter's old decorations, all that survives is the *splendid marble tomb* of the naval heroes Johann and Cornelis Evertsen (who fell in the battle against the English in 1666); dating from 1680–2, it is the last of Rombout Verhulst's great works. Both churches have organ cases on loan from the Rijksmuseum in Amsterdam; the delightful organ case (1692) with doors painted by Philip Tiedeman comes from the old Lutheran church in Amsterdam and that (1478–81) of the main organ in the Koorkerk came from St.-Nicolaaskerk in Utrecht and is the work of Peter of Utrecht. 'Lange Jan,' the octagonal *tower* some 280 ft. tall, rising from the S. wall of the Koorkerk, probably originally dates from the second half of the 14C (it can be climbed Easter–Sept., Mon.–Sat., 10 a.m.–5 p.m.

Engelse Kerk (Stadhuisstraat): Originally the chapel of the Cellebroedersklooster, this attractive little building from the 15C and 17C has a mid-17C pulpit and an organ and gallery (1761) by G.Stevens.

Gasthuiskerk (92 Lange Delft): This small church, dating from 1493 and going back to a 13C structure, was built as the second chapel of the hospital. The façade is topped by a hexagonal bell turret.

Lutherse Kerk (Zuidsingel): This

Middelburg, Stadhuis, detail ▷

small single-aisled church with simple stuccoes was completed in 1742 to the plans of Jan de Munck, town architect. The organ (1707) is by J.Duysschot from Alkmaar.

Oostkerk (Breestraat): This church begun in 1647 by Bartholomeus Frans Drijfhout (town craftsman) and Pieter Post has an octagonal dome. After Drijfhout died in 1649, work continued under Arent van 's-Gravesande, whose Marekerk in Leiden probably influenced the original design. After the death of van 's-Gravesande, the church was completed by Louis Jolijt in 1667. The rich exterior articulation with Ionic pilasters is echoed inside the building. The Louis XVI organ front forms one unit with the pulpit; the organ itself (1783) is by W.Lotens. Open to the public in July and Aug., Thur. 10 a.m.–4 p.m.

Secular buildings
Stadhuis: This splendid example of a S. Dutch late-Gothic town hall was completely burned down in 1940 but has now been most skilfully restored. The building has three wings at right

angles to one another, a central tower, and a staircase tower (the Choertoren) on the corner with Noordstraat. Its architectural history is more complicated than might appear from the façades, which look so uniform. Begun in 1452, from 1456 onwards the brothers Andries and Matthijs Keldermans worked on the façades along the Noordstraat and today's market. After the roof of the large hall burned down in 1492, rebuilding and alterations followed. In 1506, another phase of construction began under Anthonis Keldermans and this was continued by his son Rombout in *c.* 1512, from which phase the tower, the top of the staircase tower and the two gables in Noordstraat and the Markt all date. The building was probably completed *c.* 1520. The figures of the Counts and Countesses of Zeeland were added in 1518 by Michiel Ywynszoon from Mechelen (these were replaced by new figures in late-19C restoration work). The old subdivisions of the town hall were preserved inside the building. Some sections which had been altered over the years were returned to their

Middelburg, Abdij (abbey)

original in the restoration work. Opening times: Easter–Sept.: Mon.–Fri. 10 a.m.–12 noon and 1.30–4.30 p.m.

St.-Jorisdoelen (Balans): The guild house (1582) of the civic guard company of St.George was destroyed in 1940 but the stone gabled façade was rebuilt as part of a new inland revenue building.

Kloveniersdoelen (by the Lange-viele bridge): This former guild house of the Arquebusiers was built in 1607–11 and it has been a military hospital since 1795. The gable over the central section was built in accordance with old engravings during the last restoration, when it was decorated with scrolls and obelisks in the manner of Vredeman de Vries.

Stadsschuur (Hoogstraat): The town barn with its two stepped gables probably dates from the first quarter of the 17C.

Fortifications: Surrounding ram-parts and bastions (1595; altered 1692) have mostly remained intact. Gardens attached to the ramparts were laid out in *c.* 1840 to the designs of Karel George Zocher. None of the town gates survive except for the free-standing *Koepoort* (1735) in Molenwater.

Windmills: There are four round stone corn mills within the town. Two of them, 'De Hoop' (1736) and 'De Seismolen' (1728), stand on bulwarks. The other two are 'Ons Genoegen' (1847) and 'De Koning' (1882).

Houses: Only a few 16C façades sur-vive, e.g. that of *29–31 Lange Gist-straat*. Houses at *22 Nieuwstraat, 9/11 Brakstraat* and *36 Dam* are late 16C/ early 17C. Pilastered façades survive at *17 Spanjaardstraat* (1646) and *51 Vlasmarkt* (1665). The façades of the houses at *53 Spanjaardstraat* and *6 Koepoortstraat* are 18C. *37 Lange Noordstraat* has a richly decorated façade (1733). The *house in Zuidsingel* where Jan de Munck lived dates from 1736. The *provincial court of justice* (Arrondissementsrechtbank) in the

Middelburg, Kloveniersdoelen

Hofplein was built by J.P. van Baurs-cheidt the younger as a residential house (1765). The interior is unfortunately not open to the public.

Museums

Zeeuws Museum (Abdij): Exhibits related to the history and culture of Zeeland. Six 16C wall tapestries depict sea battles fought during the Eighty Years' War. Opening times: Mon.–Fri 10 a.m.–5 p.m.; May and Oct.: also Sat. 1.30–5 p.m.; June–Sept.: also Sat. and Sun. 1.30–5 p.m.

Walcheren in miniature (Molenwater): A model of Walcheren built on a scale of 1:20 comprises all the well-known buildings, streets, harbours, dykes, dunes, etc. Opening times: Thur. before Easter–1 Oct.: 9.30 a.m.–5.30 p.m. daily.

Also worth seeing: The pretty Vismarkt has a Louis XIV stone *pump* and a *gallery* with Doric columns. The *former office of weights and measures*, the IJkkantoor, (Zuidsingel) is by Jan de Munck (1739) on a site occupied by a concert hall in the 18C.

Goedereede (Middelharnis), tower

The *Kuiperspoort* (probably *c.* 1586), the coopers' guild house, stands at the end of a row of warehouses near the Domplein.

Events: *Son et lumière* presentations are held in the abbey complex every Wed., Thur. and Fri. June–Sept.

Environs: Biggekerke (10 km. NW): The tower (*c.* 1400) of the *Dutch Reform church* adjoins the S. side of the church and has a rose window and flying buttresses. The choir is also *c.* 1400, while the nave is probably somewhat later. The pulpit (first half of the 17C) is an outstanding work in copper. The white, round, stone *corn mill* dates from 1712.

Koudekerke (8 km. SW): *Huis der Boede,* formerly a medieval castle, is a mansion dating from *c.* 1740, possibly by J.P. van Baurscheidt the younger. *Slot ter Hooge* (*c.* 1300) dates in its present form from 1755. One of the two octagonal turrets comes from an older building; the other was erected for the sake of symmetry.

Zoutelande (10 km. W.): The oldest part of the neat little *Dutch Reform church* is a brick tower (*c.* 1400). The 15C nave is single aisled and there is a pretty S. portal. The choir no longer survives. The organ (*c.* 1700) came from the church in Heerlen.

Middelharnis
South Holland   p.288□F 6

This town forms a double village with Sommelsdijk and lies at the agricultural centre of Goeree-Overflakkee.

Dutch Reform church: In *c.* 1500, a N. aisle was added to this late Gothic church from the second half of the 15C which had previously been single-aisled. The tower's original appearance (the top was removed in 1811) is recorded in the painting 'Laantje van Middelharnis' ('The Avenue of Middelharnis') by Meindert Hobbema (1636–1709) which is now in the National Gallery, London.

Raadhuis: The town hall (1639) is built in a form transitional between Renaissance and baroque. The tripartite main façade by Arent van 's-Gravesande has an external staircase and a plain triangular gable. There is a small domed turret in the middle of the roof.

Environs: Goedereede (20 km. NW): This little town, which was granted a charter in 1312, was left behind by Middelharnis in the 16C when the harbour silted up. The *tower* (probably 1466–1512) is all that survives of the old parish church which fell into disrepair and was replaced by the present simple church in 1708. The front section of the Gothic *Hotel de Gouden Leeuw* (11 Markt) dates from *c.* 1550, while the rear is probably a little later than 1482. Tradition has it that Adriaan Florisz (later Pope Hadrian VI 1522–3) lived here.

Nieuwe Tonge (4 km. S.): The tower of the picturesquely located *church* (*c.*

1500) is crowned by a 17C upper storey, with pilasters, balustrade and a short spire.

Ooltgensplaat (15 km. SE): The former *Fort Prins Frederik* on the S. of the harbour has a square stone tower (built shortly after 1811) and is surrounded by ramparts and a ditch. The *town hall* (1618) has a broad main façade and stepped gables.

Oude Tonge (7 km. S.) The choir and sacristy of the *Dutch Reform church* (1499) date from the time of building, whereas nave and tower were built during enlargements in the first half of the 16C. On the S. side there is a strange little neo-Gothic brick portal.

Sommelsdijk (1 km. W.): The originally *late Gothic church* was rebuilt after fires in 1632 and 1799. The Gothic tower on the W. side dates from 1635; after the second fire its spire was not rebuilt.

Mill

North Brabant   p.291 □ L 6

This village on the W. side of the Peel

Mill, Huis de Alden Driel

forms a single parish along with the villages of St.-Hubert, Langenboom and Wilbertoord.

Roman Catholic church: The neo-Gothic basilican church (1877–8) by C.van Dijk has a tower with no spire.

Huis de Alden Driel: A rather plain house from the first half of 17C, partly surrounded by a ditch. Altered in 1763, parts of walls dating from *c.* 1500 survive near the main building.

Also worth seeing: Parts of the walls of the 16C *chapel of Marie ten Hove* survive in *Kapelweg*. The stone '*De Korenbloem*' corn mill (1847) is in *Molenstraat*.

Environs: St.-Hubert (1 km. SE): In 1924 the *Roman Catholic* church was enlarged with the addition of transept and new choir; the simple 15C tower and the 16C single-aisled nave survive. The church has an early-16C figure of St.Catherine and statues of St.Hubert, St.James and St.Barbara (late-18C).
Kasteel Tongelaar (3 km. N.): A

ditch surrounding a square marks the site of the former castle. Of the castle buildings, only a *gatehouse tower* (probably early-15C) survives. This has a barrel vault in the lower storey and a groin vault in the upper storey.

Monnickendam
North Holland   p.286□ 4

This pretty little town on the IJssel-meer dates back to the 13C when monasteries were founded on the site—there is a monk in the town coat-of-arms. It was granted a charter in 1355 and developed rapidly thanks to its favourable location on what was then the Zuiderzee. Great damage was caused by fires in 1500 and 1513.

Grote or St.-Nicolaaskerk: A large late Gothic hall church founded in the early 15C. Nave and two aisles are 17C up the W. tower which was built *c.* 1520. There is a Renaissance gable (1626) between two late-Gothic portals on the N. side. Inside the church

Monnickendam, portal at Noordeinde

is broad and airy with a splendid late-Gothic choir screen (*c.* 1530) and a fine 15C font.

Stadhuis: The town hall (1746) was built as an elegant residence and has a beautiful façade. Inside there is an ornate room for weddings.

Waag and Speeltoren: The weigh-house (*c.* 1600) has a canopy and received a pilastered façade in *c.* 1660. Behind the building stands the charming early-16C Speeltoren with an open wooden top (1591) to which a carillon of 16 bells was added in 1596. Mechanical horsemen in a niche on the S. side turn around every full hour; above them an angel blows the trombone.

Museum De Speeltoren (4 Noordeinde): Archaeological finds, tiles, clay pipes, documents to the town's history. Open: Wed., Thur., Fri. 1–3 p.m., Sat. 2–5 p.m., Fri. also 7–9 p.m.

Also worth seeing: The gable on the right of the *Gemeenlandshuis van Waterland* (23 De Zarken) dates originally from 1619, although it was completely rebuilt in 1908. In *Kerkstraat* there are some stepped gables, and a gable with scrolls and pilasters (early-17C).

Environs: Marken: (8 km. above the dyke): Marken was formerly on the mainland until the flood of St.Julian in 1164 turned it into an island. Since 1957 it has again been joined to the mainland, this time by a dyke. Floods were frequent in former times and hence the little houses are built on man-made hills and wooden piles. Traditional costumes still worn here are an attraction to visitors. The *Museum Marken* (44–47 Kerkbuurt), built by combining four so-called Rookhuisjes (houses which only had a hole in the roof to let out the smoke), gives a fascinating impression of the inhabitants' former way of life.

Montfoort
Utrecht   p.289☐H 5

This little town on the Hollandsche IJssel was built in the second half of the 12C around a castle founded by Bishop Godfried (1156–78) to defend the bishopric.

Dutch Reform church: A large late-Gothic church (probably mainly *c.*1500) with a basilican nave and a slender tower. Inside, the columns with foliate capitals show damage probably caused by a fire in 1629. The chapel on the S. side of the nave has a stone vault with remains of decorative painting.

Former Commanderie: This complex of buildings belonging to the Order of St.John (founded in 1544) was built in late Gothic and Renaissance styles. There is a delightful chapel (today used as a storehouse) and a colonnaded gallery around the courtyard.

Slot Montfoort: The core of the

Montfort, Dutch Reform church

castle was probably a round building. Most of the castle was destroyed by the French in 1672 except for parts of the barbican. The surviving section of the gatehouse has two towers; to the left of this there are remains of the surrounding wall (probably 15C).

Stadhuis: This town hall on the IJsselpoort dates from *c.* 1500; some 18&19C alterations were removed during restoration work in 1965. A painting (1649) by Hendrik Heerschap hangs in the council chamber. The *local museum* houses cultural and historical documents of the region.

Muiden

North Holland   p.286□ 4

Muiderslot: The *castle* occupies a strategic location at the mouth of the Vecht. It was built or an existing structure was enlarged in *c.* 1280 by order of Count Floris V and is almost square with round corner towers and a square gatehouse tower. The rebellious nobles held Count Floris

prisoner here for a time in 1296, fleeing with him to nearby Naarden where he was murdered. The castle was probably destroyed shortly after and rebuilt in *c.* 1350. In 1508, Duke Karel van Gelre captured and plundered the castle. It was only under Pieter Cornelisz Hooft, who was appointed bailiff of Muiden in 1609, that the castle experienced a more peaceful period. Hooft, poet and historian, spent every summer in the castle until his death in 1647. He gathered around him a circle of learned men who became known as 'Muiderkring'. Joost van den Vondel, Constantijn Huygens and Jacob Cats were guests here. From this time until 1795 the castle was used by castellans who also administered justice; at this time it was official lodging, court house and prison. In 1825, King William I prevented the building, then in ruins, from being completely demolished. The Muiderslot was given the status of *Rijksmuseum* in 1875, and was restored in 1885–1909 (restoration work continued and was completed after 1955). Good 16&17C interior decorations were added over

Muiden, Muiderslot

the years and today the castle houses memorabilia of P.C.Hooft. There is a charming little herb garden opposite the entrance gate. Opening times: 1 Apr.–30 Sept.: Mon.–Fri: 1st guided tour 10 a.m., last tour 4 p.m.; Sun. and holidays: 1 and 4 p.m.; 1 Oct.–31 Mar.: Mon.–Fri., Sun. and holidays: 1 and 3 p.m.

Dutch Reform church: The Romanesque tufa tower (probably *c.* 1200) has now sunk deep into the earth. The late Gothic nave and two aisles and the choir date from *c.* 1400. Inside the church there are columns with fine foliate capitals, wooden vaults and wall paintings which include the legend of the three living and the three dead. Renaissance decorations.

Also worth seeing: The *Roman Catholic church* (1822) in 'Waterstaatsstijl' was given a Romanesque extension in the E. in 1894.

Environs: Muiderberg: (5 km. E.): The 15C *Dutch Reform church* was rebuilt in 1686 after a fire in 1623. There was another fire in 1934. The church, with the exception of the tower which had remained undamaged, was restored the same year. In the choir there is a memorial stone donated on the occasion of a requiem mass to Floris V celebrated in 1324 in the then church of Muiderberg.
Weesp (5 km. S.): A small old fortified town in the border district between Holland and Utrecht. Porcelain was manufactured here for a short time (1759–70) and this was followed by the manufacture of Loosdrecht porcelain. The large late Gothic *Dutch Reform church* is basilican in style with a nave, tall choir and a Romanesque tower (part 13C, part 16C). The church (probably completed in the 16C) has a splendid choir screen (*c.* 1530). The fine *town hall* (1772–6) with its sandstone façade was designed by Jacob Otten Husly. The partly stuccoed interior is as fine as the exterior.

Naaldwijk
South Holland p.288□F 6

This town in the centre of a horticultural area is known as the 'Glass Town' because of its innumerable greenhouses.

Dutch Reform church: A collegiate church since 1307. Restored after a fire in 1472, the oldest part of this Gothic church is the tower, with its late Romanesque pilasters and mid-

Weesp (Muiden), town hall

13C friezes of arches and toothed projections. The upper storey dates from the first half of the 15C. Transept, choir and nave were built and enlarged *c*. 1350–*c*. 1500. Side aisles are separated from the nave by octagonal pillars and moulded arches. The lower storey of the annex on the S. side of the choir has a stellar vault and was probably the sacristy, while the room above, reached by a spiral staircase, is a library. The late Gothic choir screen is early 16C; in front of it is the Renaissance pulpit.

Heilige-geest-hofje: Founded in 1496 by the noblemen of Naarden, it consists of small gabled houses around a square. Friedrich Heinrich, the stadholder, ordered these houses to be rebuilt in 1627. The chapel, now the district museum, was the gift of the stadholder (1641).

Also worth seeing: The attractive *village square* has a *pump* dating from 1629; the *town hall* was built in 1632 and redesigned in 1688.

Environs: Wateringen: (6 km. NE):

The early-14C tower of the *Dutch Reform church* was later altered and increased in height. The nave is 1532. The modern *town hall* (1938) is by the Dutch architect A.J. Kropholler.

Naarden
North Holand   p.289□l 5

History: The present town of Naarden was completely rebuilt in *c*. 1350 after the old town a little further to the NE had been destroyed. Fortifications (1675–85), which survive almost unaltered, were built by the stadholder William III and make the town one of the most extraordinary and complete examples of a fortified town in the Netherlands.

Grote or St.-Vituskerk: Side aisles and ambulatory of this large late-Gothic basilica (*c*. 1500) are vaulted in stone, while the choir and nave have wooden barrel vaults. The tall tower is somewhat older. The capitals of the columns in the choir have carvings of men, animals and monsters, while the

Huizen (Naarden), farmhouse

Naarden, Grote Kerk

columns in the nave have foliate capitals. The barrel vaults of the choir and nave are painted with scenes from the Old and New Testaments. These 20 panels date from 1518 and are by an unknown artist.

Comeniuskapel (Kloosterstraat): This late-Gothic 15C chapel originally belonged to a monastery and was restored in 1934 in honour of Johann Amos Comenius, the Czech theologian and pedagogue who was buried here in 1670.

Spaanse Huis (27 Turfpoortstraat): On the site of the town hall associated with the Spanish troops' slaughter of the population in 1572. The building was converted into a weigh-house in 1615. A stone relief on the façade depicts the murderous event.

Stadhuis: The town hall is a fine Renaissance building (1601) with two richly designed stepped gables. Inside, a painting depicts the plundering of Naarden in 1572.

Comeniusmuseum (27 Turfpoort-straat): The museum has occupied the Spaanse Huis since 1892 on the occasion of the third centenary of Comenius's birth. Large library, maps and portaits. Opening times: Tue.–Sun. 2–4 p.m.

Vestingmuseum (6 Westwalstraat): The museum in the Turfpoortbastion documents the history of the town. Opening times: Apr.–Oct.: Mon.–Fri. 10 a.m.–4.30 p.m., Sat. and Sun. 12 noon–5 p.m.

Environs: Blaricum (6 km. E.): This village in Gooiland with fine old farmhouses has preserved its rural character. The *Dutch Reform church* of 1696, which is single aisled with a tower, replaces the medieval church which burned down. Famous painters, like Jozef Israels and Piet Mondrian, lived in the village.

Bussum (2 km. SE): The *Roman Catholic St.-Vituskerk* (*c.* 1895), a neo-Gothic basilica, shows the influence of Petrus Josephus Hubertus Cuypers.

Huizen (5 km. E.): Traditional costumes are frequently worn in this

Naarden, Grote Kerk, interior

former fishing village, especially on Sundays. The *Dutch Reform church* stands higher than most of the village. The oldest part is the tower which is probably early 15C; choir and nave from the second half of the 15C were altered later.

Laren (5 km. E.): One of the oldest villages in Gooiland, it developed from Saxon and Frisian settlements. There is a pond for washing and watering sheep beside the pretty village green. The *Dutch Reform church* (*c.* 1500) has a tower and a nave but no choir. On the Sunday after the feast of St.John (24 June) each year, a large procession starts from the *Roman Catholic St.Jansbasiliek,* which dominates the landscape with its two tall towers. The *Singermuseum* (1 Oude Drift) was founded in 1956 by the widow of the American painter William Henry Singer jr. There are paintings by Singer, 19&20C Dutch and French paintings, sculptures and Asian ceramics. Opening times: Tue.–Sat. 10 a.m.–5 p.m., Sun. and holidays 1–5 p.m. The *Geologische Museum Hofland* (8a Zevenend) is open Tue.–Sun. 1–4.30 p.m.

Nederhemert

Geldern   p.289☐I 6

Dutch Reform church: The 14C tower was destroyed in 1944 when the nave was also severely damaged. Today only the choir (*c.* 1550; restored 1955) is used as a church. Marble tombs monuments include a Louis XIV tomb of Otto Frederik van Vittinghoff (d. 1726) by N.Seunties; memorial tablets commemorate Stephania Anna Amaranta van Lynden-Vittinghoff and her husband Adrianus van Lynden and date from 1750 & 1773.

Kasteel Nederhemert: This

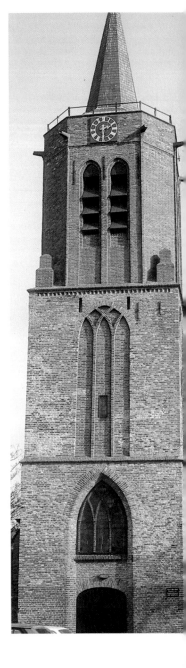

Laren (Naarden), Dutch Reform church ▷

Ammerzoden (Nederhemert), Kasteel

14&15C house occupies a fine position amidst old canals. Altered several times, it was completely gutted by fire in 1944. The massive keep and the octagonal wing on the E. side are probably the oldest sections, while the staircase tower and the towers at the front are probably somewhat later (*c.* 1500). Today the building is cared for by the 'Vrienden der Geldersche Kastelen' foundation.

Also worth seeing: The octagonal *mill* (1716) with stone coat-of-arms.

Environs: Ammerzoden: (4 km. E.): *Kasteel Ammersoyen* consists of four buildings around a courtyard and four round towers and was probably built for Johan van Herlaer in *c.* 1300. The castle was damaged by fire in 1590 and rebuilt in the early 17C; redesigned in Dutch Renaissance style in 1640–67. The entrance wing has a stone portal in Flemish baroque style. Opening times: 1 June–1 Sept.: Tue.–Sat. 10 a.m.–5 p.m., Sun. 1–5 p.m.; 1 Sept.–1 Dec. and 1 Feb.–1 June: only Sun. 1–5 p.m.

Nieuwegein
Utrecht   p.289☐l 5

Dutch Reform church: (N.-Noord): A small single-aisled church (1819–20) in the traditional manner, ending in a triangular apse. Pointed-arched windows.

Roman Catholic St.-Nicolaaskerk (N.-Noord): This neo-Gothic cruciform basilica (1874–5) has an ornate *organ case* (*c.* 1500) from the former Nieuwezijdskapel in Amsterdam. The late Gothic *altar retable* with the fourteen saints is a German work (*c.* 1500).

Huis Oudegein: A house of 1633 surrounded by a moat, it occupies the site of a medieval manor. Its drive is flanked by two lions bearing coats-of-arms.

Kasteel Rijnhuizen: Another old manor. The present house dates from the mid-17C and stands opposite the former village of Jutphaas by the Vaartse Rijn. Altered in the 18C, the house is surrounded by a charming landscaped park with a picturesque pavilion (1731).

Also worth seeing: The oldest *water mill* (1640) in Utrecht stands by the Hollandsche Ijssel.

Nieuw-Loosdrecht
Utrecht   p.289☐I 5

Nearby there are a series of small lakes, the Loosdrechtse Plassen, which go back to the 14C and resulted from peat-cutting. The town itself was founded in the late 13C, probably by Willem van Sypestein.

Dutch Reform church: The interior of this church (*c.* 1500) is light and airy. The massive tower was restored in 1937.

Kasteel Sypestein: In the early 20C, Jonkheer C.H.C.A. van Sypestein had a castle-like mansion built (mainly in old materials) on the medieval foundations of an old castle which he regarded as his family's ancestral seat (today historians do not share this opinion). The interior and its surroundings were designed with loving care and the *rose garden* has become famous. While still living, the owner bequeathed it to a charity which keeps the house open as a museum, with a porcelain collection and a set of family portraits. Guided tours: 1 May–15 Sept.: Tue.–Sat. 10.15 and 11.15 a.m., 2.15 and 4 p.m., Sun. 2, 3, and 4 p.m.

Nijmegen/Nimwegen
Geldern   p.291☐L 6

History: Members of the Germanic Batavi tribe probably lived on the S. bank of the Waal in pre-Christian times. The later Roman settlement of *Noviomagus* was of greater significance. Nimwegen was a Carolingian county palatine in the early Middle Ages, and became an imperial town in 1230 and a member of the Hanseatic League in 1364. It was of importance as a fortified town until the 19C, but thereafter it was only of regional significance. Today Nimwegen is the picture of a flourishing industrial town. The severe devastation suffered in World War 2 was quickly overcome, although some parts of the old town have vanished for ever.

St.-Stevenskerk: The simple W. pillars of the nave are remnants of the first large church built 1254–73. Much of the lower part of the tower (probably completed *c.* 1307) survives. In the late 14C/early 15C the basilican building was made into a hall church with a stone portal on the S. side. The choir, unusually sumptuous for Holland, with an ambulatory and a ring of chapels, was built in the course of the 15C by Gisbaert Schairt van (Zalt)Bommel, architect from Xanten. The three-aisled transept (16C) has a chapel of the Holy Sepulchre in the N., and a *S. portal* of a design unique for Holland (probably completed 1559). The tower had to be rebuilt in 1592–3, and 1604–05 it was given a new spire (restored in 1953). Individual scenes from the 16C *wall paintings* survive in the ambulatory and in the chapel of the Holy Sepulchre. The late Gothic monument to Anna Catharina of Bourbon, set up in 1512 by her son Karel van Gelre, is by Wilhelm Loemans from Cologne. Parts of the pews on the S. side of the high choir are by Graedt Dulcken (1577). The richly carved pulpit (1639) is by Joost

Jacobs from Amsterdam. Sculptures (1773) on the monumental organ are by J.Keerbergen and J.Otten.

Valkhof: Founded by Charlemagne as a county palatine, it was first destroyed in 1047, but rebuilt by Friedrich Barbarossa in 1155. The castle was largely destroyed in 1796–7. *St.-Nicolaaskapel* survived. This centrally planned building with a sixteen-sided ground plan and a tall octagonal main structure is probably later than 1030. There is a vaulted portal on the W. side, and the E. side has the remains of Gothic altar niches. The late-Romanesque *St.-Maartenskapel* survives from Barbarossa's castle which has otherwise been entirely lost.

Kerkboog: A vaulted double passage (1542–5) by Claes de Waele, it leads from the Grote Markt to the Stevenskerkhof and was originally part of the cloth hall (Gewandhuis). The upper storey (1605–6) is probably by Thomas Singendonck, and has a Flemish Renaissance gable on the side facing the Markt.

Protestants-Kinderen-Weeshuis (Begijnengas): The 16C orphanage was rebuilt in baroque style by Salomon de Bray and Symon Bosboom in 1644. The façade has a colossal order of pilasters, windows with triangular gables, and a relief of orphans in the tympanum of the portal.

Stadhuis (Grote Burchtstraat): The Renaissance town hall (1554–5) by Herman van Herengrave, the town architect, was destroyed in World War 2, except for the front and side façades; reconstructed and restored in 1951–3. Three series of 17C wall tapestries have survived—being restored in another town at the time of the destruction wrought during World War 2.

Former Stads- or Latijnse School (Stevenskerkhof): This school building (1544–5) is by Herman van Herengrave. The main façade has a mixture of Gothic and Renaissance forms, broad arches within which there is trefoil decoration, and Renaissance friezes. The carved details, restored in the sixties, are the

Nijmegen, St.-Stevenskerk

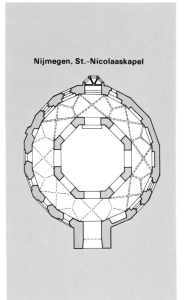

Nijmegen, St.-Nicolaaskapel

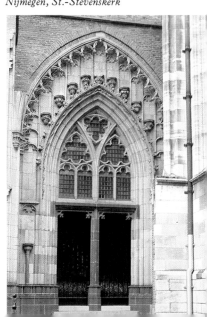

work of Hendrick Cornelisz, Meister Wylhelm and Peter van Utrecht.

Fortifications: The bold *Kronenburger tower* (1425–6) in the W., and the *Belvedere* in today's Hunerpark in the E., survive from the old 15C ring of defences. In 1646 town architect Peter van Blokhout increased the height of the Belvedere and converted it into a lookout tower. Part of the *town wall* survives between the Belvedere and St.-Jorisstraat.

Waag (Grote Markt): Dating from 1612 in Amsterdam Renaissance style, with an outdoor staircase and gable façades, this building was designed as a weigh-house and meat hall.

Houses: A number of late medieval *canons' houses* have been reconstructed on the N. side of St.-Stevenskerk. In the Steenstraat, *Besiendershuis* is in Lower Rhine late-Gothic style, the *Zeilmakerij* has late-Gothic stepped gables and *Brouwershuis* dates from 1621. *Jezuïtenhuis* (26 Lage Markt) has a classical pilastered façade from the mid 17C. There are a number of 16&17C houses between Lage Markt and Waalkade.

Rijksmuseum G.M. Kam (45 Museum Kamstraat): Finds from the time of the Batavian oppidum and Roman Noviomagus. Opening times: Mon.–Sat. 10 a.m.–5 p.m., Sun. and holidays 1–5 p.m.

Nijmeegs Museum 'Commanderie van St.Jan' (Franse Plaats): Formerly the building housed the Order of St.John. Parts are medieval. Today it is a *historical museum*. Opening times: Mon.–Sat. 10 a.m.–5 p.m., Sun. and holidays 1–5 p.m.

Also worth seeing: The *Cellenbroedershuis* (Anthoniusplaats) has two late medieval wings with tall saddleback roofs and stepped gables. The *former synagogue* (Nonnenstraat) dates from 1756 and has an entrance dating from 1798. Only the exterior has been restored. The free-standing *chapel of the former convent of Mary of Mons* now stands in the square of the same name. This large 15C hall struc-

Nijmegen, former Stads- or Latijnse School

ture with rib vaults was converted into the *district museum* in 1919.

Environs: Batenburg (17 km. W.): The nave and two aisles of the *Dutch Reform church,* and also the massive base of the tower, were rebuilt in the first half of the 17C after being devastated in the Eighty Years' War. Inside there are 17&18C memorial panels, a 13C stone font (restored) and a baroque pulpit (1655). The *castle* standing on the N. edge of the little town was once the most important castle between Maas and Waal, but it is now only a picturesque ruin. Built in *c.* 1600 on earlier foundations, this large structure was gutted by fire in 1794 and later fell into disrepair. The *windmill* on the way to Bergharen may be 16C.

Bergharen (12 km. W.): The *Dutch Reform church* is beautifully situated and has a large 15C nave and a 13C tower.

Ewijk (13 km. NW): A 12C *tower,* charmingly decorated with friezes of arches, survives from the Roman Catholic church demolished in 1918. The new *Roman Catholic church* was built *c.* 1920. *Huis Doddendael* is a small castle (probably 14C) with an early-17C NE annexe. The arched bridge across the castle moat is mid-19C.

Hernen (11 km. W.): The four residential wings (12C–early 16C) of *Kasteel Hernen,* surround an almost square courtyard. A residential tower stood at the SE corner until about 1850 when it was torn down. The other corners have a round tower and overhanging corner turrets. Some 19C additions were removed in restoration work in 1943–57 and the castle once again has a compact form which it probably possessed in the 18C.

Leur (11 km. SW): The 13C *Dutch Reform church* stands on rising ground. The tower still has its original masonry. The church's nave is 14C and the choir 15C.

Wychen (10 km. SW): In 1853, a neoclassical church was added to the Romanesque tower of the former *Roman Catholic church.* The *former castle,* built in Dutch Renaissance style 1609–26 on top of the walls of a previous building, was converted into a town hall in 1933. Three wings open on to a courtyard and a sturdy staircase tower stands at the NE corner. The round stone *windmill* dates from 1799.

Norg

Drente   p.287□N 2

Norg is one of the most beautiful villages in Drente, picturesquely located in enchanting countryside with streams, woods and fields of grain.

Dutch Reform church: This mainly 13C church has survived in good condition, consisting of a simple Romanesque saddleback tower, nave (with a flat roof today) and a choir ending in a semicircular apse. The choir has dome-like vaulting and a stellar vault at the end. Vault paint-

Nijmegen, weigh-house

Norg, Dutch Reform church

St.-Oedenrode

North Brabant   p.290☐K 7

Dutch Reform church: This small single-aisled church dates in the main from 1808. The tower (19C top) and some columns and arches in the nave survive from the former parish church (15C), the aisle walls of which church are now churchyard walls. There are missal desks dating from *c.* 1660, 1733 and 1734, (the last two are by Claude Demeny from 's-Hertogenbosch).

Kasteel Dommelrode: Originally 15C, the castle was rebuilt in 1605 mainly in brick (also ashlars e.g. window frames) by Jonkheer Marcus van Gerwen, mayor of the district of Peelland. In 1961–3 the castle was restored and made into the town hall. 19C monastery.

Kasteel Henkenshage: Lies on the way towards Best, outside the centre of the village. The main building is 17C; the two round towers with spires date from a major reconstruction in *c.* 1840. Romantic castle courtyard.

St.-Paulusgasthuis: The hospital (1434) in Kerkstraat now houses a *museum* in which archaeological finds and also traditional bonnets and muffs from Brabant are on display. Opening times: 1 Apr.–mid-June: Mon.–Sat.

ings were restored on the basis of traces of the original along with the rest of the restoration work in 1969–70. The church has a carved pulpit (1678) and a carved lectern.

Mills: Buildings beside the village green include not only the church, but also two attractive, typically 19C upright mills, 'De Noordenveld' (1878) and 'De Hoop' (1857).

Also worth seeing: *A megalithic tomb* in nearby Westervelde.
The *Westervelde* 'castle' is late 18C. A barn was added in 1804, and an extra storey in *c.* 1870.

Environs: Een (2.5 km. W.): The *Zwartendijkster Schans* (1593–4) has a ditch and a bastion.
Zuidvelde (2 k. S.): The picturesque old *farmhouse at 78 Asserstraat* may be from the first half of the 17C.

St.-Oedenrode, Kasteel Henkenshage

1.30–4 p.m., mid-June–Sept.: Mon.–
Sat. 10 a.m.–12 noon and 1.30–4 p.m.,
Sun. 1.30–4 p.m.

Environs: Breugel: (7 km. S.):
Roman Catholic church with nave, net-
vaulted choir, and W. tower with flying buttresses, all dating from the
second half of the 15C. The transept
was knocked down in 1822 and rebuilt
in a different form in 1960.
Son (7 km. S.): A stone tower dating
from *c.* 1500, richly articulated in
stone, is all that survives of the *late
Gothic church,* which fell into disrepair after a fire in 1958 and was
eventually demolished. The middle
part of the *town hall,* built *c.* 1760 and
restored and enlarged in 1920, has a
small bellcote and an upper window
decorated with a radiant sun.
Uden (15 km. NE): The 18C Maria
Refugie, a Brigittine abbey, was built
on what are probably the remains of a

small former castle. The chapel of
1720 was slightly altered last century.
The *Roman Catholic church* by
C.Weber and consecrated 1890, takes
the form of a cruciform basilica in
Romanesque and Gothic style, with a
trefoil apse in the E.
Veghel (8 km. NE): The *Roman
Catholic church of St.Lambert,* a neo-
Gothic cruciform basilica by Petrus
Josephus Hubertus Cuypers, has a
tall tower, rib vaults, and an ambula-
tory. The main façade is decorated in
stone with sculptures and baldachins.
Neo-Gothic interior decorations, also
by Cuypers, survive.

Oirschot
North Brabant   p.289□ l 7

St.-Pieterskerk: This large late-
Gothic basilica whose tower was com-

Oirschot, Raadhuis

pletely gutted by fire in 1944 (since rebuilt) is a magnificent example of Kempen Gothic. The former building was devastated by fire in 1462 and another building with a nave, two aisles, transepts, choir with ambulatory and a ring of chapels, was built in the decades following. Inside there are columns with simple capitals, stellar vaults over the crossing, and rib vaults above the aisles; ambulatory and choir chapels. All that survives of the decorations is a black marble tombstone commemorating Richard van Merode (d. 1552), now in the tower portal. The four lions, formerly part of this slab, now support the font. After 18C restoration, the Roman Catholic church had a baroque high altar (*c.* 1700) and two pretty side altars (1766).

Dutch Reform church: This former chapel of the Virgin Mary (probably early 12C) was turned into a weigh-house for butter in 1648. Since 1801 it has been a Dutch Reform church. The Gothic choir was shortened in 1880 and given a straight end. There is a turret (1786) above the W. façade. The pulpit (1756) is by Claude Demeny.

Raadhuis: The town hall, rebuilt after a fire in 1513, was much altered in the 18C. The only original sections are the stepped gables and the flat-vaulted cellar, which is the council chamber today.

Also worth seeing: The *main façade* (1775) of the former *Kasteel Oud Beysterveld* stands between the modern annexes of the Missionaris-senklooster monastery. *St.-Francis-cushof* has a pilastered façade (1663). Tall linden trees stand in the pretty *Kempische market square*.

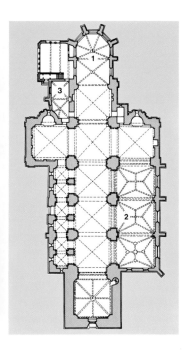

Oldenzaal, statue of St. Plechelm

Oldenzaal, St.-Plechelmuskerk 1 Gothic extension (c.1450) of choir **2** Gothic side aisle (1480) **3** Sacristy (c.1500)

Oldenzaal

Overijssel   p.287☐O 5

This town in beautiful Twente countryside was mentioned in 893. The right to hold markets was granted in 1049, and the town was granted a charter in *c.* 1249.

St.-Plechelmuskerk: A Roman Catholic church dedicated to St.Plechelm who proclaimed Christianity here in the 8C, it was formerly one of the most important collegiate churches in the bishopric of Utrecht. The cruciform Romanesque sandstone basilica from the second half of the 12C has a sturdy 13C tower. The Romanesque choir apse was replaced

by a Gothic choir in the 15C; the large S. aisle dates from 1480. Apart from the abbey church of Rolduc, the church of St.Plechelm is the finest example of a high Romanesque vaulted basilica in the metrical system (where the unit of measurement employed in the crossing is used for all parts of the ground plan) in the Netherlands. The interior is rather more ornate and has a baroque pulpit from Germany, a Crucifixion painting (*c.* 1500), and a triptych from Antwerp (*c.* 1525). The best item in the church treasure is a 15C gilded *reliquary* of St.Plechelm.

Museum Het Palthehuis (13 Marktstraat): The museum, which occupies a building with a Renaissance gable façade dating from *c.* 1660, houses a complete 19C pharmacy, an old private library and rooms decorated in different styles.

Opening times: Tue.–Fri. 10 a.m.–12 noon and 2–5 p.m., Sat. and Sun. 2–5 p.m.

Also worth seeing: The *Michgorius-huis* (10 Marktstraat) has a fine Renaissance gable from *c.* 1660.

Environs: Weerselo (7 km. NE): The *Dutch Reform church* survives from a Benedictine abbey founded *c.* 1150 (later a charitable foundation for women). It is likely that the walls of this small single-aisled structure are 14C or even older. The upper sections probably date from alterations in *c.* 1500. Inside: Romanesque font (*c.* 1200) and 16&17C tombstones. The *priest's house*, which has a charming entrance, was formerly part of a charitable foundation (1731). In *Volte* there is the *palace of Het Everloo* (17C) which is now a museum.

Ommen
Overijssel   p.287□N 4

Ommen was built in *c.* 1200 beside a

Oldenzaal, Museum

ford over the Vecht. Granted a charter in 1248.

Dutch Reform church: This late-Gothic building (15C) has old parts from *c.* 1300 in the choir. The present belfry (18C) on the W. side of the N. aisle has two bells by Heinrich of Dortmund (1517).

Kasteel Eerde: Originally built in the 13C, the building has been besieged and burned down more than once. Today it appears as an elegant mansion dating from 1715. Around the entrance there are coats-of-arms and heraldic figures.

Oudheidkamer 'Den Oordt' (7–8 Den Oordt): A *museum* with prehistoric finds, costumes etc. housed in a mill and the adjoining customs house. Opening times: 15 June–31 Aug.: Mon.–Fri. 10 a.m.–12 noon and 2–5 p.m., Sat. 2–4 p.m.; 1–15 Sept.: Mon.–Fri. 2–4 p.m.

Environs: Hardenberg (14 km. NE): Part of the *town wall* (38 Voorstraat) survives as testimony to the town's former strategic importance. The *Oudheidkamer* (34 Voorstraat), in the former community hall, has agricultural implements, Saxon costumes, old coins etc. Opening times: 1 Apr.–1 July: Mon., Wed. and Fri. 2–4 p.m.; 1 July–15 Aug.: Mon.–Fri. 2–5 p.m., Thur. also 7–9 p.m.; 15 Aug.–19 Sept.: Mon., Wed. and Fri. 2–4 p.m.

Oosterbeek
Geldern   p.291□L 6

Dutch Reform church: The church was badly damaged in the war. Later investigations showed that the building originally consisted only of a nave with three identical apses at the E. end which were probably pre-Romanesque. The Romanesque choir was replaced by a Gothic choir, probably in the 15C. During restoration work, a new choir was built following the ground plan of the Romanesque choir—outlines of the three pre-Romanesque apses are indicated on the floor. The tower is 14C or 15C.

Huis Mariendaal: This country house stands in a scenic park with a large arbour surrounded by beech trees, on a site formerly occupied by the old abbey of Marienborn.

Environs: Doorwerth (1 km. W.): *Kasteel Doorwerth* was mentioned in 1260 when it was owned by the van Dorenweerd family. The oldest section is the E. wing. In the course of restoration work necessitated by war damage, an old entrance in the E. wing was discovered. A second phase of construction took place in the late 14C, and there was another rash of building after 1400 (N. wing with bartizans). The S. wing and gate are from the second half of the 15C, while the large corner tower is 16C. Later alterations were ignored in the extensive restoration work. Part of the building now houses the *Nederlands Jachtmuseum* (hunting museum) which

has interesting exhibits. Opening times: 10 a.m.–5 p.m. daily except Tue., 1–5 p.m. on Sun. and holidays, closed on 25 Dec. and 1 Jan.

Oosterhout
North Brabant   p.290□H 7

St.-Janskerk: A Gothic church from the second half of the 15C, it has a nave and two aisles. Parts of the old building survive in the choir and transepts. 1881–3, the church was enlarged into nave and four aisles to plans by Petrus Josephus Hubertus Cuypers.

Dutch Reform church: The simple church (1810) with a Greek cross ground plan has a richly carved pulpit (probably 1639).

Monastery of St.Catharinadal: In 1647, when the Premonstratensian convent moved from Breda to Oosterhout, the house called De Blauwe Kamer (first half of 16C) was acquired to accommodate it (today the pro-

Doorwerth (Oosterbeek), Kasteel

Oosterhout, St.Janskerk

Ootmarsum, Roman Catholic church

vost's house). At the front of the building, the square tower is flanked by gables (one of which is stepped). 17C monastery buildings. The neo-Gothic chapel is by J.van Gils (1905).

Huize Limburg: is one of the three *country houses*, known as 'Slotyes', on the S. side of the town. The early-15C building is roughcast in white and has turrets at the corners of the façade. Two more wings were added in 1460 and the building was redesigned and enlarged in classical style in 1789.

Environs: Dongen (5 km. E.): When the *Dutch Reform church* was restored in 1932, only the choir and transept (late 15C) were rebuilt, the nave (1640) being preserved as a ruin. The brick tower with flying buttresses at the corners is probably somewhat older than the church. 17C pulpit.

Ootmarsum
Overijssel   p.287☐O 4

This small old town, first mentioned in 917 in a description by Bishop Radboud, has been well restored and the medieval layout has survived.

Roman Catholic church: A mid-13C basilican structure built of stone from Bentheim in Westphalian Romanesque-Gothic style. The E. end of the choir and the two chapels between the choir and the transepts, date from 1491. The sandstone tower in the W. was pulled down in 1842 and replaced with a wooden turret on the roof. The original polychrome style has been restored in the interior, where there are ornate capitals and rib vaulting.

Dutch Reform church: By Gerrit Hagels (1810) the building has an elegant pilastered façade. Renaissance pulpit (1674) and a fine organ.

De Hunenborg: Today, all that can still be seen of the former Carolingian castle with ramparts (SE of the town) are earthworks and some stone foundations.

Also worth seeing: The *town hall* (1778) has rococo ornaments on a sandstone façade. The *house at A67 Marktstraat* has a fine Renaissance gable façade (1658).

Orvelte
Drente   p.287☐N 3

The village of Orvelte is a kind of large *open-air museum* carefully restored to its original condition. Buildings open to the public include the *Tolhuis* (customs house) with a historic living-room, the *Bruntigerhof* (1729; 8 Lintenweg) with old decorations and farming implements, a

Orvelte, open-air museum, farmbuildings

small *village shop* (2 Schoolstraat) as it was in 1919, a *mill* (6 Schoolstraat) with an exhibition of mills in Drente, *craftsmen's shops* (Dorpsstraat) with a smithy, clog-maker's and a sawmill, a hand-operated *dairy* from 1899 (3 Melkwegje), various *studios* where ceramics, knitwear and hand-carved utensils are produced, and also *painters' studios*. Trips by covered waggon or horse-drawn tram can also be made; cars are not allowed. Opening times: Apr.–autumn holidays and 26–30 Dec.: Mon.–Fri. 9.30 a.m.–5 p.m., Sat. and Sun. 11 a.m.–5 p.m.; Easter, Ascension Day, Whit. and 1 July–26 Aug.: until 5.30 p.m.

Environs: Beilen (8 km. W.): The small 16C *church* has a tall 15C tower. *The gold treasure of Beilen* was discovered nearby in 1955. Today the 22 coins from AD 364–395 are in the Provinciaal Museum in Assen. The *Oud-*

heidkamer (4 Kampstraat) has a collection of Frisian earthenware and Chinese porcelain, gold and silver utensils, and local costumes from Drente. Opening times: Fri. 4.30–6 p.m.

Westerbork (3 km. W.): The 15C *Dutch Reform church* is a harmonious Gothic structure. The lower part of the tower is likely to be older, while the upper section was probably rebuilt in the late 18C. The '*In de Ar*' *farm museum* has fine old interior decorations. A meal of brown beans can also be sampled here (for groups of at least six persons). Opening times: Mon.–Sat. 9 a.m.–5 p.m. The *Museum van de Knipkunst Wiecher Tjeert Lever* (Burg, 15 van Weezelplein) is devoted to origami and cut paper work from Europe and the Far East (post 1700). Opening times: Apr.–Oct.: Mon.–Sat. 9 a.m.–12 noon and 1–5 p.m.

Oss

North Brabant   p.289□K 6

Oss was granted the status of a town in 1399, and from then on it was one of the main towns in the area drained by the Maas. It developed into an industrial town in the 19C.

Roman Catholic church: This cruciform neo-Gothic basilica (1857–9) by H.J. van Tulder has a nave, two aisles and an ambulatory. Unusually the tower does not have a helm roof. The stained-glass windows (1881–9) are by J.B.Capronnier from Brussels; the figures of the Apostle are by H.van Geld.

Gemeentemuseum: The local museum occupies a house built in 1889 by Van den Bergh, a margarine manufacturer, and subsequently bought by Jurgens, his competitor.

Environs: Berghem (2 km. E.): This village has become well known for excavations carried out in 1955, when finds from the Iron Age and Roman and Merovingian periods were discovered.

Geffen (3 km. SW): The *Roman Catholic church,* damaged by fire several times, has a strong 15C tower and an early-16C basilican nave five bays of which are original. The church was enlarged by C.Franssen in 1893. 16C wooden statue of St.George.

Lith (9 km. NW): The book 'Dorp aan de rivier' by the Dutch author Antoon Coolen made this town famous; the former Doktorshuis (1686) features in the book. The round stone *'Zeldenrust' corn mill* dates from 1800.

Oijen(7 km. N.): The small *'Waterstaatsstijl'* church dates from 1837. Of the *castle* pulled down in 1837, two round late-16C corner towers in the barbican and parts of older walls survive .

Oudenbosch

North Brabant   p.290□G 7

Basilica of St.Agatha and St.Bar-

Oudenbosch, basilica of St.Agatha and St.Barbara

bara: This church (1865–80) by Petrus Josephus Hubertus Cuypers is modelled on St.Peter's in Rome, although simpler and on a smaller scale (the height of the dome is 223 ft.). The main façade was built in 1892 under the supervision of G.J. van Swaay and was based on S.Giovanni in Laterano in Rome. Inside altar retable and sculptures are by the Antwerp sculptor Frans de Vriendt.

Institut Saint-Louis: The façade and dome of the chapel of this institute for boys are based on the same Roman models as the basilica. The chapel was built in 1865–6 and completed in 1889.

Zuavenmuseum: In the 19C, Dutchmen (Zouaves) were among the troops defending the Pope and Papal States during the time just prior to the unification of Italy. During 1860–1870, S. Netherlands provided 4,000–5,000 troops, many of whom came from the Institut Saint-Louis.
Opening times: May–Sept.: Tue., Thur. 1–3 p.m., Sun. 2–5 p.m.

Oudewater, Dutch Reform church

Also worth seeing: The simple classical *town hall* (*c.* 1775).

Oudewater
Utrecht   p.289☐H 5

In the 12C, the attractive little town of Oudewater was a flourishing settlement at the point where the Linschoten flowed into the Hollandse IJssel. It was probably granted a charter in 1265. An epidemic of plague befell the town in 1574 and it was conquered by the Spanish in 1575.

Dutch Reform church: The tower dates from shortly after 1300 and still has its original half-hipped roof, a very unusual form for S. Holland.
The formerly Romanesque church was made into a hall church during the first half of the 15C (the choir had been altered in the late 14C). Inside the church, a fascinating spatial impression is created by the light flowing into the building, particularly in the E. section.

Stadhuis: Remnants of the previous

Oudewater, Arminiushuis

building were used in the construction (1588) of the town hall, which has a Renaissance stepped gable.

Waaghuis: This building of 1595 is famous as a *witches' weigh-house*. At the time of the persecution of witches, suspects were weighed here (it was alleged that witches had no weight) and given a certificate of their weight. Today it is a *museum*. Opening times: 15 Apr.–14 Sept.: Mon.–Sat. 9 a.m.–5 p.m., Sun. 12 noon–5 p.m.

Houses: There are numerous 17C *houses* with S. Dutch stepped gables and decorative window arches and niches e.g. the houses at *4 Havenstraat* and *3 Donkeregaard*, and the *Arminiushuis* (1601) by the Markt, which has the figure of Fortuna in a niche.

Environs: Lopik (8 km. SE): The *Dutch Reform church,* a single-aisled brick building, is mainly 15C. It was shortened in 1818 by the removal of four bays; the tower was probably pulled down at the same time (the present turret dates from 1968).

Poortugaal
South Holland   p.289□G 6

Dutch Reform church: This attractive cruciform church has a slender tower (partly 14C). During the late 15C it was increased in height and flying buttresses were added. Nave and two aisles are early 16C. On the wall of the S. transept a painting of the Last Judgement dates from *c.* 1500. A wall panel with the Ten

Beemster (Purmerend), 'De Eenhoorn'

Commandments is dated 1687. The pulpit is dates from 1774.

Environs: Oud-Beijerland (5 km. S.): The *Dutch Reform church* (1650) has a wooden barrel vault. The E. section was enlarged *c.* 1925. The slender tower dates from 1604. The *town hall* (1622) has an attractive gable above the central entrance section.

Rhoon (3 km. E.): The choir of the *Dutch Reform church* (early 16C) has the marble tomb (1740) of the two wives of Hans Willem Bentinck, designed by Daniel Marot. The church also has the tombstone of Adriana van Room, abbess of Leeuwenhorst (d. 1527), and three rococo panels commemorating members of the Bentinck van Roon family. *Kasteel Rhoon,* founded in the 12C and redesigned and rebuilt in 16&17C, suffered a period of neglect but has now regained its old splendour. Today it is a cultural centre and a restaurant. The *''t Hert' corn mill* N. of the village is a round mill (1849) built in brick.

Spijkenisse (2 km. W.): The tower of the late-Gothic *Dutch Reform church* is mid 15C. The choir and transept are a little later, and the single, very broad aisle dates from 1521.

Purmerend

North Holland   p.289□H 4

Purmerend lies between the polders of Beemster, Wormer and Purmer. It was built here in *c.* 1212 after the original town of Purmer had been flooded. The right to hold markets here was granted by Count Jan van Egmond in 1424. The cattle market held on Tuesdays is still one of the largest markets in the Netherlands today.

Purmerend's Museum (2 Kaasmarkt): This museum is housed in the neo-Renaissance town hall (1912) designed by Jan Stuyt. It has documents relating to the cheese trade and whale fishing, both of which were formerly important in this region, as well as archaeological finds, paintings and 19C earthenware.

Also worth seeing: The *weigh-house for cheese and butter. Grote Kerk* with an organ from 1742. *Lutherse Kerk* (1612). *Former orphanage* (1789) with a pretty façade.

Environs: Beemster (3 km. N.): The low-lying land was drained in 1609 under the supervision of Jan Adriaansz. Leeghwater from De Rijp. However, there was a storm flood which the dykes were unable to withstand, and it was only in 1612 that drainage was successfully achieved with the aid of 47 mills. In the beautiful countryside around Beemster there are various old *farmhouses* with pyramidal roofs so typical of the area, e.g. '*De Eenhoorn*' (1682) and '*De Lepelaar*' (1683). The small single-aisled *Dutch Reform church* at *Midden-Beemster* has a very slender tower, built *c.* 1620 in the style of Hendrick de Keyser. The height of the tower was increased in 1661 to drawings by Pieter Post. The *Museum Betje Wolff* (178 Middenweg) in the former priest's house (1666) preserves the study of Betje Wolff, the authoress who lived here from 1759–77. Opening times: 1 May–1 Oct.: Tue. and Thur. 10 a.m.–12 noon and 1.30–5 p.m., Sat. and Sun. 2–5.30 p.m.

Jisp (6 km. W.): The attractive *town hall* (1650), with three gables and fine interior decorations, was probably built by J.A. Leeghwater. The small single-aisled *Dutch Reform church* dates from 1822.

Raalte
Overijssel   p.287☐M 4

Dutch Reform church: This single-aisled Gothic village church has a 15C choir, a nave (somewhat wider and built later) and a tower of 1697. The fine pulpit and two noblemen's pews date from *c.* 1700.

Roman Catholic church: This slender neo-Gothic building (1890–2) is by A.Tepe.

Raalte, Dutch Reform church

Also worth seeing: *Kasteel Schoonheten* (SE of the village) was originally a simple country house which was later enlarged—most recently in the 19C. *Hof van Luttenburg* NE of the town can be traced back to the 14C. The *Strunk farmhouse* is a well-preserved Saxon building (1796). The old inn, '*De Duke of Portland*', is picturesquely situated near to Schoonheten.

Public events: The *Stöppelhaene*, Salland's sumptuous harvest festival, is held here Tue.–Sat. in the last full week in August.

Renswoude
Utrecht   p.289☐K 5

Dutch Reform church: The ground plan of this church (1639–41) is a Greek cross with truncated arms. Above the crossing there is an octagonal dome on a square base, which is supported inside the building by Ionic pilasters and columns with a wooden architrave. It is not known who built the church, although it was commissioned by Johan van Reede.

Kasteel Renswoude: This enormous Renaissance structure (1654) by Gijsbert van Vianen and Peter van Cooten was built for Gerard van Reede, probably on the foundations of an older house.

Rheden
Geldern   p.287☐M 5

The district on the left bank of the IJssel includes a large section of the National Park of Veluwezoom with areas of forest and moorland inhabited by red deer, roe deer, badgers, martens, wild boars and rare species of birds.

Dutch Reform church: The 12C

Romanesque tower of this church has typical decorations including round arches and rectangular strips. 15C rib-vaulted choir; net-vaulted basilican nave and two aisles date from *c*. 1505.

Environs: Rozendaal (2 km. SW): The oldest surviving section of the *Kasteel Rozendaal* founded in the early 14C is the massive keep. The adjoining residential complex (1615) was altered in the 18C, while the space formerly occupied by the courtyard is now taken up by 19C wings. Gardens date from the first half of the 18C, and large sections have survived even after J.D.Zocher's redesigning of the grounds as a landscape garden in 1836–7. Parts to have survived include ponds, laid out in several stages, and the various grottoes and waterworks. A summer-house by Daniel Marot (probably 1722–3) also survives in good condition. Today the castle is the head office and museum of the Internationalen Kastelen Instituut.
Opening times: Tue.–Sat. 10 a.m.–5 p.m., Sun 1–5 p.m.

De Steeg (3 km. NE): The originally medieval *Kasteel Middachten* (1572) was rebuilt and enlarged in 1643 after severe damage. It was destroyed again in 1672 and finally given its present form by Steven Vennecool and Jacob Roman in 1694–7. Splendid features inside are the panelled vestibule and the central stairwell which has an ornate carved double staircase and galleries with balustrades. Stucco ceilings.

Rhenen
Utrecht   p.290☐K 6

St.-Cunerakerk: This late Gothic hall church has a stone vault, transept, choir and an enormous tower. The church is unexpectedly large because the relics of St.Cunera are preserved here and in consequence it has become a place of pilgrimage. All that is known of the church's architectural history is that an indulgence for it was granted in 1451 and that the *tower* was begun in 1492 and completed in 1531. This tower, one of the finest late-

Rozendaal (Rheden), grotto

Gothic works in Holland, is similar to the far older cathedral tower in Utrecht and also to the somewhat older tower in Amersfoort (the Lange Jan). The best feature inside the church is the early Renaissance *rood screen* (probably *c.* 1550–60) which divides the wall between choir and nave. The arch spandrels in the minstrels' gallery, which is supported by columns, show the Virtues and allegories of Faith, Hope and Charity. Fine Renaissance choirstalls (1570). Opening times: 15 June–1 Sept. Church: Mon.–Fri. 1–2 p.m., Thur. also 10 a.m.–12 noon. Tower: Mon.–Sat. 2 p.m., Thur. also 11 a.m.

Environs: Lienden (3 km. SW): The stone vaulting of the 15C late Gothic *Dutch Reform church* probably dates from the 16C. The stellar vault in the nave is supported by bundled pillars with leaf capitals, while the choir, which is narrower, has a net vault. The small chapel adjoining it in the N. has a stellar vault with corbel stones decorated with figures. 15C wall paintings, uncovered on the N. wall of the choir in 1932, depict

Rhenen, St.-Cunerakerk

St.Christopher, St.Bartholomew and a Crucifixion.

Roden
Drente   p.287☐N 2

Dutch Reform church: This 13C church was originally single-aisled. The Gothic choir is early 15C, the side aisles and tower are somewhat later. At the same time, or possibly not until the 17C, the stone barrel vault of the nave was built. The carved pulpit dates from 1717 and there is a family pew from the early 18C. The organ (1777–9) is by A.A.-Hinsch, the organ builder from Groningen.

Huis te Roden or **Mensinghe:** This farmstead standing amid drainage ditches may date back to the 16C. Enlarged in the 17C, it was more extensively altered after a fire in 1736. Beside it there is a stone dovecote.

Nederlands Museum Kinderwereld (31 Brink): Old toys (dolls, dolls' houses, tin soldiers etc.) and old educational equipment. Opening times: Mon.–Sat. 10 a.m.–12 noon and 2–5 p.m., Sun. 2–5 p.m. Closed on Mon. Sept.–Mar.

Also worth seeing: The *farm* at 1 De Spijker which may be 17C.

Environs: Eelde (9 km. E.): The *Dutch Reform church* dates in its present form from the 14C. Allegorical paintings (1715) in the wooden vaulting of the choir. The *former Schultenhuis* (1654), with a classical gabled façade, was the town hall until 1938.
Peize (3 km. E.): The *Dutch Reform church*, which was much altered in the 19C, dates originally from the 13C; the tower was built in 1803. The organ was rebuilt by A.A.Hinsch in 1757. '*Huis ter Peize*', at 2 Brinkweg, is a farm. The octagonal *upright mill* was built in 1893.

Roermond

Limburg   p.281 □ M 8

History: Roermond lies at the point where the Roer flows into the Maas. Count Gerard van Gelre founded a Cistercian abbey here in 1218. The first abbess was his mother Richardis. Roermond was granted a charter in 1234. After the Eighty Years' War, Roermond fell to Spain, and later to Austria. Since 1815 it has been part of the Kingdom of the United Netherlands. The bishopric of Roermond was founded in 1559, abolished in 1801, and re-established in 1853.

Onze-Lieve-Vrouwe-Munsterkerk: French trooops destroyed the Cistercian convent in 1797 and only the church of the Virgin Mary, a showpiece of Rhineland late Romanesque style, survived. This church was probably begun shortly after the founding of the convent. The E. section of this rib-vaulted cruciform basilica is trefoil; the W. section soars far aloft. The church was restored 1863–*c*. 1890 by Petrus Josephus Hubertus Cuypers, during which restoration the two W. towers (it is likely that they were planned in the 13C, but not built owing to the poor condition of the soil) were constructed on the site of an 18C bell-tower. At the same time, square upper storeys were added to the E. towers. This church of the Virgin Mary is among the richest and most harmonious Rhineland churches from the first half of the 13C, probably in part because it was not built on the remains of an older structure. It is also apparent that the structural forms became increasingly rich as building work progressed from the E. to the W. and also from bottom to top of the church.

St.Christoffelkathedraal: Begun in 1410 as a parish church on the site of an older structure. During the 15C and possibly also the 16C, two further choirs of the same size as the main choir, and two more aisles, were all added. After World War 2, the tall, slender tower incorporated into the nave was given a spire, a copy of the one-time baroque spire (1663). Except for the tower, the exterior of the church is not very impressive; the interior is not particularly pleasing in appearance either owing to the enlargements. However, the church is richly decorated, having a sacramental altar in Renaissance style (1593), 16C choir stalls, a richly early-18C carved pulpit, a painting by Rubens showing the head of the crucified Christ and an Ascension by T.Willeboorts Bosschaert. Stained-glass windows are by Joep Nicolas (1897–1972).

Former Minderbroederskerk: The polygonal choir of this former Franciscan church dates from *c*. 1400, along with the adjoining part of the nave. Remaining sections of the stone-vaulted hall church are 15&16C. The attractive interior has ornamental paintings in the vaults. Petrus Josephus Hubertus Cuypers

Roermond, Munsterkerk

executed these on the basis of traces of existing paintings during restoration work in 1906.

Former Karthuizerklooster: Surviving monastery buildings include the chapel (probably 15C with 18C stuccoed ceiling with rococo ornaments) and an 18C cloister.

Stadhuis (Markt): The town hall (*c.* 1700), rebuilt 1880 and restored 1955, has portraits of the Spanish and Austrian rulers of the S. Netherlands.

Statue of Cuypers (Munsterplein): The famous architect Petrus Josephus Hubertus Cuypers (1827–1921) came from Roermond and his statue is by August Falise (1875–1935).

Gemeentemuseum Hendrik Luyten-Dr. Cuypers (8 Andersonweg): Cuypers formerly lived and had his studio here. Opening times: Tue.–Sat. 10 a.m.–12 noon and 2–5 p.m., Sun. 2–5 p.m.

Also worth seeing: *Rattentoren* (probably 14C) near St.-Christoffel-kathedraal survives from the medieval belt of fortifications. The *bishops' burial chapel* (1887) is a centrally planned neo-Romanesque structure by Cuypers. Today's *Louisahuis old people's home* (1681–1700) in Munsterplein was originally the Prinsenhof. The house at *7 Brugstraat* has a late Gothic gabled façade (early-16C). The *St.-Josephs-Stift* in Neerstraat, a town house from 1666 has survived in good condition.

Environs: Beesel (9 km. N.): *Nieuwenbroek* on the E. side of the village is a mid-16C mansion with attractive stepped gables and surrounded by a ditch. The tower-like gatehouse in the forecourt is 18C.
Haelen (5 km. N.): A round brick tower (probably 15C) still survives from the medieval *Kasteel Aldengoor*, which has two early-18C wings.
Herkenbosch (13 km. SE): *Roman Catholic church* with 13C early-Gothic choir built in marl with arched buttresses, friezes of pointed arches, and a sexpartite rib vault.
Horn (2 km. NW): *Kasteel Horn*, first mentioned 1243, was the ancestral

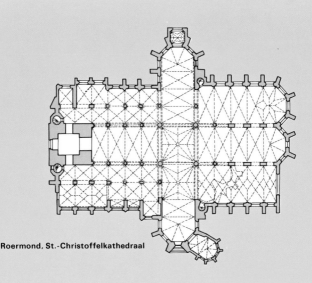

Roermond, St.-Christoffelkathedraal

castle of the rulers, later the Counts of Horn, the most famous of which was Philip de Montmorency, who was beheaded in Brussels in 1568 together with Count van Egmond. Today the castle consists of a tall surrounding wall and two semicircular 13C towers. The residential wing, after expansion and modernization over the years, was largely gutted by fire in 1948, but restored in 1547–7. The main body of the *'De Hoop' corn mill* is faced with slate.

Maasniel (1 km. E.): *Huis De Thoren* on the S. side of the village has a 16C wing with a slender turret; also a 15C square tower. *Huis De Tegeleie* on the NE side was originally a 17C nobleman's house with a square tower; today it is a farmhouse.

Montfort (8 km. SW): The *Roman Catholic church* has a Romanesque font and a late-Gothic painting of St.Anne with the Virgin Mary and the child Jesus, attributed to the so-called Master of Elsloo. The formerly significant *Kastell Montfort* was devastated by the French in 1794 and all that remains is a ruin from which the polygonal ground plan with five round towers can still be detected.

St.-Odilienberg (3 km. S.): The beautifully located *parish church,* a Romanesque cruciform basilica, was formerly a collegiate church and then belonged to a monastery. Rebuilt in the late 17C, it replaced the old parish church. The nave is probably 11C; choir and towers are likely to be *c.* 1200. The original parish church (N. side of the N. transept of today's parish church still has a wall with round arches deriving from the basilican nave (11C or 12C; restored in 1950).

Swalmen (5 km. N.): The walls of the massive octagonal tower (probably 14C) survive from the *castle of Swalmen,* which was known as Ouburg. *Huis Hillenraad,* originally 16C, has a regular appearance today with four tower-like corner pavilions dating from the 17&18C. William of Orange took up his quarters here

during the siege of Roermond in the Eighty Years' War.

Rotterdam
South Holland   p.290☐G 6

History: Rotterdam derives its name from the little river of Rotte. In the 13C a fishing village was built on the dam across the river. The village was granted a charter in 1340 and was a prosperous trading town in the 16&17C, but its economic development stagnated after this, mainly because the mouth of the Maas became silted up. The 'Nieuwe Waterweg'—the shipping link with the North Sea—and the canal links with the Rhine and Maas were built in the late 19C, at which time Rotterdam began to develop into an international port. (After World War 2, Rotterdam even outstripped London and New York in this regard.) However, the town centre was completely destroyed by German bombers on 14 May 1940, and in 1944 blasts carried out by German sappers seriously damaged

St.-Odilienberg (Roermond), church

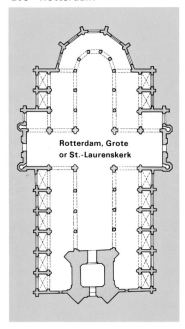

Rotterdam, Grote or St.-Laurenskerk

the harbour. The rapid reconstruction of the town and harbour was an astonishing feat.

Grote or St.-Laurenskerk: This late Gothic cruciform basilica, with chapels along the aisles and the choir and integral tower, was carefully restored in accordance with the original from 1951–68. Work on the tower was originally begun in 1440, on the nave in *c.* 1460 and the choir with its ambulatory in 1488. The only significant original features are the tracery of the windows and the delicate crowns on the staircase turrets at the ends of the transept. Features surviving inside the church include the monument to Admiral Egbert Kortenaer (d. 1665) on the N. side of the choir, and the monuments by Jan Blommendael to Johan van Brakel (d. 1690) and by Jacob Lois to Witte de With (d. 1658). New bronze doors are by Giacomo

Manzù. The church can be visited from Tue.–Sat., 10 a.m.–4 p.m.

Erasmus statue: The bronze figure of the famous humanist and theologian from Rotterdam was cast in 1622 to a model by Hendrick de Keyser and it stands in the square outside the St.-Laurenskerk. Erasmus of Rotterdam was born here on 27 or 28 October 1469 and died in Basle in 1536.

Former Gemeenlandshuis van Schieland (31 Korte Hoogstraat): The former dyke administration office (1662–5) by Jacob Lois, the architect from Rotterdam, was damaged by fire in 1864, and only the baroque façades remained undamaged. The town's *Historical Museum* is to be re-opened in 1986.

Stadhuis (Coolsingel): The largest town hall in the Netherlands, it was built in stone in 1914–20 to the plans of Henri Evers and survived undamaged. The *statue to Hugo de Groot,* a Rotterdam town councillor from 1613–18, stands in front of the building.

Statues: The famous monument to the *devastated town* (1953) by Ossip Zadkine (1890–1967) is temporarily situated in the Leuvhaven and symbolizes the destruction suffered by the town in 1940. The *war memorial* in front of the town hall is by the sculptor Mari Andriessen (d. 1897). The carved *railing* over 65 ft. high in Coolsingel is by Naum Gabo, the Russian-American sculptor (1890–1977).

Museums
Museum Boymans-van Beuningen (18–20 Mathenesserlaan): Houses fine old paintings (Hieronymus Bosch, Bruegel, Frans Hals, Rembrandt, Jan Steen, Rubens, etc.), as well as modern paintings (Dali,

Rotterdam, statue of Erasmus ▷

Rotterdam, St.-Laurenskerk

Magritte, Kandinsky, Man Ray, etc.); also glass, ceramics and a pewter collections and an extensive collection of drawings. Opening times: Tue.–Sat. 10 a.m.–5 p.m., Sun. and holidays 11 a.m.–5 p.m.; closed on 1 Jan. and 30 Apr.

Belastingmuseum Prof.Dr. van der Poel (14–16 Parklaan): A museum of taxes and customs duties with fascinating exhibits relating to fraud and smuggling. Opening times: Mon.–Fri. 9 a.m.–5 p.m.

'De Dubbelde Palmboom' historical museum (12 Voorhaven): Objects related to daily life in the area around the mouth of the Maas, both in former times and today. Opening times: Tue.–Sat. 10 a.m.–5 p.m., Sun. and holidays 11 a.m.–5 p.m.; closed on 1 Jan. and 30 Apr.

Marineinfanteriemuseum Rotterdam (119 Maaskade): History of the marines from 1665 onwards. Opening times: Tue.–Sat. 10 a.m.–5 p.m., Sun. and holidays 11 a.m.–5 p.m.; closed on 1 Jan. and 30 Apr.

The Museumschip Buffel (Leuvehaven): This restored ramming-tower belonging to the Dutch Royal Navy was built in 1868. Opening times: Tue.–Sat. 10 a.m.–5 p.m., Sun. and holidays 11 a.m.–5 p.m.; closed on 1 Jan. and 30 Apr.

Stichting Atlas van Stolk (12 Aelbrechtskolk): Photographs, drawings and leaflets on the history of the Netherlands from *c.* 1500. Opening times: Tue.–Sat. 10 a.m.–5 p.m., Sun. and holidays 11 a.m.–5 p.m.; closed on 1 Jan. and 30 Apr.

'Toy-Toy' (41 Groene Wetering): A collection of ancient dolls, miniatures and toys. Opening times: 11 a.m.–4 p.m. daily except Sat.

Zakkendragershuisje (13–15 Voorstraat): A tin foundry has been set up in this 17C corn porter's cottage. Articles of daily use are manufactured here in old foundry moulds. Opening times: Tue.–Sat. 11 a.m.–5 p.m., Sun. and holidays 10 a.m.–5 p.m.; closed on 1 Jan. and 30 Apr.

Windmills: The *'De Ster'* snuff and spice mill (1866) at 316 Plaszoom. *'De Speelman'* corn mill (1712) at 175 Overschiese Kleiweg. *'Prinsenmolen'* (1648) in Bergse Voorplats. *'De Zandweg'* (1723) in Kromme Zandweg. *'De Vier Winden'* (1776) in Terbregse Rechter Rottekade. The opening times of the first two mills can be obtained from the VVV tourist office.

Also worth seeing: In the picturesque *Delshaven district of town*, which was spared from devastation, there is a late-Gothic *church* with alterations dating from 1761. The *former town hall* (17C) has stepped

Ruurlo, Kasteel Ruurlo

gables, and was restored in 1968–71. Delfshaven is the birthplace of the maritime hero Piet Hein (1577–1629), who captured the Spanish silver fleet in 1628. His monument (1870) in Piet Heinsplein is by Joseph Graven. The *Hillegersberg district of town* has a *Dutch Reform church* (*c.* 1500) and the remains of a castle (mentioned 1269) which was devastated by the troops of Jacoba van Beieren in 1426.

Ruurlo
Geldern   p.287☐N 5

Dutch Reform church: The 14C single-aisled Gothic church has arched buttresses which penetrate into the inside of the building and form deep, pointed-arched niches. The choir is narrower than the nave. It is likely that the tower was added in the 15C, while the N. aisle, which is probably a little later, was replaced in 1845 by a larger structure. The nave was increased in height and redesigned in the 16C.

Kasteel Ruurlo: This castle in splendid parkland was first mentioned in 1312 as being owned by the van Roderlo family. In the 15C it passed into the possession of the Van Heeckerens who owned it until recently. The present state of the building derives from the Van Heeckerens. A massive Renaissance tower (1572) rises on the outer corner of the two wings which are at right angles to one another, while the much thinner tower standing diagonally opposite was built in 1627 and increased in height in the 18C. The entrance wing was redesigned in *c.* 1720, and the stepped and ridged gables at the rear are 19C.

Sassenheim
South Holland   p.289☐G 5

The Bollenstreek, the bulb-growing area, extends N. from Sassenheim along a belt of porous, calcium-rich soil. The first bulbs were brought from Turkey in *c.* 1600 and they grew particularly well here, even becoming the object of speculation. Bulb growing still flourishes here and the seemingly endless rows of blossoming tulips attract countless visitors in April and May.

Dutch Reform church: A single-aisled Romanesque tufa building (12C) with richly articulated walls. The belfry atop the mid-13C Romanesque brick tower was added in the early 16C. The church was devastated in 1573 and the nave was restored in 1594. The E. annex dates from 1684.

Teylingen ruins: This castle was once of strategic importance in the defence of the Rhine dyke but began to fall into disrepair in the late 17C. Remnants of the residential tower (*c.* 1250) and parts of the surrounding wall and wall passage still survive. Foundations of a gatehouse have been discovered.

Environs: Hillegom (7 km. N.): The early-15C tower of the *Dutch Reform church* was increased in height in the 16C; the slender onion roof is 17C. The nave and parts of the choir were rebuilt in 1929, and at the same time the rest of the old choir was restored. The *town hall* occupies the old court of te Hillegom, which in the 14C was used by the landgrave as a resting place. The town hall was given its present appearance in the 19C and today it has an attractive garden.

Lisse (3 km. N.): The *Keukenhof* ('kitchen court') is famous for its tulip park which should be visited early Apr.–late May. The *castle* is a mid-19C neo-Gothic conversion of a 17C country house.

Noordwijk aan Zee (4 km. W.): The former *Dutch Reform church* (1647) is used for weddings and funeral services today.

Noordwijk-Binnen (3 km. W.): The large Gothic *Dutch Reform church* (1450) has a sturdy tower which is probably mid 13C. The stone font is 15C and the carved choir stalls date from 1636.

Noordwijkerhout (3 km. NW): A picturesque *Dutch Reform church*. In *c.* 1619 a nave was added to the slender mid-13C tower, whose height was increased in *c.* 1500. The *town hall* was built by A.J.Kropholler in 1928.

Schagen
North Holland   p.286☐H 3

In the early Middle Ages the settlement was known as *Scagha*. The town was granted a charter in 1414 and afterwards became the most significant trading centre in the area.

Slot van Schagen: Two round corner towers are all that survives of the square *castle* founded here in *c.* 1394 by a bastard son of Albrecht van Beieren. The rest was pulled down in 1820. One of the towers was restored in 1931 and today it houses a *war museum* and has documents relating to the Battle of the Somme fought in

World War 1. Opening times: Tourist season only: Tue.–Sat. 10 a.m.–12 noon and 2–4 p.m.

Museum Vreeburg (14 Loet): This museum set up in a 17C farmhouse conveys the impression of daily life in earlier times. Opening times: 1 June–1 Sept.: Tue.–Fri. 1.30–4.30 p.m., Sun. 9 a.m.–4.30 p.m.

Public event: A *folk market* with a procession in traditional costumes, etc., is held 10 a.m.–2 p.m. every Thur. in July and Aug.

Environs: Barsingerhorn (2 km. E.): This village is situated in beautiful surroundings. The *town hall* (1622) has a gable and balustrades.

Kolhorn (5 km. E.): This picturesque village was a fishing port until the middle of last century, and was also the home of many whale fishermen. Today it is an agricultural village. A model of a ship in the single-aisled *Dutch Reform church* (17C) reminds the visitor of the villagers' former activities.

Schagerbrug (2 km. NW): The *Oudheidkamer* (97 Schagerweg) has a collection of old maps and etchings. Opening times: Wed. 2–4 p.m.

Schiedam
South Holland   p.289☐G 6

Schiedam has now almost become part of Rotterdam, although it still retains its original character. Built in the mid-13C around the castle founded on the Schie by Aleidis van Avennes (sister of William II of Holland), it was granted a charter in 1275. The inhabitants originally lived by fishing and shipping but in *c.* 1700 they began distilling gin, and this is still of economic importance today.

St.-Janskerk: Little is known of the architectural history of this hall church which has a nave and two aisles. A miraculous figure of the Virgin Mary was documented in 1380 and the church was consecrated in 1425. The main choir, the N. side choir and the tower with its alter-

Schiedam, Louis-Seize house

Schiedam, Stadhuis

nately round and pointed arched niches, are among the oldest sections, probably going back to the 14C. The nave and N. aisle are *c.* 1400; the S. aisle and S. choir *c.* 1500. The weigh-house on the N. side of the tower was converted from a former chapel.

St.-Johannes de Doperkerk: This Roman Catholic church (1822–4) of St.John the Baptist was built by A.-Tollus in 'Waterstaatsstijl'.

Former Beurs (145 Lange Haven): The large building which housed the former stock-exchange was built by Jan Giudici in 1786–92; restored after a fire in 1840.

Huis te Riviere: The *castle* (*c.* 1250) of Aleidis van Avennes was severely damaged in 1350 and then rebuilt. It again fell into ruin after devastation of 1574. Surviving ruins include the brick tower, staircase and barrel vault.

Stadhuis: The free-standing late-Gothic town hall from the mid-16C has a tall roof and two gables. Repaired after a fire in 1604, it was completely rebuilt in 1782, probably by Rutger van Bol'es, the town architect. The charming bell tower was built at the same time.

Zakkendragershuis (Oude Sluis): The house of the guild of grain porters, it dates from 1725. In the wooden turret there hangs the bell which summoned the porters to work.

Windmills: Of the 19 tall stone mills which formerly stood around the town and were used to grind cereal for the gin distilleries, four have survived along Noordest and Nieuwe Haven, namely *'De Drie Korenbloemen'* (1770), *'De Walvisch'* (1794), *'De Noord'* (1707), and *'De Vrijheid'*. .

Houses: The wealth of the gin distillers is testified to in the many splendid façades, mainly in Louis XVI style, along *Lange Haven, Tuinlaan* and *Lange Nieuwstraat*. The finest example is the *house at 65 Lange Haven,* built by Jan Giudici in 1803–4 for C.Nolet the gin distiller. It has a large hall with Corinthian columns and today functions as the district court of justice.

Stedelijk Museum (112 Hoogstraat): This museum occupies the St.-Jacobs-Spital, a hospital dating from 1787 by Jan Giudici. The hospital church has a façade in the style of an early Corinthian temple. The *Nationaal Gedistilleerd Museum* is in the same building. Opening times: Mon.–Sat. 10 a.m.–5 p.m., Sun. and holidays 12.30–5 p.m., closed on 25 Dec. and 1 Jan.

Also worth seeing: The *Luthersе Kerk* at 219 Lange Nieuwstraat, a classical building from the mid 19C has a small tower. The neo-Gothic cruciform *Basilika Onze Lieve Vrouwe van de Rozenkrans* (1880–1) at 106 Singel is by E.J. Margry. The *parish church* and *Oud-Katholieke Kerk* (28–30 Dam) date from *c.* 1860.

Schiermonnikoog/Skiermuontseach (I)

Friesland   p.287☐M 1

Cars are not allowed in Schiermonnikoog, the easternmost of the West Frisian islands. The visitor should park in Lauwersoog on the mainland and use the ferry.

History: The island derives its name from the 'schier' (grey) monks of the Klaarkamp monastery in Rinsumageest who owned the island. Formerly much nearer to the mainland, monks in Anjum on the mainland were able to hear the island's. Schiermonnikoog was taken over by Friesland in 1580, sold in 1638, and belonged to the German Counts von Bernstoff-Wehningen from 1892–1945.

Schoonhoven, Kanal with St.-Bartholomeuskerk

Schiermonnikoog: This, the only village in the island, was built in 1760 after an older settlement had been swallowed up by the sea. *Dutch Reform church:* Dating from 1860, the church stands in its churchyard. There are many old gabled *houses* in the village, including *No. 42 Langestreek* (1759). The only older houses, which go back as far as 1724, include some in *Middenstreek.* In *Voorstreek,* as in Hindelopen, there are some *Likhusen,* or summer lodgings for fishermen's wives. *Bezoekerscentrum De Centrale* (Torenpad): Mussels, sea birds, etc., as well as dioramas of the sea, beach and mud flats, are on display here. Opening times: 1 Apr.–1 Oct.: 2–5 p.m. daily. *Also worth seeing:* A *statue* in memory of the 'schier' monks, and a *whalebone* commemorating Willem Barentsz the sailor. To the E. of the village is the *Vredenhof sailors' cemetery.* The old *lighthouse*

(1854) is now a water tower. In the W. of the island are the *nature reserves of Kobbeduinen* (6,200 acres) and *Kapeglop* (40 acres) .

Schoonhoven

Schoonhoven lies at the confluence of the Vlist and the Lek. Built around an early-13C castle owned by Jan van de Lede, it was granted a charter in 1281. This pretty little town still has 17C ramparts and today these are planted with trees. A silver industry developed here at an early date.

St.-Bartholomeuskerk: The oldest part of this Dutch Reform hall church is the choir (*c.* 1400); side choirs were given polygonal apses in *c.* 1500. The nave walls date from the time of the church's enlargement in the 16C; another reconstruction was completed in 1658. The tower was begun in the mid-15C and extensively rebuilt 1648–50. In 1927–34, it had to be massively shored up on the E. side (inside the building) owing to a dangerous tilt. 16C choir screens were converted into noblemen's pews in the 17C; reliefs have scenes from the life of Christ as well as scenes from the Old Testament. In the S. choir there is a monument to Olivier van Noort (1558–1627), the first Dutchman to sail around the world.

Stadhuis: A former late Gothic tufa building (1452–4) with a balustrade dating from 1604. The old form was not reconstructed when the building was restored in 1927–9. Instead, windows, entrance and staircase were added in a plain modern design. Ground floor rooms have net vaults supported by columns.

Stadskorenpakhuis (Koestraat): The stepped gable (1566) of the town granary has an ornate relief with the town's coat-of-arms.

Veerpoort: This gate (1601) through the ramparts has a small guard-house above. On the river side there is a richly articulated stone portal.

Waag: The picturesque weigh-house (1617) overlooks the harbour.

Houses: The house at *82 Haven* (early 15C) has a façade dating from 1608. The house at *13 Lopikerstraat* has a stepped gable (1571). *37 Lopikerstraat* has two stepped gables (1642). The houses at *109, 130* and *134 Koestraat* are also worth seeing.

Nederlands Goud, Zilver- en Klokkenmuseum (7 Oude Haven): This museum houses gold and silver objects from the 17–20C, as well as tools used by silversmiths, clockmakers, etc. Opening times: Tue.–Sat. 10 a.m.–5 p.m., Sun. 1–5 p.m.;

closed on Easter Day, Whit Sunday and Christmas Day.

Environs: Nieuwpoort (2 km. SE): This is the smallest fortified town in Holland. The 17C *ramparts,* with six bastions, have survived in good condition and are planted with trees today.

Sittard

Limburg   p.290☐L 8

Sittard, an old trading centre, was in the process of being surrounded by ramparts and ditches when it was granted a charter in 1243. In 1676 soldiers of Louis XIV devastated the defences. Today remains of the ramparts can be seen surrounding the oval which contains the old town centre.

St.-Petruskerk: This large Gothic cruciform basilica with a tall tower is a dominant feature of the town. From 1299 to 1802 it was a collegiate church. Partly ruined *c.* 1380, it was later rebuilt. The church was restored after a fire in the tower in 1857. Petrus Josephus Hubertus Cuypers contributed to the restoration work. At the same time the tower was given a neo-Gothic upper storey. The nave is probably mainly early 14C, while the transept, choir, and choir chapels all probably date from after 1380. The beautiful *stellar vault* above the crossing is probably late 15C. The tower with has flying buttresses at the corners and probably dates from the early 16C. The Gothic choir stalls have beautifully carved misericords and somewhat more coarsely carved ends (possibly 14C).

St.-Michaelskerk: This former Dominican monastery church (1659–61) in the Markt has a baroque brick façade and decorative relief panels in marl. The gable has a large *relief* of St.Dominic receiving the rosary from the hands of the Virgin Mary. Inside, stuccoed rib vaults, fine oak panelling and oak confessional boxes, an early-18C baroque high altar and a pulpit from 1668. Large *paintings* of the Immaculate Conception, the Nativity, the Mysteries of the Rosary and St.Dominic with the Rosary are by an unknown artist and date from the second half of the 17C. A fine mid-17C brass candelabra hanging in the nave shows the abduction of Ganymede.

Streekmuseum 'De Tempel' (27 Gruizenstraat): This regional museum occupies the former town bailiff's house (1652). Opening times: Mon.–Fri. 10 a.m.–12 noon and 2–5 p.m., Sat. and Sun. 2–5 p.m., closed on holidays.

Also worth seeing: The *Dutch Reform church* in Gruizenstraat, a small single-aisled church of 1681 with a slender tower of 1684. Neo-Gothic cruciform *Basilika Onze Lieve Vrouwe van het H.Hart* (1875–6) by J.Kayser.

Environs: Beek (8 km. SW): This village has a small single-aisled *Dutch Reform church* (1835–7) and a *priest's house* with a stepped gable (1723), as well as a *local museum*.

Born (5 km. NW): Born means 'fountain', and the name probably refers to the many springs in the area. *Huis Born* (1647–66), with tower-like corner pavilions, burned down in 1930, and only the annexes survive. Today this picturesque ruin stands in the middle of a rather overgrown park amidst an area of broad canals. The annexes have already been restored, and the ruin is to be rebuilt in 1986. The small 16C *Grasbroek castle* is also in a picturesque state of dilapidation.

Geleen (2 km. S.): Formerly a coal-mining town, today it is important for chemical and processing industries. The beautiful 14/15C tower of the *Roman Catholic church* is mainly built of marl. 17C *Huis Maes* (4–6 Leurstraat) belonged to Willem de Gavarelle, captain of the Bokkenrijders, in the 18C. The *St.-Jans-Kluis* hermitage (1699) has rather a strange appearance. The walls between the hermits' dwelling and the chapel were removed in restoration work in 1936

Sittard, St.-Michaelskerk, gable

Meerssen (Sittard), baptismal chapel

Limbricht (Sittard), former parish church

and today this room is a devotional chapel. The *community hall* (1921) with its tall hip roof and large central projection is by Jos Cuypers.

Limbricht (3 km. N.): *Former parish church* with a nave in part dating from the 11C or 12C, a late Romanesque choir, and a late Gothic S. aisle with a squat tower on its W. side. The building is no longer used as a place of worship. The new *Roman Catholic church* has a 16C late-Gothic winged altar and a carved reliquary with painted wings. *Kasteel Limbricht*, built *c.* 1630 on a hill probably on the site of a previous building, has been restored and is now an elegant building.

Meerssen (16 km. SW): A residence of the Frankish kings formerly stood here. (Charles the Bold concluded the treaty of Meerssen here in 870.) The 14C *Roman Catholic cruciform basilica* which now occupies the site is one of

the finest Maas Gothic churches. Originally part of a Benedictine priory church, this large church is also a place of pilgrimage, two miracles having taken place here—the miracle of the Holy Blood (1225) and a miracle of burning (1565).

Obbicht (7 km. NW): *Huis Obbicht* (1780), built by Jacques-Barthélémy Renoz, an architect from Liège, in a style of obvious French influence, stands on the site of an older castle. The back and front have projecting central sections.

Stein (8 km. SW): Gallery tomb (2500–2000 BC) discovered in 1963. The *Archeologisch Reservaat* has ancient ceramics, Iron Age urns, and Roman archaeological finds. Opening times: 1 May–1 Oct.: 4–6 p.m. daily; other months: only Sat. and Sun. The neo-Gothic *Roman Catholic church* has a marl tower (probably *c.* 1400), simply decorated with corner pilaster strips and friezes of arches on the E. and S. sides of the top storey. The romantic *ruins of the castle of Stein* stand near the village in the grounds of the Paters Missionarissen van het H.Hart.

Urmond (8 km. W.): The simple single-aisled *Roman Catholic church* (1793) has a late Gothic Christ Crucified. The *Dutch Reform church* (1685), also single-aisled, has a heavy marl brick cornice supported by Ionic pilasters. *Schippershuis*, a house with a splendid Renaissance façade (possibly 16C) stands beside the Roman Catholic church. An *upright mill* dates from 1803.

Slochteren
Groningen   p.287☐O 2

Fraeylemaborg: This elegant country house dating mainly from the second half of the 16C is beautifully located in a wood and surrounded by a canal. Its present appearance results from reconstruction in 1782 and the 19C. Around the forecourt there are buildings of 1783 and 1889. Inside a number of rooms have good decorations, including some from the 17C when Henrik Piccardt, syndic (local official) of the Ommelanden, lived here. A curious character, during his youth in Paris, he spent his days working as a street musician and his evenings enjoying the brilliant life of the court. Opening times: 1 Apr.–1 Oct.: 10 a.m.–12 noon and 1–5 p.m.; Oct., Nov., Dec. and Mar.: Tue.–Sun. 10 a.m.–12 noon and 1–4 p.m.; closed in Jan., open only at week-ends in Feb.

Dutch Reform church: An enormous 13C Romanesque-Gothic church. Since the second half of the 16C, only the transept has survived—despite being much altered, it is very impressive. The free-standing tower dates from *c.* 1300.

Also worth seeing: In the 17C the *Hoogehuis* was a court-house and the village inn. The three *mills* by the Groenedijk include the *Fraeylema mill* (1786) and the *watermills* of the former Ruitenpolder (1935) and the former Grote Polder (1783).

Environs: Noordbroek (6 km. E.): The *Romanesque-Gothic church* and free-standing tower go back to the first half of the 14C. The choir vault was painted with a Last Judgement in the late 15C. The very ornate pulpit of 1757 is by W.E. Struve. The organ (rebuilt 1894) was built by A.A. Hinsch in 1768. Many interesting *farmhouses* nearby.

Schildwolde (2 km. N.): The *Dutch Reform church,* built in old brick in 1686, was later altered and roughcast. The free-standing tower (*c.* 1250), known as Juffertoren, has a spire in Groningen style. On 31 December, following an old tradition, the bells are rung non-stop from 8 p.m. until 8 a.m. on New Year's morning (the so-called Thomas bell-ringing). The house at *217 Hoofdweg* has a fine entrance door with a relief above.

Slochteren, Fraeylemaborg, statue

Siddeburen (5 km. N.): Nave and choir of the *Dutch Reform church* date from *c.* 1200. The tower (probably also 13C) was newly roofed and reduced in height in 1832.

Sloten/Sleat
Friesland   p.286□K 3

History: With 650 inhabitants (in 1714 there were 523), Sloten is the smallest of the eleven Frisian towns. It is, however, also one of the finest, with ramparts, bastions and a beautiful canal lined with trees. Lying at the intersection of waterways and land routes, it was fortified in the 13C and granted a charter in 1426. The fortifications withstood enemy attacks in 1420 and 1486, but in 1523 the Burgundians were more successful and razed the defences to the ground.

Menno van Coehoorn, the famous fortification architect, built a new and stronger system of defences in 1672.

Dutch Reform church: This single-aisled church (1647) with a splendid gable and ridge turret has fine interior decorations including a richly carved pulpit.

Stadhuis: The town hall was built in 1759 as an elegant town house; town coat-of-arms above the ornate entrance. Stucco work inside the building. In the council chamber there are documents relating to the town's past.

Museum Laterna Magica (48 Heerenwal): Magic lanterns, projectors and stereoscopes. Opening times: Tue.–Fri. 10 a.m.–12 noon and 2–5 p.m., Sat. and Sun. 2–5 p.m.

Waterpoort: Only the *water gates* (*de Woudsender* of 1768 and the *Lemster Waterpoort* of 1821) survive of the fortifications.

Also worth seeing: By the Lemster-

poort there is an octagonal *mill* with a revolving roof (1795). The town has a number of old houses, the best being the *priest's house* with two stepped gables (1610 and 1671).

Environs: Balk: (5 km. W.): This picturesque town is surrounded by a moat, along which there are linden trees and old houses. The *Dutch Reform church* (1728) was by Roelof Saegman, a carpenter. The *town hall* (1615) has a stepped gable and colourful sculptures.

Wijckel (Wikel, 2.5 km. W.): An old village in Gaasterland. The *Dutch Reform church*, standing high up in the middle of a graveyard, has a simple Gothic nave (1671), and a ponderous 16C tower with saddleback roof. The church contains the lavish marble tomb of Menno van Coehoorn (1641–1704) who had a country house nearby. The monument, designed by Daniel Marot, has a recumbent figure of the warrior who played a glorious part in the siege of Kaiserswerth and Bonn in 1689 and in the War of Spanish Succession. The church also has other tomb monuments, an oak

Sloten, Voorstreek canal

pulpit and two family pews. Enter through left side door.

Sluis

Zeeland   p.288☐D 8

Sluis, on a bay in the SW of Zeeuws-Vlaanderen, was founded in *c.* 1280 to serve as the outer port of Brügge. Originally called *Lamminsvliet*, it was granted a charter in 1290.

Raadhuis: The most striking feature of the late-14C town hall (rebuilt after severe damage in 1944) is the large tower, which has four projecting corner turrets on the model of the Flemish belfry. The wrought-iron railing (by J.P. van Baurscheidt the younger) in the council chamber came from the court-room of the Middelburg town hall. Opening times: Mon.–Fri. 10 a.m.–12 noon and 2–5 p.m. May–Sept.: also open on Sat. and Sun. (closed on Mon.).

Fortifications: The foundations of the *Westpoort* still survive from the medieval town walls. Of the 17C outworks, improved by Mennor van Coehoorn in 1702, the *main rampart* with its six bastions, and the *Zuidpoort*, rebuilt in 1781, can be seen. Trees were planted on the main rampart in 1948.

Environs: St.-Anna ter Muiden (1 km. E.): This village has a pretty square with linden trees and a Louis XVI pump. The *Dutch Reform church* (1653) stands to the E. of the massive 14C tower, which probably formerly rose over the crossing of the old church destroyed by the Spanish. The *town hall* in the village square is a simple 17C building with a ridge turret and stone coat-of-arms.

Sneek/Snits

Friesland   p.286☐K 3

Sneek was probably built beside the terp on which the Martinikerk now stands. Ramparts were erected around the settlement in 1300. The town was granted a charter in 1446

Balk (Sloten), Raadhuis

Sluis, Raadhuis

and in the second quarter of the 16C it was expanded into a fortified town. With the exception of the water gate the fortifications were razed in the 18C.

Grote Kerk or Martinikerk: A new W. side (a choir) was added to this mainly late Gothic basilica after the two-towered Romanesque façade had collapsed in 1681. The choir (originally built 1499–1501) was increased in height at the same time. The bell tower dates from 1771 and has modern bells. The 15C wooden *bell-house* N. of the church was given its present appearance in the 18C and restored in 1968.

Stadhuis: The town hall was built in 1550 on the foundations of two older buildings. In the 18C it was increased in height and the ornate façade was added. The impressive *town hall* has gold leather wall hangings and in the small council chamber there are silver items and memorabilia of Henriette Catharina, daughter of Friedrich Heinrich the stadholder, who became an honorary citizen of the town in 1696.

Waterpoort: A picturesque building (1613) consisting of two octagonal fortified towers on both sides of a covered bridge. Above the bridge there is a complex of roofs and pretty gables.

Paleis van Justitie: The palace of justice (1838) by the town architect G.Rollema has a severely classical façade with Corinthian pilasters.

Fries Scheepvaart Museum (14 Kleinzand): Ceramics, model ships, and memorabilia of the legendary Grote Pier, an early-16C freedom fighter. The *Sneeker local museum* and the *Schutterskamer* are in the same building. Opening times: Mon.–Fri. 9 a.m.–12 noon and 2–4 p.m.

Environs: IJsbrechtun (2 km. W.):

This village is situated in a beautiful part of Friesland. The *Dutch Reform church* (1865) has a late-17C marble memorial stone. *Epemastate* originally a 17C country house, is beautifully sited amidst trees. 20C alterations. The gatehouse (1652) has stepped gables and a staircase tower. The building is surrounded by ditches. The house is open 10 a.m.–4 p.m. on Tue., Wed. and Thur. 15 June–1 September.

Soest
Utrecht   p.289□l 5

Dutch Reform church: This single-aisled church with a narrower choir dates from *c.* 1400, while the large and beautifully proportioned tower is early 16C. On the N. side between nave and tower there is a staircase tower. The corresponding section on the S. side has a baptismal chapel in the lower storey. During restoration in 1957, the nave regained its wooden barrel vault, which had been built according to old descriptions.

Petrus en Pauluskerk: The Roman Catholic church has now been replaced by a modern building, but the towered façade (1852–3;Waterstaats-stijl style) by Th.Molkenboer has survived.

Environs: Baarn (10 km. NW): This town, situated in a region of woods and parks, was granted a charter in *c.* 1350. The 14C brick tower of the *Dutch Reform church* was increased in height in the early 16C. Shortly thereafter, a wide S. aisle was added to the nave and to the some-what narrower 15C choir. *Kasteel Groeneveld*, a stately country house built in 1737 has side wings of a later date. *Kasteel De Hooge Vuursche*, in a fine park outside the town, is by E.-

Sneek, Waterpoort ▷

Baarn (Soest), Huis Groeneveld

Cuypers (1912). There are pretty gardens in *Cantonpark* in Faas Elias-laan and in *Pekingtuin* in the town centre.

Eemnes (15 km. N.): A parish consisting of the two villages Eemnes-Binnen and Eemnes-Buiten. There are several fine *farmhouses* on the dyke between them. The late Gothic *Dutch Reform church* in *Eemnes-Binnen* is single-aisled with a narrower choir to which the tower was added in *c.* 1500. The 15C *Dutch Reform church* in *Eemnes-Buiten* has a stately tower probably finished in 1521. The beautifully decorated interior has a charming pulpit (1604) and fine choir screen (1618).

Soestdijk (2 km. NW): In 1672, king and stadholder William III of Orange bought a country house and in 1674 he commissioned Maurits Post, son of Pieter Post, to enlarge it into the *Paleis Soestdijk*. The palace fell into

disrepair in the early 19C and was rebuilt in Palladian style from 1816 onwards under the supervision of Jan de Greef. In 1815, the State dedicated it to the later King William II for his courageous effort in the battle of Waterloo, at which time the splendid landscape garden was also laid out by Zocher and his son. At the end of Koningslaan, opposite the palace, an *obelisk* commemorates the battle of Waterloo in 1815, at which Napoleon I, the French Emperor, was finally defeated.

Staveren/Stavoren/Starum
Friesland   p.286☐K 3

Staveren on the IJsselmeer is the oldest town in Friesland, being documented in 313 BC. In the 10C it was an export harbour for Frisian salt.

Eemnes-Binnen (Soest), church

Eemnes-Binnen (Soest), church

Staveren, granted a charter in 1060, became a member of the Hanseatic League in the 14C. Tradition has it that rich merchants ordered the doorsteps of their houses to be covered with gold during this period of prosperity. Another legend, known as the 'Vrouwtje van Staveren' ('the little woman of Staveren'), gives a quaint explanation for the silting up of the harbour. A wealthy merchant's wife commissioned a ship captain to bring back the richest cargo he could find. Imaginatively he returned with a load of grain but this did not fit in with the rich woman's expectations and, much annoyed, she ordered it to be thrown into the sea rather than be distributed to the poor. However, the grain grew on the sea bed and caused a sand bank and this in turn led the harbour to silt up. The statue standing by the lock gate commemorates the legend. After the harbour silted up, Staveren became a fishing village. The completion of the Afsluitdijk dam accelerated the village's economic decline. Today it is a water sports centre.

Stadhuis: The town hall has a fine *council chamber* with 18C paintings. In the mayor's room there is a portrait of Prince William V.

Environs: Warns/Nijefurd (3.5 km. E.): In 1682 the *Dutch Reform church* was added to a 12C tufa tower. A *monument* near the Rode Klif (red cliff) commemorates the battle of Warns (1345).

Stedum

Groningen   p.287☐N 2

Dutch Reform church: The Roma-

Soestdijk (Soest), Paleis Soestdijk

nesque-Gothic church from the third quarter of the 13C has a massive, somewhat older tower and a sacristy from the first half of the 16C. The end of the choir is 15C. The tower becomes narrower towards the top and has a saddleback roof; on the W. wall there is the original round window, but other decorations are later and of a different style. The domed vault of the nave, and the Gothic stellar vault at the end of the choir, are both late 15C and have paintings of Adam and Eve along with tendrils, and various symbols and sayings.

The marble tomb (1672) of Adriaan Clant is by Rombout Verhulst. Baroque pulpit (1671) with carvings; the organ dates from 1680, but was later altered.

Some very interesting tombstones in the choir and transept, including a Gothic memorial panel in sandstone (1471) commemorating Andelof Nittersum.

Steenbergen
North Brabant　　　　　　　p.288☐F 7

Dutch Reform church: Dating from 1832, this church was probably built by P.Huysers and has a nave and two aisles, white roughcasting and a classical gabled façade. The tower is very like that of the St.-Anthoniskerk in Breda.

St.-Gummaruskerk: This large Roman Catholic church (1900–02) by P.J.H. Cuypers, J.Cuypers and Jan Stuyl is a neo-Gothic cruciform basilica with a round tower over the crossing.

Environs: Nieuw-Vossemeer (8

Steenwijk, weigh-house

km. W.): The original façade of the *Dutch Reform church*, a simple single-aisled structure (1649), was rebuilt during restoration work in 1969. The ridge turret was also rebuilt based on old drawings. The *'Assumburg' corn mill* (1780), brought here by Assendelft in 1897, today houses the *Molenmuseum Nederland* and has many interesting items related to mills, including models and photographs. Opening times: 15 May–1 Sept.: Sat., Sun. and holidays: 2–5 p.m.

Steenwijk
Overijssel   p.287☐M 3

Steenwijk, fortified at an early date, was granted a charter in 1255. Much damaged by the Gelderlanders and Zwolleners in 1523, the town successfully defended itself aganst the Spanish in 1580 and 1581.

Grote Kerk or **St.-Clemenskerk:** This Dutch Reform church is a late Gothic hall church with a nave and two aisles. Work on it continued from *c.* 1400 until the 16C. The picturesque tower was begun in 1467; the top was altered during restoration work in 1913–15. The S. side choir has fine net and stellar vaults, while the nave is barrel-vaulted in wood. The large organ dates from the first half of the 19C, fine 17C chandeliers and sconces, and well-preserved tombstones.

Kleine Kerk or **Lieve-Vrouwekerk:** This late-Gothic Dutch Reform church (1477) has a large roof over the nave and the lower aisles.

Stadhuis: The only Art Nouveau town hall in the Netherlands, it was built by J.C. van Gendt in 1899 and has a fine entrance of unusual design.

Susteren, St.-Amalbergakerk

Oudheidkamer (64 Markt): Archaeological finds, utensils and documents on the town's history.

Also worth seeing: The SW section of the tall rampart with its bastions and ditches survives in good condition. The *weigh-house* in Waagstraat has an attractive stepped gable (1642). Fine 17C *façades* in the Markt and *Oosterstraat*.

Environs: Oldemarkt (11 km. W.): In the 16&17C, the old Markt was a trading centre for butter, pigs and other commodities. The *Dutch Reform church* (1648) with its fine organ, and some *façades* bear witness to the town's former prosperity.
Paasloo (9 km. W.): This town flourished after the right to hold markets here was granted in 1437. The *Dutch Reform church* (probably first half of 16C) looks very like a farmhouse,

mainly because of the wooden supports inside. The visitor must stoop to enter the church through the so-called Normans' door.
Steenwijkerwold (3 km. W.): The late-Gothic *Dutch Reform church* sits on a small hill. The triumphal arch was rebuilt in the old pointed arch form; the richly carved pulpit dates from *c.* 1700.

Susteren
Limburg   p.291 ☐ L 8

St.-Amalbergakerk: The present parish church was formerly the abbey church of a monastery probably founded by Benedictines in *c.* 700, but mentioned as a convent in the late 9C and later a charitable institution for women. Little is known of the architectural history of this cruciform

of the Virgin Mary and St.John in a Crucifixion are probably early 14C, while the Christ is rather more coarsely worked and later. The church *treasury* has a Evangeliary with 9C miniatures, and some sumptuous silver. (*c.* 1100).

Environs: Ohé en Laak (5 km. N.): *Huis Hasselholt* (also known as Het Goedje) is a richly decorated late Gothic main building (1548) with a long Renaissance E. wing (1651). The Meierhof (1629) is at right angles to this, and has a half-timbered wall on the courtyard side. All the buildings, which are of considerable architectural value, were extensively restorated in 1970–2. The *Roman Catholic church* (1867) by A.C. Bolsius is a cruciform basilica in Romanesque/Gothic style with an octagonal tower over the crossing.

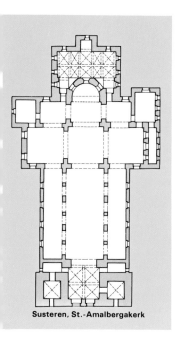

Susteren, St.-Amalbergakerk

Romanesque basilica, but it is thought that it was probably built mainly in the second half of the 11C, with work proceeding from E. to W. The unusual crypt around the choir apse may be copied from that of the minster in Essen, which was consecrated in 1051. The W. tower, possibly 12C originally, consists of a squat central tower (now hardly recognizable, owing to the 19C saddleback roof) with two side towers. The nave walls are supported alternately on rectangular pillars and columns with cubiform capitals. The rectangular choir has round arches leading to chapels on both sides. These chapels give access to the *crypt* which, although lower than the church, is not actually underground. Groin vaults are supported on square pillars with shaped bases and capitals. Tombstones (15–18C), including those of abbesses, line the inner walls of the church. Figures

Ten Boer

Groningen   p.287☐N 2

Dutch Reform church: The church is all that remains of a deserted Benedictine monastery; traces of the adjoining buildings can be seen on the side walls. Fine choir walls, both inside and out, are a splendid example of Groningen Romanesque-Gothic at its best (mid–late 13C).

Environs: Ten Post (5 km. N.): The *'Olde Widde' corn mill* (earlier than 1828) on the picturesque Damsterdiep.

Thesinge (6 km. SW): Much of the choir survives from the *church of the former Benedictine abbey of Germania*, but other parts of the church were pulled down; the choir itself was reduced in height and, in 1786, given a hip roof with a ridge turret. The attractive *'Germania corn mill'* (1852) is still in operation.

Woltersum (2 km. E.): The W. end of the simple *Dutch Reform church* dates from 1765, while the E. part from 1837–8. The pulpit has 16C paintings. *'De Fram'*, a saw- and corn-mill dating from 1867 has barns attached on both sides.

Ter Apel

Groningen   p.286□O 3

Former Bethlehemite monastery: A ruined monastery founded by the Premonstratensians in the 13C and taken over by the Bethlehemites

Ter Apel, Bethlehemite church, font

in the 15C. It stands in the middle of a wooded area in the southernmost corner of Groningen. The Bethlehemites left the monastery during the Eighty Years' War and in 1604, it was taken over by Protestants. Some of the buildings were pulled down over the following centuries, but the monastery regained much of its former splendour in a thorough restoration. A richly decorated choir screen divides the church (consecrated 1501) into a part for the congregation and a priests' choir. The latter has tripartite choir stalls and a built-in tabernacle, while in the congregation's section there is a pulpit (1711) with the town's coat-of-arms. There are pointed-arched windows and rib vaults in the surviving sections of the cloister. Other parts to have survived include the remains of traceried ceiling panelling, a carved rococo wall (1851), a Renaissance bay window (1554), and a small gate (1561). Today the whole complex is a museum open to the public. Opening times: Tue.–Sat. 9 a.m.–12 noon and 1.30–5.30 p.m., Sun. 1.30–5.30 p.m.

Environs: Sellingen (8 km. N.): The nave of the *Dutch Reform church* is probably 13C (the large windows were later additions). In the choir, which is slightly later, vaults decorated with plant ornaments and Evangelists' symbols date from *c.* 1500. St.Christopher and St.Margaret can be seen on the W. side of the triumphal arch. Sandstone font; 17C pulpit.

Ter Haar (2 km. N.): An unusual wooden *windmill,* the only one of its kind still to be seen in the N. Netherlands, was moved here from Bourtange in 1831.

Terschelling/Skylge, Skylgeralân (I)

Friesland   p.286□I-K2

Holland and Friesland quarrelled

over this, the largest of the West Frisian Islands, from the Middle Ages onwards. In the 15C it came under the control of Popmas for a short time, and then fell to the Arembergs in 1609 and to the Republic of the United Netherlands in 1615. It has been part of Friesland since 1942. Terschelling was at its most prosperous from the 16C to the 18C as a result of shipping and whaling. There are nature reserves in the varied landscape with dunes, moors, woods and polders.

West-Terschelling: The island's charming main town and the ferry port. The town has various *gabled houses*, mainly from the second half of the 17C. Here and there in front of the entrances there are 'Stoeppalen' (pavements on stone piles). The *Brandaris lighthouse* (1594) is the largest in the Netherlands; until 1920 it was operated with a real flare. In clear weather the light is visible at a distance of 40 km. *Cultuurhistorisch Museum ''t Behouden Huys'* (32 Commandeurstraat): The museum is housed in various buildings dating from 1668. Opening times: Apr.–Dec.: Mon.–Fri. 9 a.m.–5 p.m., 15 June–15 Aug.: also Sat. 9 a.m.–5 p.m.

Formerum (7 km. NW of West-Terschelling): Willem Barentsz, the well-known sailor who gave his name to the Barents Sea (part of the Arctic Ocean near Spitzbergen) was born in this village . Splendid *farms* on the W. and S. sides of the village, some with 18C façades. Fine *corn mill* (1876).

Hoorn (9 km. NW of West-Terschelling): The W. section of the *Dutch Reform church* is probably 12C; the choir was added in the second half of the 13C. 19C spire on the sturdy tower.

Midsland (5 km. NW of West-Terschelling): 18C *gabled houses* around the churchyard and on houses along the main road which runs parallel.

17C *tombstones* in the old Strieper graveyard in the SW.

Texel (I)
North Holland   p.286□H 2

Texel, the largest of the Dutch islands on the mud-flats, was inhabited in the Neolithic period and also in Roman times. The island can be reached by boat from Den Helder.

Den Burg: The island's charming main town. The large late-Gothic *Dutch Reform church*, dates back to the mid 15C (the lower, ornate part of the tower); the upper part of the tower was probably built later than 1539, while the spire was built in 1604.

Den Hoorn (5 km. SW of Den Burg): The picturesque *Dutch Reform church* (*c.* 1500) has a short nave and a slender white tower.

Oosterend (7 km. NE of Den Burg): The *church* stands on high ground.

Tholen, Onze-Lieve-Vrouwekerk, entrance

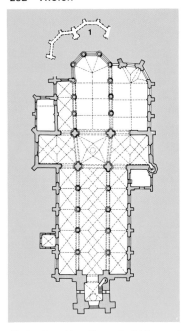

Tholen, Onze-Lieve-Vrouwekerk 1 Excavated foundations of the ambulatory (c. 1460)

Nave originally early Romanesque; 15C tower (altered in the 17C & 19C).

Tholen
Zeeland   p.288□F 7

The little town of Tholen in the S. of the peninsula of the same name probably owes its origin and its name to tolls once levied on ships using the port.

Onze-Lieve-Vrouwekerk: A cruciform basilica in mature Brabant Gothic style with nave and two aisles, transept, and choir with an ambulatory on the N. side (all built 1460–1520). The 14C tower was increased in height in the 15C (helm roof and balustrade date from the restoration of 1947–60). The broad chapel on the S. side of the choir is probably early 15C. Stone columns with excellent leaf capitals catch the eye in the nave; the choir and S. chapel have wooden barrel vaults. Simple 17C decorations.

Stadhuis: The town hall, with a tall façade and hexagonal turret, was probably rebuilt shortly after a fire in 1452. A rococo staircase (1758) leads to the large hall, whose vaulted anteroom and two columns support the tower.

Ramparts: Part of the regular surrounding ramparts (*c.* 1620) which have seven bastions was converted into a park in 1846/7. The remaining section of the ramparts with four bulwarks survives in good condition.

Environs: Oud-Vossemeer (4 km. N.): The *Dutch Reform church* has a slender tower with a vaulted lower storey (first half of 15C). The single-aisled interior ends in a triangular apse which was added later that century. The transept is late 15C. In 1769, a lectern by Johannes Specht from Rotterdam was added to the 17C pulpit. The *court of justice* (1767–71) has old panelling and decorations.
Poortvliet (6 km. E.): The choir of the large Gothic *Dutch Reform church* was pulled down and now the church consists of a basilican nave from *c.* 1450, a massive mid-14C tower and a late-15C chapel between nave and N. transept. The organ (1805) by Abrahams Meere came from Utrecht.

Thorn
Limburg   p.291–L 8

Roman Catholic church: Once the collegiate church of a Benedictine abbey for both men and women, it was founded shortly before 995 by Ansfried, then bishop of Utrecht, and his wife Hereswit (or Hilsondis). Their daughter Hildewardis was the first abbess. In the 12C the monastery was presided over by an abbess holding the rank of princess, who was supported by a chapter of noblewomen, as well as canons for liturgical duties. Dissolved 1797. The Gothic cruciform basilica (mostly 14C) has a crypt beneath the choir and crossing, and an elevated 'princess's choir' in the S. transept. The lower part of the W. section (12C), and the crypt beneath it, both survive from the previous Romanesque building. Chapels were built along the nave in the 15C, and the stellar and net vaulting of nave, crossing and N. transept is probably 16C or 17C. In the 18C, F.Dukers, an architect from Liège, redesigned the interior in classical style. The exterior was restored by Petrus Josephus Hubertus Cuypers in 1860–85, and at the same time the W. end was given a neo-Gothic storey. Fortunately, the elegance of this lavish collegiate church was not altered when it became a parish church. In 1786, the charming *high altar* (1769) by F.X.Bader was brought here from the Karthuizerkerk in Roermond. Stuccoes on the side walls of the E. choir are also by Bader. The best of the side altars is the Renaissance altar with a painted copy of the Deposition by Rubens. In the N. transept there is a fine baroque monument to Clara Elizabeth van Manderscheid-Blankenheim (d. 1688). The collegiate church *museum* is open daily from 9 a.m.–6 p.m. from 1 March–1 November.

Kapel van Onze Lieve Vrouw onder de Linden: The Loreto chapel outside the town was founded by Clara Elizabeth van Manderscheid-Blankenheim in 1673. The building was enlarged on the W. side in 1811 and has stuccoes inside.

Grathem (5 km. N.): The *Roman Catholic church* has a late Romanesque tower built of marl bricks with 13C pilaster strips and friezes of round arches, 15C Gothic nave, and a late-Gothic choir also built in marl.

The church was enlarged during restoration work in 1954.

Heel (6 km. NE): The fine Romanesque tower and four columns with foliate capitals are the only remnants of the *old church* to have survived in the *new church*. The latter also has a Romanesque font with tendril-like reliefs and a richly carved pulpit (1705). The whitewashed 17C *castle* has two low 18C wings.

Linne (7 km. E.): The *Roman Catholic church* (1897) has a ornate rococo pulpit (1759) and a Romanesque font with animal figures.

Tiel

Tiel on the Waal and the Amsterdam-Rhine canal is one of the oldest trading towns in Holland and was at its most prosperous in *c.* 1000.

Grote Kerk or **St.-Maartenskerk:** Dutch Reform church with a tower begun in 1440. In the second half of the 15C an additional S. aisle was

Thorn, Roman Catholic church

added to the existing two aisles of the nave. The choir, begun by Cornelis Frederiks from Gouda in 1588, was not finished and was actually pulled down in the 18C, as was the transept. A baptismal chapel, and above it, the library, were built in the W. bay of the outer S. aisle in 1554.

Lutherse Kerk: What is now the Dutch Reform church was the chapel of the former convent of St.Cecilia. The tall choir is early 16C; the nave is probably a little older. Capitals of the short semi-columns supporting the net vault in the choir are decorated with angels playing musical instruments.

Amtbmanshuis: This double house, fomerly occupied by the bailiff, is now the office responsible for the polders of Tielerward. Originally built in 1525–6, it was enlarged in 1562–3.

Fortifications: A much-rebuilt section on the *Waalkade* still survives from the medieval defences. Of the 17C fortifications, the *Singel canals*

Tiel, Grote Kerk

and the *Oliemolenwal* (oil mill rampart) on the N. side survive. The gate at the end was devastated in World War 2 but rebuilt in 1983.

Residential houses: The house at *47–49 Weerstraat* is built in Lower Rhine late-Gothic style and has a stepped gable; the side portal bears the date 1623. The *house at 17 St.-Walburgstraat* is probably 15C and has a late-18C façade in Louis XVI style. **The houses at** *20 Gasthuisstraat* and *1-9 St.-Walburgstraat* are good examples of 19C architecture.

Also worth seeing: The *stone pump* (1768) in the Groenmarkt has Louis XV decorations. *Korenbeurs*, the corn exchange, has neo-classical colonnaded galleries (1849) on both sides of Beursplein. In the *Vismarkt*, the classical colonnaded gallery was given its present form in 1789.

Environs: Geldermalsen (12 km. W.): The *Dutch Reform church*, a stately 15C Gothic village church, has a tower possibly dating back to the 13C, which was increased in height when a N. aisle was added to the church. *Corn mill* (1840) and two *polder mills*.
Zoelen (3 km. N.): The choir of the *Dutch Reform church* (*c.* 1500) is flat-ended, with a wooden ceiling and panelling throughout. The elevated *Kasteel Zoelen* was built in its present form in *c.* 1642, using medieval masonry. The gatehouse is partly 16C and partly later; 19C Gothic annexes.

Tilburg
North Brabant   p.290□I 7

Heike Kerk: Built in 1828 by N.van der Waals in Waterstaatsstijl. The late-15C tower was restored in 1895. The marble high altar by G.Kerriex (1699–1700) came from the abbey of St.Michael in Antwerp.

Stadhuis (Stadhuisplein):   This

white palace (1847–9) was built by King William II in English neo-Gothic style. Today it is part of the modern town hall (1967–71). Large pointed windows were added during rebuilding in 1934.

Nederlands Textielmuseum (23 Gasthuisring): Documents the history of textile manufacture; interesting collection of old textiles.
Opening times: Mon.–Fri. 10 a.m.–5 p.m., Sat. and Sun. 2–5 p.m., Mon. also 7–10 p.m.

Schrift- en Schrijfmachine Museum (54 Gasthuisring): A collection of typewriters, pens, inkwells and many other writing utensils. Open by arrangement.

Natural history museum (26 Kloosterstraat): Geological specimens, flora and flora (mainly related to North Brabant). Opening times: 2–6 p.m.

Also worth seeing: Neo-Gothic *St.-Jozefskerk* (1872–89) by H.J. van Tulder. The *Tongerlose Hof,* formerly the Maierhof of the abbey of Tongerlo, consists of a reed-thatched 17C building with a tithe barn, cart-shed, bakery and a reconstructed sheep pen. The building was restored in 1969 and is now open to students.

Environs: Berkel-Enschot (4 km. NE): The *Roman Catholic church* was in ruins by 1788 and until restorations in 1938 and 1960 only the early-15C tower was standing. On each side of the tower one bay of the original survives.
Hilvarenbeek (13 km. S.): The Roman Catholic church has its origins in a 12C building, followed by a 14–16C church in late Gothic style, which was itself rebuilt in 1615 and restored in 1929. The brick tower is a fine piece of Kempen Gothic; fine old interior decorations. The small single-aisled *Dutch Reform church* (1809) is a classical building by L.van

Heijst. *Huis Groenendaal*, an early-19C country house, is in Empire style.
Moergestel (5 km. E.): The old 16C *Roman Catholic church* was replaced by a new church in 1931; only the tower (*c.* 1500) survived. The *upright mill* was moved to its present site in 1860.
Oisterwijk (6 km. E.): Tilburg was granted a charter in 1213, but retained its village character. 'De Lind', the village square, is most picturesque. The oldest *house* (1633), in *Kerkstraat*, has a stepped gable. The small single-aisled *Dutch Reform church* was built in 1811 in classical style. The neo-Gothic *Roman Catholic church of St.-Petrus' Banden* (1897) by Petrus Josephus Hubertus Cuypers is a combination of a centrally planned and longitudinally oriented building.
Udenhout (6 km. NE): The well-proportioned *St.-Lambertuskerk* (1840–1) takes the form of a hall church in Waterstaatsstijl style. Four grisaille paintings of the Evangelists (1696) are by Jan de Bray from Haarlem. The *town hall* (1849) is a small neo-Gothic building.

Oisterwijk (Tilburg), oldest house

Uithuizen

Groningen   p.287□N 2

Menkemaborg: This imposing building is one of the finest castles to have survived more or less intact in the province of Groningen. It is now a *museum*. The castle consists of three rectangular buildings, joined together and with saddleback roofs, which were built in several phases during the 15–17C. The entrance is flanked by corner turrrets, and the bridge is guarded by stone lions bearing coats-of-arms. The 18C sandstone vases were brought here from the former castle of Dijksterhuis in Pieterburen. Most of the interior decorations date from renovation in *c.* 1700. Exhibits from the Groningen Museum van Oudheden have been set up in both storeys and in the park. A complete old Groningen style kitchen can be seen in the cellars. The gardens are entirely 18C in style, with famous rose walks. Opening times: Apr.–Oct.: 10 a.m.–12 noon and 1–5 p.m.; Oct.–Apr.: 10 a.m.–12 noon and 1–4 p.m.; closed in Jan.

Dutch Reform church: This building (13–15C) is impressive for its vaults and interior decoration (*c.* 1700). The ornate pulpit (1711) is by Albert Meyer, Groningen's town architect. The choir ends in a gallery (1702) with a noblemen's pew; the organ of 1701 is by Arp Schnitger.

Environs: Oldenzijl (5 km. E.): The mainly Romanesque *brick church* from the mid-13C has a fine semicircular apse. Inside, paintings date from 1570 and even earlier.
Oosternieland (8 km. E.): The 13C *Dutch Reform church,* has a simple exterior and fine vaults within.
Uithuizermeeden (4 km. E.): The *Dutch Reform church* has a fine interior. The nave dates from *c.* 1250 and the choir is Gothic while the transepts were added *c.* 1705 and the tower (1717–26) was rebuilt in 1896–7. The richly decorated pulpit (1708) was by Albert Meyer, Groningen town architect, and the organ (1785) is by A.A.-Hinsch. The tomb of Rudolf Huinga op Ungersma (d. 1574) has a wooden figure of the deceased.

Urk

Flevoland   p.286□K 4

Urk is the oldest town in the new, twelfth province of the Netherlands, which has existed since 1 January 1986. Formerly an island in the Zuiderzee, today Urk is a fishing village standing on a loam hill above the floodwater and surrounded on three sides by the broad lands of the new province. Documented since 966.

Dutch Reform church: The present appearance of this simple building dates from rebuilding of 1786. Inside there are models of ships, and a bell dating back to 1461. The dome on top of the tower was added during restoration in 1955.

Museum Oud Urk (near the lighthouse): This museum, housed in a former farmhouse has exhibits of dolls in Urk local costumes and temporary exhibitions on the theme of

Utrecht, cathedral cloister ▷

local history. Opening times: 1 June–
1 Oct.: Mon.–Fri. 9 a.m.–1 p.m. and
2–6 p.m.; 1 Nov.–1 May: 2–6 p.m.

Visserijmuseum 'Hulp en Steun'
(44 Westhavenkade): Mainly houses
folk art and models of fishing vessels,
as well as various other exhibits.
Opening times: Mon.–Fri. 9 a.m.–1
p.m. and 2–6 p.m.; 1 Nov.–May: only
2–6 p.m.

Environs: Emmeloord (11 km.
NE): This town was founded in 1942.
The *polder tower* (1957), some 213 ft.
tall, has one of the largest carillons of
bells in the Netherlands, with 48
bells.

Utrecht

Utrecht   p.289□l 5

Utrecht, the main town of the province of the same name and the fourth
largest city in the Netherlands, is
situated on the Kromme Oude Rijn
and on the river Vecht which subsequently flows into the IJsselmeer. A
centre of commerce and communications, Utrecht is also an intellectual
centre, with a university, and the seat
of both Catholic and an Old Catholic
archbishoprics.

History: The Roman fortification,
Trajectum ad Rhenum stood here in 48
BC. After the expulsion of the
Romans, it was the site of a Frankish
castle built in the 7C. Utrecht was
later chosen by St.Willibrord as his
diocesan seat, which was occupied by
St.Boniface in the 8C. The church
was a dominant feature of the town
for centuries. The town was granted a
charter in 1122. The town's political
significance declined after the princi-
pality of Utrecht was taken over by
Emperor Charles V in 1528, but it
subsequently regained influence
during the Dutch struggle for liberation from Spanish rule. An added
impetus came in 1636 with the foundation of the university, and again in
1713 with the Peace of Utrecht which
brought about the end of the War of
Spanish Succession. Utrecht prospered in the 19C, thanks to its favourable location in the heart of the
Netherlands.

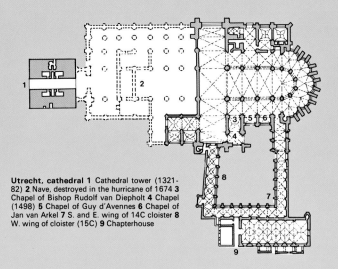

Utrecht, cathedral 1 Cathedral tower (1321-
82) **2** Nave, destroyed in the hurricane of 1674 **3**
Chapel of Bishop Rudolf van Diepholt **4** Chapel
(1498) **5** Chapel of Guy d'Avennes **6** Chapel of
Jan van Arkel **7** S. and E. wing of 14C cloister **8**
W. wing of cloister (15C) **9** Chapterhouse

Religious buildings
Cathedral: In 1254, Bishop Hendrik van Vianden laid the first stone of the choir of a new church on the site of the Romanesque cathedral of St.Martin, which had been damaged by fire in 1253. The ring of chapels around the choir was probably finished in the late 13C; other parts of the choir were built shortly after. The main body of the Romanesque church survived until a hurricane of 1674 destroyed it (ground plan visible in the cathedral square) and now the magnificent *cathedral tower* (1321–82) stands isolated. Begun by Master Jan from Hennegau, this fine building was inspired by French cathedral Gothic; the square lower storey has deep niches but the rest is rather plain. The tower is topped by an airy octagon with a short slate spire. Inside, there are two chapels, that of St.Michael, mentioned in 1328, above which is the flat-roofed chapel of St.Egmond. The tower has seven old bells (1505/6) by Geert van Wou, and six new bells; also a carillon (1663/4), mainly by the brothers Hémony.

The nave has not survived, but the interior remains impressive. Interesting architectural details include the bases of pillars, foliate capitals in the ambulatory and vault keystones (second half of 13C). Wall paintings dating from *c.* 1300 decorate the chapels of Jan van Arkel and Guy van Avennes on the S. side of the choir; there are elegant niches in the chapel of Rudolf van Diepholt (*c.* 1455). In the N. aisle of the choir, a delicate late-Gothic gate leads to the sacristy. *Wall painting* (*c.* 1430) of Christ on the Cross in the chapel of Guy van Avennes. Surviving parts of a Holy Sepulchre (1501) can be seen between the two central pillars of the ambulatory; the splendid figures are by Gherit Splintersz. In the chapel of Jan van Arkel, there is a stone retable (*c.* 1500), which unfortunately has been badly damaged. The following things are also of interest: the black marble tomb of Guy van Avennes (d. 1317), parts of the tomb of Jan van Arkel (d. 1378), an early-Renaissance cenotaph (1549) of Bishop Joris van Egmond, and a monument (1676) to Admiral Willem Jozef van Gendt by Rombout Verhulst. In the transepts

Utrecht, cathedral cloister

there are the remains of the beautiful Renaissance choir stalls (1563).

E. and S. wings of the *beautiful cloister* date from the second half of the 14C; the W. wing is 15C. The fountain (1913) with its bronze figure is by Jan Brom. The cathedral chapterhouse (probably mid-15C) is now the university's assembly hall. During 1495–6, it was given a new vault with fine corbels decorated with figures. The cathedral is open to tourists from 1 May–30 Sept., Tue.–Sat. 2–4 p.m.

Former Agnietenklooster (Agnietenstraat): The chapel (1512–16) and former kitchen and refectory wing survive from the former convent of St.Agnes. The complex was enlarged in 1916–21 and converted into the *Centraal Museum* (see Museums).

St.-Augustinuskerk (Oude Gracht): The neo-classical Roman Catholic church (1839–40) by K.G.Zocher has a monumental temple façade.

Buurkerk (Steenweg): The present hall church (14&15C) stands on the

University, statue of Count Jan

GRAAF
JAN VAN NASSAU

site of a cruciform Romanesque basilica damaged by fire in 1253. During the early 16C, two short aisles were added to the existing nave and two aisles (1435–56). The entire choir section was pulled down in 1586 after the Reformation. The late-14C tower was probably intended to be given a crown on the model of the cathedral tower, but only the spire was built. Twelve very fine 13C *columns* survive inside the building. The church also has *wall paintings* (*c.* 1500), a fine carved *pulpit* (second half of 16C), and a curious panel (1612) banning any coming and going during divine service. Converted into a museum in 1984 (see Museums).

St.-Catharinakerk (Lange Nieuwstraat): This late-Gothic cruciform basilica with stone vaults and arched buttresses inside was begun in *c.* 1470 as the church of the Carmelite monastery. It was completed in 1551 by the Order of St.John of Jerusalem, which had taken over the monastery and associated hospice in 1528. It became a Roman Catholic cathedral in 1853, and was enlarged towards the W. in 1898–1900, the old gable being faithfully copied.

Doopsgezinde Kerk (Oude Gracht): A small, simple single-aisled Mennonite church (1772–3) by Willem de Haan from Haarlem.

Geertekerk (Geertekerkhof): This church dedicated to St.Gertrude of Nivelles was once one of the town's four parish churches. Today it is the Remonstrants' church. The tower (probably second half of 13C) has pointed niches, pilaster strips and friezes of round arches; the choir and transept are probably early 14C. The aisles are probably a 15C addition to an older nave.

Jacobikerk (Jacobsstraat): Today, a Dutch Reform church, it was formerly another of the town's four parish churches. In the 15C, the early

Gothic cruciform basilica was converted and enlarged into a stone-vaulted hall church with incorporated tower. The three W. bays of the nave survive from this building. The ornate round-arches and corbels decorated with figures are features of the central choir. All three choirs have good choir screens; the late Gothic screens in the southern H.Kruiskoor and the northern Onze Lieve Vrouwekoor are by Jan van den Ende from Mechelen (1516–19), and the middle screen (1566), in Renaissance style, is by Jan de Clerck from Amsterdam. Fine Renaissance pulpit (c. 1600).

Janskerk (Janskerkhof): Tradition relates that the former collegiate church was founded by Bishop Bernoldus (1027–54), but 11C features have not survived as well as in the Pieterskerk. A new late Gothic choir with ornately vaulted side chapels was built in 1508–39. The Romanesque W. tower was pulled down in 1681 and the W. façade later rebuilt. Inside are interesting monuments, including the tomb with a life-size figure of Provost Dirk van Wassenaar.

Lutherse Kerk (Hamburgerstraat): Formerly the late-Gothic chapel of the convent of St.Ursula, which was rebuilt in 1745.

St.Mary' Cloister (Mariaplaats): The *cloister* is all that survives of this Romanesque collegiate church dedicated to the Virgin and built c. 1090–1150. Arches are supported on columns, whose pillars have cushion capitals. The wooden roof is a 20C restoration.

St.-Nicolaaskerk (Nicolaaskerkhof): Formerly one of the four parish churches and now a Dutch Reform church. Originally a 12C Romanesque cruciform basilica (on the outside only the Romanesque towers survive and even the S. tower was increased in height in 1586), it was made into a hall structure in the 15C and vaulted in stone throughout.

Utrecht, Pieterskerk 1 Former W. façade with 2 Romanesque towers, destroyed in the hurricane of 1674 **2** Wall paintings (c. 1325) **3** Fragments of wall paintings (possibly 15C) **4** 12C Romanesque reliefs **5** 14C Gothic chapel with corbel stones supporting the vault decorated with figures

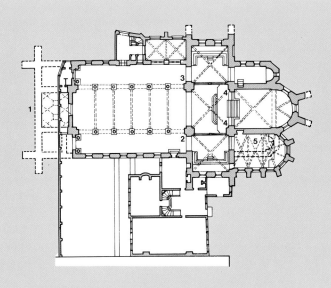

St.-Pauluskerk (Hofpoort, on the Nieuwe Gracht): 11C church. The façade of the S. transept came to light during extensive building work on the Palace of Justice in 1954 and much of it has been retained in the N. façade of the today's court-house.

St.-Pieterskerk (Pieterskerkhof): Formerly a collegiate church (today it belongs to the Walloon Confession), this early Romanesque colonnaded basilica has a cruciform ground plan. Founded by Bishop Bernoldus, it was consecrated in 1048 and the 11C church has survived almost unaltered. The nave is roofed in wood and there are sturdy sandstone columns with cushion capitals. The choir has a crypt beneath it and chapels on either side of it. The more southerly of these chapels was replaced in the early 14C by a Gothic chapel, larger than the previous one. Transept and choir received rib vaults in the late 13C. The W. façade was rebuilt after the hurricane of 1674. *Wall paintings* inside the building include the Crucified Christ with the Virgin Mary and St.Peter and part of the figure of

Paushuize

St.John (*c.* 1325; SW pillar of the crossing) and two badly damaged paintings which may be early 15C (NW pillar of the crossing). 12C *reliefs* of Christ before Pilate, Crucifixion and Resurrection have been re-attached to both sides of the steps leading to the high choir. Transept vaults have good 13C paintings of abbots, angels and prophets.

St.-Willibrorduskerk (Minderbroederstraat): A large neo-Gothic cruciform basilica (1876–7) by A.Tepe.

Former Gasthuis Leeuwenberg (corner of Servaasbolwerk and Schalkwijkstraat): Formerly a hospice founded in 1567, it became a church of the Dutch Protestant union of Utrecht after its restoration in 1930. Still of medieval appearance, the building has two saddleback roofs between gables and pointed windows.

Secular buildings
Bartholomeigasthuis (corner of Lange Smeestraat and Pelmolenweg): The hospice was founded in 1407, the right wing and the chapel date from *c.* 1500, and the left wing was added in 1838. Fine *tapestries* (1642–5) in the 17C warden's room.

Fundatie van Renswoude (Agnietenstraat): A charitable foundation dating from 1757 and built to the plans of Joan Verkerk; imposing central section. The large warden's room is rococo with panelled walls and a stucco ceiling. Nearby there are two attractive almshouse complexes, *Beyerskameren* (1597) in Lange Nieuwstraat and, next door, *Hofje van Pallaes* (1651).

Huis Drakenburg (Oude Gracht): This late-13C house incorporates the remains of a 12C tufa house. The façade has been rebuilt.

Huis Zoudenbach (Donkerstraat):

The main façade dates back to 1467–8 (restored in 1903 & 1964).

Paleis van Justitie (Hamburgerstraat): Neo-classical Palace of Justice (1834–7) by Christiaan Kramm with a figure by J.Rijnbout representing Legislation above the entrance.

Paushuize (corner of Pausdam and Kromme Nieuwe Gracht): This elegant house, begun in 1517, was built for Hadrian VI, the Pope from Utrecht (1459–1523). The part along the Kromme Nieuwe Gracht, with the exception of the entrance gate which may be late-Gothic, is 16C.

Schröderhuis (50 Prins Hendriklaan): Built in 1924 by Gerrit Rietveld, this house expresses the new functionality of the De Stijl group. Rietveld also built two residential blocks in Utrecht (Erasmuslaan and Robert Schumannstraat).

Stadhuis (Stadhuisbrug): The town hall originally consisted of the medieval houses Hazenberg and Groot and Klein Lichtenbergh, which were

spanned by a large classical sandstone façade in 1824–47. Parts of the façade of the early-15C house, 'Het Keyzerrijk' have survived on the left.

Statenkamer (between Janskerkhof and Minderbroederstraat): Formerly part of the Minorite monastery (founded 1247). After the Reformation, from 1581 onwards, it was used as the council chamber of the States of Utrecht. The fine gate dates from 1643; the roof dates from *c.* 1900. Now part of the university.

Other houses: 8 *Achter St.-Pieter*, rather an unusual house dates from 1664. *14 Achter St.-Pieter* has a well-preserved classical façade (*c.* 1640). *20 Achter St.-Pieter*, today a local government office, has a façade with a colossal order (*c.* 1650). *20 Janskerkhof* (*c.* 1640) dates in its present form from *c.* 1725. *13 Janskerkhof* was built in 1648. *18C façades* in *Nieuwe Gracht* and *Kromme Nieuwe Gracht*.

Museums
Centraal Museum (1 Agnietenstraat): Houses art, including decora-

Huis Oudaen

House with stepped gable at 2 Hoogt

tive art, up until 1850. Opening times: Tue.–Sat. 10 a.m.–5 p.m., Sun. and holidays 2–5 p.m. The *Provinciaal Oudheidkundig Museum,* has prehistoric, Roman and early medieval finds, and occupies the same building.

Rijksmuseum 'Het Catharijne Convent' (63 Nieuwe Gracht): A museum of religious art, it documents the history of Christianity in Holland. Opening times: Tue.–Sat. 10 a.m.–5 p.m., Sun. and holidays 2–5 p.m., Tues. also 8–10 p.m.

Hedendaagse Kunst Utrecht (14 Achter de Dom): International modern art. Opening times: Tue.– Sun. 12 noon–5 p.m.

Nationaal Museum van Speelklok tot Pierement (Buurkerk, 10 Buurkerkhof): This museum has musical boxes, barrel organs etc. from the 18C to the present day. Guided tours are held every hour on the hour from 10 a.m.–4 p.m. Tue.–Sat., and 1–4 p.m. on Sun. and holidays.

Het Kruideniersmuseum 'Erven Betje Boerhave' (6 't Hoogt): A museum of colonial produce in rooms above an old grocer's shop. Opening times: Mon. 2–4.30 p.m., Tue.–Sat. 10 a.m.–4.30 p.m.

'Utrecht' Museum (10 Archimedeslaan): Museum of insurance. Opening times: By agreement: Mon.–Fri. 9 a.m.–12 noon and 2–5 p.m.

Also worth seeing: The earlymedieval defences were torn down in 1829, and fine *gardens* were laid out. The best of these are those by J.D.Zocher (1843) between Mariaplaats and Lange Smeestraat, and by S.A. van Lunteren (1859–60) beside the Lepelenburg.

Environs: De Bilt (3 km. E.): This area (which includes Bilthoven, a village of villas) was documented as a hunting ground in 1308 and even now

it is an area of woods and estates, with 18&19C country houses and parks. The local government office occupies the *Jagtlust,* a former country estate. The Royal Dutch Metereological Institute has been in De Bilt since 1893.

Houten (7 km. S.): The *Dutch Reform church* has a nave and choir (probably 13C) and a massive late Gothic tower (*c.* 1500). *Heemstede castle* (1645) has an octagonal ground plan and pentagonal turrets on four sides. Interior decorations are in Louis XIV style.

Vleuten (4 km. W.): The *Dutch Reform church* with its late Gothic nave and two aisles has a fine, simple tower (*c.* 1300). To the S. of it there are some picturesque whitewashed 17C cottages with small stepped gables and roofs thatched with reeds. In the E. of the village, there are the remains of the *Den Ham manorial estate* survive: the massive square tower is probably 15C; the gatehouse dates from 1642.

Vaals
Limburg   p.291 □ M 9

Vaals, on the border with Germany and Belgium is 1058 ft. above sea level, and the highest point in the

Houten (Utrecht), Heemstede castle

Valkenburg, ruined castle

Netherlands. From this point *Drei-landenpunt*, where three countries meet, there is a good view of Aachen, part of the Eifel, the pre-Ardennes, and the Limburg mining district. The cloth trade flourished in the town in the 18C, under the von Clermont family from Aachen.

Lutherse Kerk: This unusual brick building (1737) is basically square with bevelled corners and a tent-like roof. Inside the church, eight columns surround the octagonal central area. The mainly 18C decorations are probably the work of a craftsman from Aachen. Interesting noblemen's pews are usually locked up behind glass.

Stadhuis: Fine palatial house (1761) in classical style with a courtyard; built for J.A. v.Clermont by Joseph Moretti from Aachen.

Environs: Lemiers (2 km. NW): The *old parish church* is probably dates back to the 11C or 12C. *Huis Lemiers*, a 17C mansion, resembles a castle.

Valkenburg
Limburg   p.291 □ L 9

St.-Nicolaaskerk: (Roman Catholic) The tower of this modest late Gothic basilican structure is possibly 14C; the nave was enlarged in 1891 and choir and transepts were lengthened in 1904. Inside a triptych (*c.* 1600) has scenes from the life of St.Remigius.

Ruined castle of Valkenburg: The Valkenburg, the only mountain fortress in the Netherlands, probably began with an early-12C tower. The castle was later surrounded by paved roads known as Dwingel, some of which actually ascend within the mountain itself (the soft marl being very easy to work). The castle was repeatedly besieged, devastated and rebuilt and was finally destroyed in 1672. 20C excavations have uncovered foundation walls of widely different dates.

Town wall: Two castle gates built in marl and possibly going back to the 14C, survive from the town fortifications which joined on to the outermost castle walls. The *Grendelpoort* on the W. side has round towers, and the *Berkelpoort* in the E. is roughly square. Considerable remains of the wall itself survive in the W.

Houses: *Huis Den Halder* is mainly 17C and has a small staircase turret. *Huis De Guasco* (13 Grotestraat) has a fine 17C gable decorated with volutes. The *Spaanse Leenhof* (1661), 5 Th.Dorrenplein, has a marl façade of unusual design.

Environs: Houthem-St.-Gerlach (2 km. W.): The present *parish church*

Veere, Stadhuis

(*c.* 1725), originally the church of the foundation of St.Gerlach, consists of a single large room with Corinthian pilasters. Paintings on ceilings and walls in the W. part are by Johann Adam Schöpff, a rococo painter from S.Germany (1702–72). The Last Judgement behind the organ is probably also his work. After the dissolution of the convent, the former *monastery* (*c.* 1713) to the E. of the church became a nobleman's house.

Klimmen (3 km. E.): The nave and tower are the only parts of the *Roman Catholic church* to have survived in the original Romanesque. The rest of this cruciform basilica dates from restoration work of 1904–06. The N. transept has a large late Gothic altar triptych with a Crucifixion, Calvary Procession, Deposition, Entombment and Resurrection, probably painted in the mid-16C in Utrecht.

Oud-Valkenburg (about 1 km. E.): Roman Catholic church with an elegant rococo high altar. The tower is possibly medieval, the choir dates from 1757, while the nave is mid-19C. *Kasteel Oud-Valkenburg* or *Genhoes* occupies the site of a building which possibly preceeded the Valkenburg. The present building consists of a residential wing, a large tower (*c.* 1500), and a low 18C wing with the entrance.

Veere

Zeeland   p.288☐D 7

The walls defending this little harbour town were built in 1358. Standing on the Veerse Meer (an arm of the the sea which the Veersegat dam has turned into a lake), the town experienced its peak period in the 15&16C as the result of trade with Scotland in wool and cloth.

Onze-Lieve-Vrouwekerk: This massive late Gothic cruciform basilica was begun in 1479 under Anthonis Keldermans, who was succeeded by his son Rombout in 1512. A fire broke out in the church in 1686 and in 1809 it was a target for English fire. In 1811–13, under Napoleon, it was divided up into storeys (now no longer present) for use as a hospital.

Campveerse tower: This tower (*c.* 1500) is the only surviving section of the old town wall. When restored in 1950, it was once again given its tall roof and stepped gable decorated with pinnacles. The side of the adjoining *Zuidhavenpoort* facing the harbour was designed in the 16C. The other side facing the town was altered in 1738.

Stadhuis: The town hall attributed to Evert Spoorwater from Antwerp was begun in 1474 and has projecting turrets at the front and another tower (dating from 1594–9 in its present form) at the rear. The seven figures of men and women by V.des Michiel Ywijns (1517) are today in the Schotse Huizen museum; the figures now visible on the façade are copies. The town hall's interior decorations date mainly from 1699. The most

valuable possession in today's Oud-heidkamer, the former court-room, is a silver-gilt goblet, the gift of Maximilian of Burgundy, with scenes of the heroic deeds of Maximiliaan van Egmond-Buren. Opening times: 1 June–15 Sept.: Mon.–Sat. 10 a.m.–4 p.m.

Schotse Huizen (25–27 Kade): The Scottish houses (1561), two fine late-Gothic buildings, today are used as a museum. Opening times: Apr.–Sept.: Tue.–Sat. 10 a.m.–12.30 p.m. and 1.30–5 p.m.

Velp

Geldern   p.291☐L 6

Dutch Reform church: This church has a simple Romanesque nave with high round-arched windows and a N. chapel with early-16C net vaulting. A choir was added to this structure in 1949–52 while the war damage was being repaired. The slender Romanesque tower with its pilaster strips and friezes of arches (12C) was

Veere, Onze-Lieve-Vrouwekerk (left), fountain outside church (right)

increased in height in the Gothic period when a low brick storey was added.

Kasteel Biljoen: The present form of the castle, which was founded in 1531 by Duke Karel van Gelder, is pre-1731 and has four round corner towers. Portal, entrance section and bridge are 19C. The Flemish wall tapestries (first half of 17C) came from Simon Bouwens, a weaver and trader from Antwerp. The ballroom has ornate stucco decorations on the walls and ceiling.

Venlo
Limburg   p.291 □ M 7

Parochiekerk van St.-Martinus: The parish church of St.Martin, a Gothic hall church with rib vaults, was begun in c. 1400 as a cruciform structure, and completed in its present form during the second phase of construction. The present tower dates from after 1945, and replaces former towers on the site, including one by Petrus Josephus Hubertus Cuypers. Sides and misericords of the late Gothic choir stalls (late-15C) have carvings decorated with figures. The monumental font (1619–21) is by Herman den' Potgieter.

Minderbroederkerk (Pothoofdstraat): This single-aisled church survives from a Franciscan monastery of 1614–18. Mainly late Gothic, there are some Renaissance features.

Dutch Reform church (Gasthuisstraat): Built in 1718 by P. van Bolnes from Dordrecht, it takes the form of a large T. The late Gothic choir of the former hospice chapel was incorporated into the building.

Stadhuis: The almost square *town hall* (1596–1601) by Willem van Bommel from Emmerich is a free-standing building in the Markt. The front is flanked by two charmingly dissimilar octagonal corner towers. The external double staircase and the entrance porch with columns both date from 1609. Bartizans on the corners at the back were added during the rebuilding of 1888 during which the façade received its Renaissance form. The ceiling of the market hall on the ground floor is supported on four Doric columns. (The hall is now a district archive.)

Gemeentelijk Museum van Bommel-van Dam (8 Deken van Oppensingel): Collection of 20C Dutch painting. Opening times: Mon.–Fri. 10 a.m.–5 p.m., Sat., Sun. and holidays 2–5 p.m.

Goltziusmuseum (21 Goltziusstraat): A museum of local history. Exhibits include archaeological finds. Opening times: Mon.–Fri. 10 a.m.–12 noon and 2–5 p.m., Sat. and Sun. 2–5 p.m.

Environs: Broekhuizenvorst (15 km. N.): The late Gothic *Roman Catholic church* (possibly dating from 1535) has a low 15C choir and a tower of c. 1500 which may have 13C foundations.
Kessel (13 km. SW): Excavations carried out after the castle was destroyed in 1944 brought to light foundation walls of a residential tower dating from c. 1000. This tower was destroyed at an early date and the castle hill was later increased in height. In the 12C a wall surrounding the top of the hill was built. Another building was added in the 14C, and a squat gatehouse tower in the 16C.
Lottum (12 km. N.): The new *Roman Catholic church* has some late Gothic figures of saints figures (repainted), the best of which are St.Michael, St.Gertrude and St.Catherine. '*De Borggraaf*', is like a small-scale castle with 16C buildings around a small courtyard.
Reuver (14 km. S.): The *Roman-*

Catholic church (1878–80), a neo-Gothic cruciform basilica influenced by North German Gothic brick style, is by J.Kayser .

Steyl (6 km. S.): The two-storeyed *Missionary Chapel* (1882), a squat neo-Gothic structure, was built by H.Erlemann built to sketches by Prill, an architect from Cologne.

Tegelen (2 km. S.): The brick tower of the *Roman Catholic church* dates *from c.* 1500 and was extensively restored just before the neo-Gothic cruciform basilica was built by C.Franssen in 1899–1900. The tower was increased in height in 1956.

Venray

p.290☐L 7

Venray (23 km. NW): *St.Petruskerk* , a late Gothic building dates from the second half of the 15C. In the 19C J.Kayser built a new church tower to replace the old one. Church furnishings include a baroque pulpit (1679), late-16C Renaissance font, 15C late Gothic lectern, and figures of saints

(c. 1500), which may originally have come from the Lower Rhine; 16C figures of the Apostles on the columns seem Italianate in style.

Environs: Oostrum (5 km. E.): The *new church* was built to the S. of and at right angles to the old Roman Catholic church which is now used as an entrance hall. The massive lower section of the incomplete late-15C tower stands to the W. of the old nave.

Vianen

South Holland p.289☐I 6

A little old fortified town on the Lek with a very regular layout of streets. The church and town hall stand in the broad Voorstraat which runs through the town from N. to S.

Dutch Reform church: The massive tower (probably 14C) of this large late Gothic building has Romanesque pilaster strips, friezes of arches and 2 doors with pointed arches. The height of the tower was increased in the 15C.

Venlo, Romerhuis

Venlo, Stadhuis

The large main choir is mid-15C, while the two low side choirs are a little later. The nave, rebuilt after a fire in 1542, has an elegant brick portal from the mid-14C on the N. side. The N. choir has the Renaissance tomb of Reinoud III van Brederode (d. 1556) and his wife Phillippote van der Marck (d. 1537), the work of an unknown craftsman from Brussels.

Raadhuis: The fine brick town hall has a tall stone façade and dates from the mid-15C; battlements on the top storey were replaced during restoration work in 1956–62. Some of the stone mullions are original. The council chamber has good portraits of members of the Brederode and van Nassau families and a painting reputed to be the largest equestrian painting in the Netherlands (1550).

Town wall: The *Lekpoort* on the N. side is a 15C tower-like gatehouse with projecting turrets on the outer side. It is part of the old fortifications, of which there are other remnants. The *Hofpoort* (second half of 17C) survives from the former castle of the Brederodes; nearby stands a large *pump* (1648) with stone figures.

Vlaardingen

South Holland   p.290☐G 6

Vlaardingen, an important industrial town, is the fourth largest port in the Netherlands.

Dutch Reform church: A hall church with a nave and two aisles resulted from rebuilding and enlarging the medieval parish church which burned down in 1574. The brick tower (1744) with the wooden 'pepper-pot' roof is by Daniel van Stolk. The large rococo organ came from the St.-Baafskerk in Gent in 1802; the font and neo-Gothic pulpit came from the Willemskerk in The Hague.

◁ *Vianen, Raadhuis*

Raadhuis: The town hall (1650) by Bartholomeus Drijfhout is in a style transitional between Renaissance and baroque. The façade gable has a statue of Justice; on the roof there is an octagonal bell turret.

Vismarkt: The fish market (1778), an attractive building by the harbour, has an open gallery and a turret.

Visserijmuseum, Institut voor de Nederlands Zeevisserij (53–4 Westhavenkade): This fishing museum with model ships, maps, implements and paintings of sea fishing and whaling occupies a house with a monumental Louis XIV façade (1790). Opening times: Mon.–Sat. 10 a.m.–5 p.m., Sun. & holidays 2–5 p.m. Closed on 25 Dec. & 1 Jan.

Also worth seeing: The tall round '*Aeolus*' *corn mill* (1790) near the Korte Dijk.

Environs: Maassluis (5 km. W.): In 1648–50 the *Dutch Reform Grote Kerk* (1629–30) was given a tall tower built to the plans of Arent van 's-Gravesande. Fine features inside include the railing of both pulpit and font (both 1639), the choir screen (1660) and the large organ (1732) by Rudolf Garrels. The church also has two guild paintings by A.van Beyeren (1649). An elegant building houses the *dyke office* (1626). The *former town hall* probably dates back to 1676 and has colossal pilasters. The '*De Hoop*' *mill* (1792), built in brick, stands by the Zuiddijk.

Vledder

Drente   p.287□M 3

An *erratic* (a large boulder brought down by glaciers during the Ice Age) weighing 35 tonnes, stands in the village square.

Dutch Reform church: A simple

Vianen, Lekpoort ▷

Gothic building on the edge of the village. The saddleback tower with four storeys of diminishing size, has a Frisian appearance. This tower may possibly go back to the early 14C; choir and nave are 15C.

Bijenteelt Museum Hoeve Bekhof (5 De Hoek): A bee-keeping museum in a Saxon farmhouse (1651). Old implements and objects decorated with bee motifs are on display. Opening times: 15 June–end of Aug.: Wed. and Thur. 2–5 p.m.

Environs: Frederiksoord (3 km. S.): This town owes its origin to a charitable foundation which established a 'free agricultural colony' here in 1818. Little farmhouses which line the road to Noordwolde, to left and right, stand about 200 ft. apart. The *Klokkenmuseum* (17 Maj. van Swietenlaan) hass exhibits of both Dutch and foreign bells, as well as clocks and other timepieces from 1500 to 1900. Opening times: May–Sept.: Mon.–Fri. 10 a.m.–5 p.m., Sun. 2–5 p.m. The *G.A. van Swieten Middelbare Tuinbouwschool*, a splendid garden, is at the same address. Opening times: Mon.–Fri. 9 a.m.–12 noon & 2–5 p.m. Pentecost–August: also Sun. 2–5 p.m. The *Zeemuseum Miramar* at 25 Vledderweg has bivalves, corals, sea urchins, sea birds and waders from all over the world. Opening times: Easter–Oct.: Mon.–Fri. 9.30 a.m.–12 noon & 1–5.30 p.m.; June–Aug.: Mon.–Fri. 9 a.m.–5 p.m., Sat. 1–5.30 p.m. & Sun. 11 a.m.–5 p.m.

Vlieland/Flylân (I)
Friesland   p.286☐H-I 2

Vlieland is the smallest and most westerly of the West Frisian islands belonging to Friesland. No cars are allowed on the island. The ferry leaves from Harlingen.

Oost-Vlieland: Since West-Vlieland sank below the waves in the 18C, Oost-Vlieland has been the only town on the island. The *Dutch Reform church* (1605) is a single-aisled hall structure with arched buttresses; the transept was added in 1647. The beautiful interior has a pulpit (1605), an 18C organ, and many tombstones. One of the five brass candlesticks was presented by Admiral de Ruyter, who had a house on the island (as did Admiral Tromp). The *former poorhouse,* a long building which now belongs to a charitable foundation, stands beside the church. *Tromp's huis,* 99 Dorpstraat, was originally owned by the admiralty. Altered in the 18&19C, it is now open to the public as a *museum*. There is also a *museum of natural history* at 152 Dorpstraat. Opening times for both museums: May–Aug.: Mon.–Fri. 9 a.m.–12 noon & 2–5 p.m.

Vlissingen
Zeeland   p.288☐D 7

A trading and fishing port on the mouth of the Westerschelde in the S. of the Walcheren peninsula. From here, ferries leave for Breskens in Zeeuws-Vlaanderen and for England. Although the town has the only S.-facing beach in the Netherlands to be protected from the wind, it is more a busy industrial town with shipyards than a seaside resort.

St.-Jacobskerk: (Dutch Reform church) A late-Gothic hall church; the tower and the end of the choir date from an older (14C) building. The church was restored after a fire in 1911 and the destruction of World War 2. A (damaged) memorial stone of 1619 commemorates Johannes Lambrechtsz. Coolen; a black-and-white marble monument by J.Camhout from Middelburg commemorates Daniel Octavius Barwell, who was killed in a natural disaster in 1779).

Beurs: The former stock exchange (1635), whose appearance has lost much of its charm since the open galleries were walled up in 1880; hexagonal tower.

Cornelia Quack's hofje: Founded in 1634 (an attractive little side gate dates from this time) and built around a courtyard. Since 1786 it has been an almshouse for sailors.

Van Dishoeck-huis: Built for Anthonie van Dishoeck in 1733, this house has an ornate central section. 1818–1966 it was the town hall.

Oranjemolen: A round stone mill (1699) picturesquely located on a bulwark.

Statue of Admiral Michiel Adriaansz. de Ruyter: This monument of 1842 designed by L.Royeto commemorates the town's greatest son (1607–76), who saved the Netherlands from defeat in the third Anglo-Dutch war.

Fortifications and harbour build-

ings: The harbour (once known as *Oude Haven*, today the Bellamypark) was built by Count Willem III in 1315 and surrounded with ramparts in 1489. Emperor Charles V had a fort built to the W. of the harbour entrance in 1548; today this fort is a breakwater. The *Gevangenpoort*, part of the former Westpoort, also survives from this period. The *Engelse* or *Vissershaven* (surviving today as the Oranjedijk) was built 1580–1590 along the Nieuwendijk on the E. side of the Oude Haven. A new harbour (the Oosterhaven) was built to the E. of this in 1609. The W. entrance of the Oosterhaven was flanked by the surviving bulwark on which a windmill stands. After the English invasion of Walcheren in 1809 (when the town hall of 1594 was destroyed), the ramparts were reinforced under Napoleon. Most of the ramparts on the land side have disappeared since the fortifications were abandoned in 1867. The *new harbour* dates from 1870 and was enlarged in 1932 by the addition of the Petroleumhaven.

Houses: The *Lampsinshuis* (11 Nieu-

Vlissingen, Beurs (stock exchange)

wendijk) has a roof balustrade, an octagonal turret and a stone façade (1641) with a projecting middle section. The pilastered façade (1730) of the *Beeldenhuis*, 25 Hendrikstraat, is in Antwerp baroque style.

Stedelijk Museum (19 Bellamy-park): Exhibits include memorabilia of Admiral de Ruyter. Opening times: 15 June–15 Sept.: Mon.–Fri. 10 a.m.–5 p.m., Sat. & Sun. 1–5 p.m.; 15 Sept.–15 June: Tue.–Fri. 10 a.m.–12.30 p.m. & 1.30–5 p.m., Sat. 1–5 p.m.

Also worth seeing: The *Lutherse Kerk* (1735), a simple building enlarged in 1778.

Vollenhove
Overijssel   p.287□L 3

Grote or St.-Nicolaaskerk: This late Gothic Dutch Reform hall church has two aisles ending in polygonal choirs. These two choirs, probably

Vollenhove, Onze-Lieve-Vrouwekerk

14C, were followed by the four W. bays with their slender columns. The free-standing brick tower is probably early 16C.

Kleine or O.L. Vrouwekerk: A single-aisled Dutch Reform church dating back to 1434. The extension of the nave and the tower were built in 1458–61. The tower was increased in height in 1823.

Former town hall: This graceful building (1621) has an open colon-naded gallery and a richly decorated façade. It is unusual in that it adjoins the tower of the Grote Kerk.

Also worth seeing: The *former Latijnse School* (25 Kerkplein) has a stepped gable (1627). The *Marxveld country estate* (Bischopstraat) lies within the borders of the town. *Toutenburg castle* was begun by George Schenk van Toutenburg in 1524. It was pulled down in the early 19C, and the remains of two gatehouse towers are all that survive today. 17&18C *façades* can be seen here and there about this little town.

Vorden
Geldern   p.287□M 5

This holiday village in Achterhoek, in a little corner of Geldern, has more country houses than any other parish in the Netherlands. The village is known as the 'acht Kastelen van Vorden'.

Dutch Reform church: This church with its 14C brick tower was built in several Gothic styles from *c.* 1300 (the nave) until *c.* 1500 (the choir). The neo-Romanesque entrance dates from the restoration of 1897. The tombstone of Bernt van Hackfort (d. 1557) has a figure of a knight in relief. The choir has a late Gothic relief (*c.* 1540) of the Adoration.

Kasteel Vorden: An L-shaped building constructed in the mid 16C on the site of a medieval house. The outer NW corner has a powerful tower with a saddleback roof between two stepped gables. A polygonal staircase tower stands at the inner corner. The building was thoroughly restored in 1873. Today it houses local administrative offices.

Huis Den Bramel: Originally 17C, the building was converted into a brick mansion in the 18C. The neo-Gothic entrance with turret dates from 1830.

Huis Hackfort: This large house was mentioned in 1324. Its present appearance is the result of a conversion in 1788. The two round towers (probably 16C) were retained at that time.

Huis De Wiersse: This rather modest two-storeyed 18C country house was enlarged c. 1930. The entrance wing is by D.F. Slothouwer.

Huis Onstein: This elegant mansion (1711) is surrounded by a ditch. A 20C tower has been added at the rear.

Huis 't Medler: As in the case of Onstein and Den Bramel, the façade of this mansion has five bays, with the entrance in the middle. The house was built c. 1800 and enlarged 1892–3. A round piece of land nearby probably indicates the site of a medieval castle.

Huis Wildenborch: The round tower (probably early-16C) was originally the entrance to a medieval castle. Residential wings were added to both sides of the tower in 1782, and the neo-Romanesque appearance dates from 1847. The house at the rear was also enlarged at that time.

Huis De Kieftskamp: This, the last of the eight country houses, dates in its entirety from 1776. Its original condition has been well preserved.

Also worth seeing: The *water mill* near Huis Hackfort is *c.* 1700. The two charming *windmills* are characteristic of the town's appearance. The

Vollenhove, St.-Nicolaaskerk

octagonal mill dates from 1850, the round mill from 1851.

Vries
Drente   p.287☐N 3

Dutch Reform church: The ponderous, richly articulated 12C tower is the finest Romanesque tower in Drente. Romanesque windows were re-installed in the tufa-stone nave in restoration work in 1946–9, while the tall late Gothic brick choir is from 1425. The rebuilt rib vault of the choir is supported by carved corbel stones. The font is 13C, and the pulpit and some pews are 17C. The casting mould (discovered in the nave) of the bell in the tower, and also some sarcophagus lids, are in the crypt of a new church room adjoining the choir.

Also worth seeing: There are *megalithic tombs* in the nearby areas of *Tinaarloo* and *Zeijen*. Near *Zeijen* there is also a *field of burial mounds,* with large and small *tumuli* from the Bronze and Iron Ages.

Waalwijk
North Brabant   p.290☐I 6

Dutch Reform church: A late Gothic church probably begun in *c.* 1450 (including the choir) and completed *c.* 1520. The W. façade was rebuilt in 1617 after the destruction of the W. tower in the late 16C.

St.-Janskerk: H.W.Valk built this Roman Catholic church in 1926. A bold, centrally planned structure with

Vorden, Kasteel Vorden

a tall dome, it is surrounded by domed chapels. Terracotta Stations of the Cross are by Charles Eyck (1941).

Nederlands Museum voor Schoenen, Leder en Lederwaren (148 Grotestraat): This footwear museum has exhibits from many periods and cultures. Opening times: 1 Apr.–1 Oct.: Mon.–Sat., 10 a.m.–12 noon & 2–5 p.m.

Environs: Drunen (6 km. E.): The '*Hertogin van Brabant*' corn mill dates from 1842. The *Lips Autotron Collection*, housed in buildings designed by Anton Pieck, has a collection of old cars and vehicles owned by Lips, who manufactured ships' propellers. Opening times: Late Mar.–early Nov.: Tue.–Sat. 10 a.m.–6 p.m., Sun. 12 noon–6 p.m. Open only at weekends in the winter months.
Dussen (10 km. NE): Today's *town hall* occupies a former castle of medieval origin and consists of a courtyard surrounded on three sides by buildings and, on the N. side, by an entrance gate flanked by two towers. The charming arcades around the courtyard date from 1608 & 1628. The '*Het Noordeveld*' mill was built in 1795.
Heusden (12 km. NE): This little old town is surrounded by a ring of fortifications, including ramparts and canals, which are now in the process of being restored. Interesting *mills in the ramparts*. The *Dutch Reform church* was rebuilt in 1572 after a fire; the tower was destroyed in 1944. The marble tomb of Johan Theodoor Baron van Friesheim was built before 1733 to the designs of Jacob Marot. The 12C *castle* was blown up in 1667; today, parts of the foundations have been excavated.
Sprang-Capelle (3 km. S.): This town suffered greatly in the St.Elizabeth flood of 1421. The *Dutch Reform church*, which has three nave bays and a choir, was begun in *c.* 1400; the transepts are a little later. During the late 15C, work started in the W. on a

larger church with richly articulated buttresses, and now the two sections form one building; the two periods of construction can be clearly distinguished inside the church. *Upright mill* of 1811 in Oudestraat.

Wageningen
Geldern   p.291 □ L 6

This little town on the Lower Rhine is still almost completely surrounded by fortification ditches. The town's agricultural college has made it an international centre of agrarian science.

Dutch Reform church: The church has a 12C Romanesque tufa tower with pilaster strips and friezes of arches. The Gothic brick nave has a broad N. aisle and a narrower S. aisle (19C). The transept and net-vaulted choir are late Gothic. The severe damage suffered in 1940 and 1943, when the tower collapsed, has been repaired.

Town hall: The town hall was rebuilt in 1862; the stone central section (1698) with its figure of Justice survives from the previous building.

Warffum
Groningen   p.287 □ N 2

Dutch Reform church: The nave is probably 13C, while the choir with its delicate net vault is more recent; the massive tower dates from 1638. Inside there are numerous tombstones and 18/19C decorations.

Vrouw Fransens Gasthuis: This hospice was founded in 1768 in Groningen, pulled down in 1970 and rebuilt in Warffum. Today it is part of the 'Het Hogeland' open-air museum.

'Het Hogeland' museum (2

Schoolstraat): In 1959 this open-air museum was set up with the aim of preserving various aspects of domestic life in Groningen, particularly of the marsh area. The museum includes: the Vrouw Fransens Gasthuis; the 19C 'Harbarg bie Koboa' with original decorations and a shop; 'Venhoeske', a one room house from the early 19C; the 'Olle Kösterije', a stable with horse-sleighs and a fire-engine (1841); the 'Termunten Skippershoeske' (1839); and 'Huis Markus' (1834), a Jewish house and butcher's shop.

Environs: Huizinge (10 km. SE): The fine 13C Romanesque-Gothic *church* has an ornate Gothic portal (at the SW corner) most of which was rebuilt in 1847. Vault paintings with tendril-like decorations and a Last Judgement were discovered inside in 1960–3.
Kantens (7.5 km. NE): The W. half of the *Dutch Reform church* and the octagonal tower both date from *c.* 1200 (the upper section of the tower is *c.* 1500); the E. half of the church was built in the second half of the 13C on the site of a small apse. Small Romanesque windows were discovered during restoration work. The attractive stone entrances are 17C. The octagonal *'Grote Geert' corn mill* dates from 1818.
Middelstum (14 km. SE): In the village there is a late Gothic church, which is rather rare for Groningen. In 1445, transepts and a choir were built on to an already existing nave. The nave was subsequently increased in height and rib vaults were added. Finally, the strong tower was built in 1487. Inside the *church* there are vault paintings, a sandstone monument (1476) to Egbert Onsta, a beautiful pulpit (1733), and a set of ornately decorated choir stalls (1704). The bottom of a round gun-turret, (1472) surrounded by a ditch, was formerly part of *Castle Ewsum*. Part of the former Asingaborg survives in the form of a tall and narrow building,

which dates from 1611 and was converted into the gatehouse of a new house during restoration work in 1926.
Usquert (3.5 km. NE): Located in an area of mud flats most of which is polder land today. The Knights of St.John of Jerusalem had a house here until 1587. Today there are two large *farms*, 'Kruisstee' and 'Kloosterwytwerd', the latter of which has a fireplace dating from *c.* 1461 with the coat-of-arms of the Knights of St.John.

Warmond
South Holland   p.289□G 5

Oude Kerk: With the exception of the tower (probably late 15C) only ruins survive of the old parish church which was built in a magnificent position amidst splendid parkland. After a fire in the church in 1573, the Dutch Reform community rebuilt the central choir alone and they used this for worship until a new church was built in 1874; the old choir is now in a state of disrepair.

Huys te Warmont: This white building of regular design with four corner turrets, stands a little way outside the village and occupies the site of two castles, the last one of which disappeared in 1420. A subsequent building burned down in 1573 and in 1579 this was replaced by the house visible today (with alterations dating from 1870).

Windmills: There are a few old polder mills around Warmond, the oldest being the 'Boterhuismolen' (1744), while the rest are mostly early 19C; some are still in use.

Environs: Rijnsburg (3 km. W.): This village stands at the S. edge of the great flower fields. In the 12C Petronella van Saksen built an abbey which was devastated in the Spanish period. The slender 12C Romanesque tower of the *Dutch Reform church* was formerly the abbey's tower; decorations on the top of the tower date from 1830. The church itself was begun in 1578 and enlarged in the 17C & 20C. The philosopher Baruch Spinoza (1632–77) lived in *Spinoza house* at 2 Spinozastraat during 1661–3. This house was restored in 1899 & 1922 and today houses Spinoza memorabilia.

Voorhout (5 km. NW): The birthplace of Hermannus Boerhaave, physicist and botanist (1668–1738). Today the local Dutch Reform priest lives in the house where he was born. The *church*'s tufa choir, which may be 14C, was part of a former parish church; the choir was rebuilt and enlarged in 1913–14.

Wassenaar
South Holland   p.289☐G 5

Dutch Reform church: Parts of the N. wall of the aisle (11C or 12C), and also the brick base of the tower, probably came from the old church which was destroyed in 1573 in the siege of Leiden and later rebuilt in a simpler style.

Kerk van de Goede Herder: (Roman Catholic) The church of the Good Shepherd was built by J.A. van der Laan in 1931 influenced by early Romanesque basilicas .

Kasteel Oud-Wassenaar: This pompous Renaissance-style structure was built by C.Muysken in 1876–97 for Cornelis Jan van der Oudermeulen, equerry to King William III. It was later used as a hotel, and also for entertaining statesmen and ambassadors—Winston Churchill and Anthony Eden were among those to stay here.

Raadhuis: This town hall, formerly a neo-classical country house known as

De Pauw, was the residence of Prince Frederick, second son of King William I, from 1838 until his death in 1881. Petrolt designed the gardens.

Also worth seeing: The *Raephorst park* was also laid out on the orders of Prince Frederik. *Serengenberg*, a high point in the park, has an observation pavilion (*c.* 1820). 18C *Rentmeestershuis*, neo-Gothic riflemen's clubhouse belonging to the sharpshooters' company of St.Hubert; *Huis ter Horst* is also neo-Gothic.

Wieuwerd
Friesland   p.287☐L 2

Dutch Reform church: A small church in an isolated country location, it was rebuilt in 1860 and given a new tower in 1889. The church became famous 200 years ago when four mummified corpses (probably members of a religious community) along with a mummified rooster, were found in the crypt beneath the choir (rebuilt in 1609). Opening times: 1 Apr.–31 Oct.: Mon.–Sat. 9 a.m.–12 noon & 1–4.30 p.m., open only until 4 p.m. from Sept. on.

Also worth seeing: Many interesting *farmhouses* can be seen around this village. Typically, they consist of a passage linking the tall barn and stable section to the smaller and lower residential section.

Environs: Bozum/Boazum (3 km. S.): The village's *Dutch Reform church* is a 12C Romanesque building almost entirely faced in tufa. Vault paintings in the choir are among the oldest in the N.Netherlands and display a beardless Christ Enthroned surrounded by the symbols of the Four Evangelists and flanked by two standing Saints. The large organ (1791) has an ornate, richly carved case. Opening times: 1 Apr.–31 Oct.,

Mon.–Sat. 9 a.m.–12 noon & 1–4.30 p.m., open until 4 p.m. from Sept. onwards.

Wijk-bij-Duurstede

The Rhine changes its name to the Lek at this point. The town stands on the site occupied by the large harbour of *Dorestad* in the early Middle Ages. The Normans, together with a major flood, put a stop to this harbour's operations in *c*. 860. The castle and a new settlement which was granted a charter in 1300 were built to the W. of today's town in the 13C.

Dutch Reform church: The bishops of Utrecht who resided in the castle, especially David (1456–96) and Philip (1516–24) of Burgundy, probably played a large part in determining the size of this church. The present incomplete cruciform basilica (no choir) was built between 1486 and the mid-16C by altering and enlarging the original church (*c*. 1300).

Work on the massive tower proceeded only as far as the beginning of the second of the three storeys originally planned. The tower is richly articulated by arched buttresses, deep niches and delicate balustrades. The interior, with its columns and arches, is quite impressive even though the stone vaulting is incomplete.

Ruined castle: The sturdy keep (probably from the second half of the 13C), and an even stronger round corner tower of almost 50 ft. diameter (probably from the second half of the 15C; restored 1948–52) survive from the castle which has been in an ever-worsening state of repair since the early 18C. In 1727 it came into the hands of the district authority. Parts of the outer walls, with the remains of a gatehouse and a small round corner tower, have also survived. The ruins, which still have a very romantic appearance, are surrounded by the park laid out by J.D.Zocher, in *c*. 1836.

Stadhuis: The town hall, a broad

Bozum (Wieuwerd), church

Wijk, Dutch Reform church

rather plain building with a tall staircase was built by Gijsbert van Vianen and Peter van Cooten in 1666.

Town wall: The *Runmolenpoort*, one of the town's gates on which the '*Rijn en Lek*' *corn mill* was built in 1659, stands on the S. side of the town, along with extensive remains of the town wall. The mill is sometimes incorrectly thought to be that in Jacob van Ruysdael's painting 'The Mill of Wijk bij Duurstede' (Rijksmuseum, Amsterdam); of Ruysdael's mill in the ramparts, a little further to the W., all that survives are the foundations.

Willemstad
North Brabant   p.290☐G 6

Town layout: The town, with a star-shaped layout and surrounded entirely by canals, has a broad main street (Voorstraat) running at right angles to the dyke and ending in the church square. The fortifying ramparts, in the form of a seven-pointed star with seven bastions, were built by Adriaen Anthonisz., the fortress architect, between 1581 and 1597. The ramparts, only slightly altered and improved since then, have survived in unusually good condition.

Dutch Reform church: Built on an octagonal ground plan in 1596–1607; the tower in the SW corner is unfinished. The church was gutted by fire in 1950. Inside, there are a pulpit (1659) from the church in Hoogvliet and some pews (*c.* 1670) from the demolished church of Graft.

Arsenaal: The arsenal by the harbour was built by P.W.Schonck in 1793 and has two stone gates on the side towards the harbour.

Prinsenhof or **Mauritshuis:** Today the town hall, it was founded by Prince Maurice in 1623 and was probably designed by Melchior van Herbach.

Former town hall: Built in 1587 and altered in 1620, from which time the double curve gable dates, as does the tower which is square in its lower

Wijk, ruined castle

Willemstad, Prinsenhof

stories and octagonal in the upper ones.

Environs: Klundert (8 km. SE): The dominant features of the town's appearance are the two symmetrically laid-out squares, the churchyard and church, and the market place with the town hall. Some ramparts and canals, especially the *Suijkerberch crown*, still survive from the fortifications built in 1583.

Winschoten

Groningen   p.287☐O 2

Dutch Reform church: Walls and E. façade of this elongated late-13C building still have the original Romesque-Gothic articulation. The W. façade and the interior vaulting were altered in restoration work in 1906. 17&18C tombstones line the walls of the choir. A small rococo gate (1772) has been installed in the partition by the W. portal. The free-standing 13C tower was given an octagonal belfry in 1930–1.

Environs: Bellingwolde (8 km. E.): The road leading to the village is lined with fine farmhouses and the splendid trees of country estates. The simple late Gothic *Dutch Reform church* has groin vaults which were added later. The lower part of the free-standing tower dates from 1720, while the upper section is modern. The former *Rechthuis* (1643) in the main street was converted into a residential house in 1956. The round *windmill* dates from 1855. The *'De Oude Wolden' regional museum* (161 Hoofdweg) has archaeological and geological finds, and also costumes and utensils. Opening times: Apr.–Oct.: 3–5 p.m., Sat. & Sun. 2–5 p.m.

Heiligerlee (3 km. W.): The Eighty Years' War between the Republic of the United Netherlands and Spain began here on 23 May 1568. In this first battle, 4,200 Gueux led by Lodewijk van Nassau fought against 3,200 well-trained soldiers commanded by Jan de Ligne. The Gueux were victorious. 300 years later, King William III unveiled a monument commemorating this battle.

Midwolda (6 km. N.): The *Dutch*

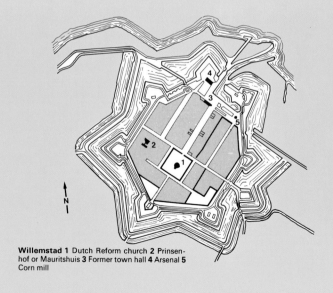

Willemstad 1 Dutch Reform church **2** Prinsenhof or Mauritshuis **3** Former town hall **4** Arsenal **5** Corn mill

Reform church is a broad rectangular hall building (1738–40) with a tower from 1708. The decorations date from the time when the church was originally built; the organ (1772) is by A.A.Hinsch. Today the *Ennemaborg* is a distinguished country house dating from *c.* 1700 in the main with a few late-14C sections. Beautiful 18C figures in the garden.
Nieuweschans (12 km. E.): This village on the border with West Germany has a *former garrison church* (1751), the upper part of which was originally an ammunition depot and hay loft. Some *soldiers' houses* can still be seen in Kanonnierstraat. The hall in the Achterweg was formerly a *synagogue*. *Vestingmuseum* (1e Kanonierstraat 2) is a small museum devoted to the fortress (fortifications built in 1628 and abandoned in 1870). Opening times: Mon.–Fri. 9 a.m.–12 noon & 1–4 p.m.
Wedde (7 km. S.): The *Dutch Reform church* consists of a 13C nave, a broader late-Gothic choir (both of which date from 1666 and were later altered), and a tower (1860) with a new spire. The splendid *Wedderborg* (*c.* 1370) was rebuilt in the 15C and consists of two wings with a connecting staircase tower betwen them. The stone with the Schenk van Toutenburg coat-of-arms is dated 1541.

Winterswijk
Geldern   p.291 □ O 6

Winterswijk is the regional centre of the SE Achterhoek. Amidst areas of woodland there are Lower Saxon farmhouses which have survived in splendid condition from the 18C and early 19C.

Dutch Reform church: The choir of this late-Gothic basilican structure was begun in *c.* 1470; the building itself was completed in 1507 when the W. sections of the nave and tower were built. Rib vaults are supported by corbel stones decorated with figures (nave and W. part of the choir) and by half-columns in the E. part of the choir. A number of good late-Gothic *vault paintings* were discovered in the course of the most recent restoration.

Museum Freriks: Collections of objets d'art, items of historical interest, and natural history and geological exhibits. Opening times: Tue.–Fri. 9 a.m.–12 noon & 2–5 p.m., Sat. & Sun. 2–5 p.m; July & Aug.: also Mon.

Environs: Groenlo (11 km. NW): Most of the ramparts of this old fortified town, along with canals, still survive; today, parks have been laid out along the fortifications. The choir of the *Dutch Reform church of St. Callixtus* was probably built in the third quarter of the 15C when the nave walls were already standing; the chapel and the staircase tower on the N. side of the choir were erected at the same time. The large nave was expanded in the 16C, and the dome over the late-14C tower was added in the 18C. Three figures of the Apostles from the late 15C survive on the N. walls of the choir. The *Grols Museum* (15 Noteboomstraat) is a 17C timber-framed building with an old kitchen and weaving room, along with exhibits concerning the town's history. Opening times: Mon.–Fri. 2–5 p.m.

Wittem
Limburg   p.291 □ L 9

Dutch Reform church: J.C.Schlaun, an architect from Aachen, built the church for the then Capuchin monastery in 1729–33. Since the late 19C the building has been a Redemptorist monastery. Essentially a large square central room with an adjoining choir in the E. and an entrance building in the W., the church is almost entirely sur-

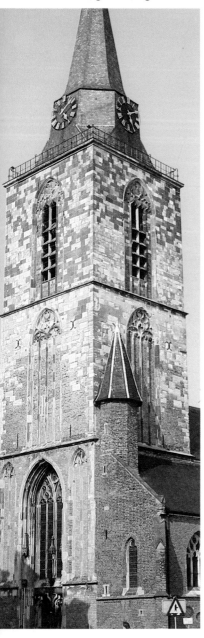

rounded by neo-Gothic extensions today. Inside there are side altars, Stations of the Cross, and 18C sculptures. The modern vault paintings are by Charles Eyck.

Kasteel Wittem: Two wings and a corner tower, restored in neo-Gothic style in the 19C, have survived from the original medieval castle.

Environs: Eys (2 km. E.): This fine *baroque Roman Catholic church* was built by J.C.Schlaun in 1732–4. It was restored in 1934–5, when low transepts were added. The fine decorations are mainly original.

Mechelen (3 km. S.): This *Roman Catholic church* (1810) was built to the plans of Mathias Soiron. It was later enlarged in the E., and a tower was added in 1837.

Wolvega/Wolvegea
Friesland   p.287☐M 3

Dutch Reform church: The church, standing in an elevated position in its churchyard, was built in Gothic style in 1646, partly using older materials. Fine mid-17C pulpit and richly decorated organ case (1723).

Landaus Lindenoord: A late-18C classical building by Onno Zwier van Haren.

'Windlust' corn mill: This 19C mill came from Zaanstreek. Today it houses a local museum. Opening times: Tue.–Fri. 9 a.m.–5 p.m., Sat. 9 a.m.–12 noon & 2–5 p.m.

Also worth seeing: The Sickengaplein with a *statue of Pieter Stuyvesant*, who was born in Scherpenzeel in 1592.

Environs: Oldeberkoop/Aldeber-

◁ *Winterswijk, Dutch Reform church*

keap (11 km. NE): This village has a beautiful square and a large *church* with a 12C Romanesque nave faced in tufa. The choir is more recent; 17C tower. Inside there is a 14C sandstone font on an octagonal pedestal. The *Bekhofschanze* entrenchment on the river Linde dates from the period when the Bishop of Münster invaded Friesland (1672). The line of defence on the Linde was too weak, but the Frisians held out at Oudeschouw. A cannon which was excavated near the entrenchment stands by the Heerenveenseweg.

Workum/Warkum

Friesland   p.286☐K 3

The beautiful appearance of Workum, one of the eleven Frisian towns, still survives from the town's heyday. The historical town centre is among the most charming in Frisia.

History: Workum, as well as Staveren and Hindeloopen, maintained a brisk trade with the Baltic countries. Coins were minted here in the 15C. Trade in live eels was pursued with London, and for this purpose the Frisian fishermen had some anchorages on the Thames. When the harbour silted up, Workum became of only local significance.

Grote Kerk or **St.-Gertrudiskerk:** The nave of this large church was left unfinished, as was the tower. The oldest part is the choir; the nave and two aisles were added about the mid 16C. The bright and spacious interior has a richly decorated pulpit (1718) with stairs and a copper lectern, remains of the choir screen (1569), a richly decorated noblemen's pew, and an organ (1697).

Stadhuis: The originally Gothic town hall was altered in 1727 and given a new roof. The elegant 18C façade has an ornate portal and decor-

Workum, Grote Kerk

ations above the windows. The external staircase did not receive its present form until restoration work was carried out in 1952. The council chamber has gilded leather wall decorations and a stuccoed ceiling with allegorical paintings (1773); the rococo fireplace shows the death of Ananias and Saphira.

Waag: This picturesque free-standing building in the market square was built by a local architect in lustrous red brick in 1650. There is a canopy on six Doric columns over the entrance on the N. side. Today the *local museum* is housed here. Opening times: 15 May–15 Sept.: Tue.– Sat. 11 a.m.–5 p.m.

Also worth seeing: The *Doopsgezinde vermaning* at 102 Noard is a Mennonite barn church (1694). Numerous *houses* with stepped gables, some decorated with mosaic friezes, survive in *Het Sûd*, *Noard* and *Dwarsnoard*. The only *Tjaskermolen* still operating in Friesland dates from (1915) and can be seen in the SE of the town.

Woudrichem

North Brabant   p.290☐I 6

Dutch Reform church: The 15C late Gothic church was badly damaged in a fire in the early 16C, and was rebuilt in 1573. The church itself looks very simple by comparison with its richly decorated tower with flying buttresses, arch niches and arch friezes.

The tower was probably built in *c.* 1530. In 1717 it lost its roof, which in 1933 was replaced by a balustrade at the top of the building.

Former Raadhuis: An earlier town hall (1592) with a saddleback roof and two stepped gables.

Waterpoort: This 16C gate with the projecting oriel on its NE corner was formerly part of the ramparts.

Also worth seeing: In *Hoogstraat* there are four houses with façades in the Dordrecht style. These are: 'In de Salamander' (1606), 'In den gulden Engel' (1593), 'In 't Hert' (1601) and 'In den vergulden Helm'.

Environs: Kasteel Loevestein (approx. 1 km. E.): A ferry across the river Maas, for foot-passengers only, leads to the castle which is in the Geldern district. It was probably founded between 1357 and 1368. Despite the modifications of the 17&18C, during which it became a State prison from which Hugo de Groot escaped inside a book-box in 1621, the castle has preserved its medieval appearance. On the E. side of the long main building there are two massive towers which were joined in the 15C by a wall with a projecting gatehouse tower. Opposite this is the round 'Kruittoren', the surviving corner tower of the former castle outworks.
Opening times: 1 Mar.–1 Nov.: 9 a.m.–5 p.m.

Woudrichem, ramparts with Dutch Reform church

IJlst/Drylts

Friesland   p.286□K 3

IJlst, the second smallest of the eleven Frisian towns, was granted the status of a town in 1268, and with it the right to a weekly market, two fairs and a weigh-house for butter.

Dutch Reform church: Rebuilt in 1830; the beautifully carved pulpit dates from 1672.

Huis 'De Messingklopper': This house has a fine stepped gable (1669) with tympana and other decorative strips including small sculpted heads. The frame around the entrance is also ornate.

Also worth seeing: Rather simple *houses* , some of which are 18C, stand along the Ee and Galama canal. On the Geeuw there is an old *saw mill* called 'De Rat'.

IJsselstein

Utrecht   p.289□I 5

Probably already settled in Carolingian times, the town developed from the 12C castle of the same name.

Dutch Reform church: Little is known of the architectural history of this large late-Gothic church. The Renaissance tower was probably begun shortly before 1532 to the plans of Alessandro Pasqualini and completed in 1535. Damaged in 1568, it was not rebuilt until 1633–5. The two lower storeys are by Pasqualini, the third dates from 1633–5; the modern fourth storey and the top are by M.de Klerk. The church has two *tomb monuments* which were damaged but have been restored. The black marble tomb is that of Gijsbrecht von IJsselstein (d. 1344), his wife Bertha van Heukelom, their son Arnold (d. 1363) and his wife Maria van Avennes. The other is a Franco-Dutch Renaissance tomb which was built in *c.* 1540 for Aleid van Culemborg, the wife (d. 1471) of Frederik van IJsselstein (d. 1522).

St.-Nicolaaskerk: This Roman Catholic neo-Gothic hall church (1885–7) by A.Tepe has a beautifully carved pulpit from the second half of the 18C, and a Virgin Mary which may be 13C.

Stadhuis: Built in the third quarter

IJsselstein, Dutch Reform church

of the 16C, the building has an attractive bell turret on the roof. The plasterwork was removed in the most recent restoration and the old stone is now visible once more. The rib-vaulted basement, originally a weigh-house, now houses a restaurant.

IJsselstein castle: Most of the building was pulled down in 1888, except for the almost square keep, which was built in *c.* 1500 in S. Brabant style.

IJzendijke
Zeeland   p.288□D 8

IJzendijke, formerly a small fortified town, has a large market square with pretty gabled houses.

Dutch Reform church: The church was built in 1612 on a regular octagonal ground plan and enlarged 1656–9. During the rebuilding the original domed roof with its delicate turret was retained, while the new section was given a saddleback roof. Fine early-18C pulpit; 19C font railing and organ. Opening times: June–Sept.: 9 a.m.–4 p.m. daily.

Streekmuseum (Markt): A regional museum occupying the former community centre. There is an interesting reconstruction of the room of a peasant from Cadzand, as well as costumes and archaeological finds from the surrounding region. Opening times: Mon.–Fri. 10 a.m.–12 noon and 1.30–5 p.m., Sat. & Sun. 2–5 p.m.

Environs: Breskens: (12 km. NW): This town, linked to Vlissingen by ferry, is situated in the middle of an area of polder land whose dykes were built in the 16C. Breskens has a good sandy beach and a fishing harbour.

Zaandam
North Holland   p.286□H 4

Westzijderkerk: Also known as the Bullekerk. Built in 1638–40, it was lengthened in the W. and E. between 1672 and 1680. There is a charming little tower above the crossing. The Renaissance pulpit dates from 1644.

Oostzijderkerk: This Dutch Reform church has been altered many times. The tower was built by L.J.Immink, the town architect, in the mid 19C. The six stained-glass windows date from the late 17C and early 18C.

Lutherse Kerk (Vinkenstraat): Built in 1699 with a saddleback roof between two ridge gables, a broad façade with pilasters and an elevated central section. The ornate pulpit dates from 1704 and the beautifully-carved organ casing from 1737.

Czaar-Peterhuisje (on the Krimp): Part of the wooden cottage where Tsar Peter the Great lived as a ship's carpenter in 1697. Extensive rebuilding dates from 1895. Opening times: Tue.–Sat. 10 a.m.–1 p.m. & 2–5 p.m.; also 10 a.m.–1 p.m. & 2–5 p.m. every second & fourth Sunday in the month.

Zaanse Schans: An open-air

museum a little way outside the town with twenty reconstructed buildings, including mills (e.g. a mustard mill, a sawmill and an oil mill), commercial establishments and shops (e.g. a bakery, a clog-maker's, and a tin foundry) as well as museums (e.g. a clock museum, a small museum of interior decoration and the reconstructed interior of an old grocer's shop). Much of the museum is open daily 1 Apr.–1 Nov. (weekends only in winter).

Environs: Heemskerk (13 km. W.): The tower of the *Dutch Reform church* is probably late 15C, while the main body of the hall church dates from 1628. An obelisk decorated with reliefs and built in 1570 by Maarten van Heemskerk (1498–1574) for his father's tomb can be seen in the graveyard.
Koog aan de Zaan (3 km. N.): The *Dutch Reform church* was built in 1685, rebuilt in 1824, partly destroyed by fire in 1920 and subsequently rebuilt. 'Het Pink', an oil mill was built as a post mill in 1620 and converted into an octagonal rotary-cap mill in 1751. A *museum of mills* (18 Museumlaan), occupies a merchant's house (*c.* 1760; enlarged in 1800). Opening times: Tue.–Fri. 10 a.m.–12 noon & 2–5 p.m., Sat. & Sun. 2–5 p.m.
Krommenie (10 km. N.): After its almost complete destruction in the Eighty Years' War, the late Gothic *Dutch Reform church* was rebuilt in 1657–8 using the old materials.
Zaandijk (4 km. N.): The *Gemeentehuis* (104 Lagedijk), built in 1752, was substantially rebuilt in *c.* 1800; the rococo hall has decorative wallpaper of 1804. In the garden opposite the house there are five statues on rococo pedestals (Bacchus surrounded by Morning, Noon, Evening and Night). The *Zaanlandse Oudheidkamer* (80 Lagedijk) in an 18C merchant's house has paintings and Chinese porcelain. Opening times: Tue.–Fri. 10 a.m.–12 noon & 2–4 p.m.; Sun. 2–4 p.m.

Zaltbommel

Geldern   p.290☐I 6

This pretty little town on the left bank of the Waal lies within its almost undamaged 17C walls (turned into gardens today).

St.-Maartenskerk: Today a Dutch Reform church. Rebuilt in 1303 after becoming a collegiate church. The oldest part is the choir which has enormous windows. The tower and the nave and two aisles, which differ only slightly from one another, were built from the mid 15C onwards. The unusually richly articulated four-storeyed *tower* is a fine example of Lower Rhine Gothic. The spire burned down in 1538 (its original appearance can be seen in a 16C painting inside the church). In the N. aisle *wall paintings* of *c.* 1500 depict a legend; also a St.Christopher (*c.* 1540). Vault paintings, in places heavily overpainted, can be seen in the side aisles and choir. The late Gothic choir stalls (mid 15C) have good relief figures;

Zaltbommel, Huis van Maarten van Rossum

the pulpit dates from 1678 and the organ from 1784.

Gasthuistoren: Formerly the tower of the 15C hospice chapel with a round staircase tower alongside. The top of the tower (*c.* 1530), which has been rebuilt, is most attractive and contains a carillon by Hémony.

Roman Catholic church (Oliestraat): A neoclassical building dating from 1837; after alterations only the nave was retained.

Huis van Maarten van Rossum (5 Nonnenstraat): An interesting building with delightful bartizans, it was probably built *c.* 1535 as the gatehouse of a castle, which was itself never built. Today it houses a *historical museum.*
Opening times: May–June: 2–4 p.m.. July & Aug.: 10 a.m.–12 noon & 2–4 p.m. Sept.–Apr.: Wed. & Sat. 2–4 p.m.

Stadhuis: Originally a late medieval building, it was altered by Anthony Viervant in 1761–3. The façade has a colossal order of pilasters and a wooden architrave with triglyphs. A small wooden bell turret rises from the middle of the roof.

Waterpoort: This gate in the medieval town wall stands at the end of Waterstraat. Nearby there is a house built within an arch in the town wall.

Houses: Houses at *2 Markt* and *6 Ruiterstraat* are *late Gothic,* while *26 Waterstraat* and *16 Kerkplein* are *early Renaissance.* Other houses have 16&17C *stepped gables: 10–12 Boschstraat, 17, 22, 23, 24 Gasthuisstraat, 26 Kerkstraat, 3 Markt, 2 Kerkplein, 14–16 Ruiterstraat* and *2 Vismarkt.*

Environs: Kasteel Waardenburg (3 km. N.): A horseshoe section of

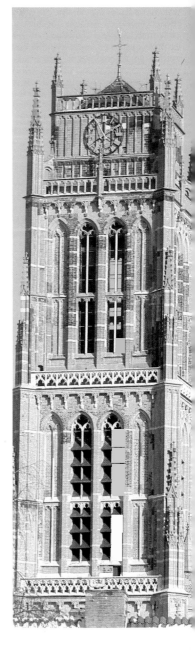

Zaltbommel, St.-Maartenskerk ▷

wall has survived from the late-13C defensive wall. In the mid 14C a large residential tower was added in the E. (this was later reduced in height and given a new roof). Residential wings were built within the surrounding wall in the 15C and these were partially rebuilt after the devastation of 1574. The dilapidated S. wing was pulled down in 1705, and the E. wing was extended *c*. 1895. A large part of the complex is still surrounded by a moat.

't Zandt
Groningen   p.287☐O 2

Dutch Reform church: This long building dates from the 15C, when a High Gothic choir was added to the 13C nave. Vaults and walls are decorated with fragments of paintings (including a Last Judgement). The free-standing 13C tower with a saddleback roof is topped by a small belfry.

Environs: Eenum: (5 km. SE): The small 12C *brick church* with an 18C tower stands on a terp.
Leermens (2.5 km SE): The *Dutch Reform church* has a 10C or 11C tufa nave, a choir of a later date and a 13C transept. Inside there are 15C figures of saints e.g. Donatus, Sebastian, Ursula and the Virgin Mary.
Zeerijp (3 km. S.): The *church* is the youngest of the Romanesque-Gothic churches in Groningen. Mostly built in the mid 14C, the enormous tower dates from the first half of the 15C. Restoration reproduced the former appearance of the inside walls, which are red and white. The baroque pulpit (1646) is by Johan Elderkamp; the organ (1651) is by T. Faber. The *'De Leeuw' corn mill* (1865) is still in operation.
Zijldijk (4 km. NE): The *Mennonite church* (Doopsgezinde vermaning), a typical barn-like hall church (1772), has pointed windows.

Zeist
Utrecht   p.289☐I 5

Castle: This elegant structure (1677–86) was built by Jacob Roman, with the assistance of Daniel Marot, for Willem Adriaan, Count of Nassau-Odijk, who had spent much of his youth at the French court, and was now building himself a 'small-scale Versailles'. The *stairwell* decorated by Marot, and the strictly classical stuccoed *hall* (first half of 19C) by J.D.Zocher the younger, are fine features of the interior. In 1746 the castle was acquired by Cornelis Schellinger, a wealthy Amsterdam merchant who made the castle a centre for the Moravian Brethren, and had stately houses built in the Broederplein and Zusterplein to the left and right of the avenue leading to the castle. The small Moravian church (1768) was built by Maurice v. Schweinitz in 1768; a bell turret from 1854. Some of the houses are still inhabited by Moravians, while the organization for the preservation of monuments is accommodated in other houses. Guided tours of the castle.

Dutch Reform church: This church (1843) in English neo-Gothic style is by N.J.Kamperdijk.

Environs: Bunnik (3 km. SW): The roughcast *Dutch Reform church* has an attractive late-Romanesque brick tower. The *Roman Catholic church* was built in 1939. 18C *country houses* lie scattered in the attractive countryside along the Kromme Rijn. *Huis Cammingha* is a manor house with wings from *c*. 15C and 16C; the house was enlarged in the 17C.
Driebergen-Rijsenburg (6 km. SE): This double parish has the beautiful, Sparrendaal country house (1754) as its *town hall*. The *Roman Catholic church of St.-Petrus' Banden* in Rijsenburg, with a curving gable façade and a colonnaded portal, was built by A.Tollus in 1809–10.

Zeist, castle

Pyramid of Austerlitz (6 km. SE): Built by French soldiers on a hill 203 ft. high to commemorate Napoleon's victory over Austria and Russia in the battle of Austerlitz in 1805.

Werkhoven (7 km. S.): The fine Romanesque tufa tower of the *Dutch Reform church* is probably late 12C. *Kasteel Beverweerd* was rebuilt in neo-Gothic style in 1835–40 on the site of a 13C residential tower (itself expanded from the 14C to the 18C by the addition of towers and wings).

Zierikzee

Zeeland   p.288□E 7

The main town of Schouwen-Duiveland, it was at its peak from the 14C to the 16C as a result of trade in salt.

St.-Lievensmonstertoren: After the fire of 1832, all that survived of the formerly large collegiate church was the free-standing tower which dominates the town's skyline from afar. Begun by Andries Keldermans in 1454, work on it was continued by his successors Anthonis and Rombout and ceased in *c.* 1535 when about half finished. The two completed storeys arched buttresses and staircase towers in the middle of their N. and S. sides, and an ornate portal on the W. side. Roof and balustrade date from restoration work in 1965–70. The building is open to the public daily from 11 a.m.–5 p.m. in summer.

Nieuwe Kerk: In 1842, G.H.Grauss, the town architect from Middelburg, built this neo-classical church on the site of the St.-Lievens minster.

Gasthuiskerk: Originally the chapel of the 14C St.-Elisabeth hospice, it

Zierikzee, Zuidhavenpoort

was enlarged in 1651 and redecorated. Opening times: Mon.–Fri. 2–4 p.m.

Lutherse Kerk: Formerly a private chapel which was rebuilt in 1713 and enlarged in 1755.

Beurs: This market hall by the Oude Haven was built as a Renaissance gallery in 1651. The upper galleried storey is in fact part of the Gasthuiskerk.

Blauwe Bolwerk: The bulwark by the Nieuwe Haven was built in 1621 to defend the harbour canal. Only remains survive.

Gravensteen: This former law court and prison (1524–6), designed by Herman van Aken from Antwerp, has survived in good condition and has a Gothic stepped gable in stone. It houses the *Maritiem Museum* which is

open to the public as follows: 1 May– 30 Sept.: Mon.–Sat 10 a.m.–5 p.m.

Huis de Haene (Meelstraat): The 14C stepped gable shows the influence of buildings in Brüggen; the windows are contained within pointed arches with trefoils. Parts of two carvings of birds can be seen in the entrance tympanum.

Nobelpoort: This, the oldest town gate, dates from the first quarter of the 14C and is flanked on the outside by two round towers.

Noordhavenpoort: Horseshoe bulwark (*c.* 1500) with building with stepped gable on the seaward side and two fine gables on the town side in Flemish Renaissance style (1559).

Raadhuis: The oldest section of this building is the late-14C octagonal tower, which was formerly the meat hall. The part to the E. of this, with a façade crowned by two gables was built from 1550–4. The court room is on the ground floor; its wooden ceiling is supported in the middle by a row of four stellar columns. Further extensions were added to the rear of this building in the 17C. Today the *Gemeentemuseum* is also in the town hall. Opening times: 1 May–1 Oct.: Mon.–Fri. 10 a.m.–12 noon & 1.30–4.30 p.m.

Vismarkt: (St.Domusstraat): Small enclosed square of small houses of the St.-Jacobshofje (altered in 1804) to which a small colonnaded gallery was added.

Weeshuis (45 Poststraat): This 17C building was converted into an orphanage in 1863. The rear façade was built in *c.* 1740. Exhibitions are held here (June–Aug., Mon.–Sat., 10 a.m.–5 p.m.).

Windmills: Two round corn mills built of stone, 'De Haas' (1727) and

'De Hoop' (1876), are to be found by the Nieuwe Haven.

Houses: There are a number of houses with 17C façades in and around the *St.-Domusstraat* and *Nieuwe Boogerdstraat*. Splendid 18&19C *façades* are to be seen by the *Oude Haven*.

Zuidhavenpoort: The second and particularly splendid *gate* by the *Oude Haven* is probably 14C and has four bartizans. The roof has an 18C domed turret. Parts of the old town wall have been rebuilt on the N. and S. based on old pictures of the town.

Environs: Nieuwerkerk (4 km. E.): The nave of the *Dutch Reform church* had to be pulled down in 1583 after a fire; the tower was destroyed in 1944. Only the large 15C choir survives.
Oosterland (6 km. E.): The *Dutch Reform church* has a late-15C choir and a 14C brick tower. The nave burned down in 1612, and today only some masonry is visible.

Zierikzee, Raadhuis

Zu dlaren
Drer te   p.287☐N 2

This beautiful village, which has ten squares including the main square with a pond used by the fire brigade, was mentioned in 1360. The village is also referred to in the 16C chronicles of the abbey of Werden on the Ruhr.

Dutch Reform church: The tower from *c.* 1300 is topped by a 15C crown. The church has a late Romanesque/early Gothic nave and a tall 15C Gothic choir. In danger of falling down in the late 16C owing to war damage, the church was rebuilt throughout in 1648–50. Inside there are old stone slabs and a richly carved pulpit (1675). The stuccoed coat-of-arms of Alexander Carel van Heiden (d. 1776) is in the choir.

Huize Laarwoud: This beautiful house surrounded by a ditch has a 17C central section and two low wings from sometime after 1750. Today it is a community centre. The ceiling in the mayor's room was painted in 1698. The former 'Schathuis' in the forecourt is today the 'Dorpshuis' (village house). A.C. van Heiden, who lived in this house, became a Drente magistrate in 1751.

Also worth seeing: Squares surrounded by splendid Saxon *farmhouses*. The house at *28 Kerkbrink* has fine wrought-iron decorations of 1750 on its doors. *'De Schipborg'*, a farmhouse built in 1914, is by H.P.Berlage.

Zundert

North Brabant   p.289□G 7

Zundert, the birthplace of Vincent van Gogh, is well known for its large *flower parade* which is held on the first Sunday in September.

St.-Trudokerk: The high altar and two side altars from the abbey of St.-Michiel in Antwerp, which was damaged in the French Revolution, were set up in a new church built in 1936. The large baroque *colonnaded altar* (1622), with a copy of Rubens's 'Adoration of the Magi', stands in the S. transept today. Associated with the altar are three large alabaster figures of the Virgin Mary, St.Michael and St.Norbert which are distributed about the church (they were probably carved by Hans van Mildert to sketches by Rubens). The N. chapel has a *marble altar* (*c.* 1655) with a painting by P.Fruytier of the Glorification of the Virgin Mary. The second marble altar (*c.* 1675, in the S. chapel) is by Artus Quellinus the younger and has a painting by Johannes Erasmus Quellinus.

Also worth seeing: A *bronze monument to Vincent van Gogh* by Ossip Zadkine. *'De Moeren'*, in the Rucphenseweg, is a beautiful country house (1818) in Empire style. Other interesting buildings nearby include the *'In den Anker' restaurant* (1653), *'De kleine Anker'* a farm from 1670, altered in 1913, the early-17C *'De Akkermolen' upright mill* and the monumental neoclassical *town hall* (1830) with a roughcast façade with a colossal order and a crown over the gable above the central projection.

Zutphen

Geldern   p.287□M 5

Zutphen, located where the Berkel flows into the IJssel, was granted a charter in 1190 and has one of the finest old town centres in the Netherlands. Formerly it maintained relations with the Hanseatic cities and was of great economic and political significance.

St.-Walburgskerk: The building which preceded the present Gothic hall church on this site was a cruciform Romanesque-Gothic basilica. Parts of this older structure survive, chiefly the choir, transept and nave with 13C vaults. Between 1370 and 1390 the old main choir was given an ambulatory as tall as the choir with a surrounding ring of chapels. Some time after 1393, the polygonal chapel of the Virgin Mary was built to the E. of this ambulatory; there are staircase turrets at the points where the two buildings join. The side aisles, equal in height to the nave, are mid 15C, while the fine *Virgin Mary portal* by the N. aisle was built in the late 15C. The chapels in the extension of the old transepts date from *c.* 1500. The famous *library* on the S. side of the ambulatory dates from 1561–3. The old tower roof (1633) was rebuilt in restoration work completed in 1970. The church looks very attractive both from the outside (thanks to the variety of roof shapes and building materials) and from the inside (owing to the various different vistas). A number of early-15C *wall paintings*, in rather poor condition, were uncovered in the choir chapels during restoration work; 15C *vault paintings* in a rather better state of preservation were found in the choir, transepts and crossing. The monumental font (1527) in late Gothic and Renaissance styles is by Gielis van Eynde from Mechelen; the pulpit dates from *c.* 1670. The organ (1637–43) is by Bader, an organ builder from Zutphen. Sandstone sarcophagus lid from *c.* 1200 in the S. aisle. Guided tours of the church and the library, with its medieval manuscripts and early printed works, are held on weekdays from May to September.

Broederenkerk (Rozengracht): The church of the Dominican monastery, founded in 1293 and built in the early 14C, is a typical church of the mendicant order, with a basilican nave and a simple choir. The roof turret dates from 1772. *Vault paintings* have tendril-like decorations, Dominican

Saints and Dominican coats-of-arms (second quarter of the 16C) have been discovered in the choir and nave. Remains of the 15C *monastery* on the N. side of the church consist of parts of the cloister, and a wing containing the dormitory and refectory. The *Stedelijk Museum voor Zutphen en de Graafschap* is housed in these remains. Opening times: Tue.–Fri. 10 a.m.–12.30 p.m. & 2–5 p.m., Sat. 10 a.m.–12.30 p.m., Sun. 3–5 p.m. Closed on Easter Sunday, Whit Sunday, Christmas Day, 1 January, Ascension Day, Good Friday & 30 April.

Nieuwstadskerk (L. Vrouwestraat): The Roman Catholic church is a modest hall church with an enormous tower from the 14&15C.

Stadhuis (corner of Lange Hofstraat and 's-Gravenhof): A sheriff's court and meat hall were built in 1450–2 on the N. side of the old town hall. These buildings were united by identical roofs and three ridge gables facing onto the Lange Hofstraat; the gables disappeared during rebuilding in

Panorama of Zutphen, seen from the IJssel

1729 and only the former meat hall regained its gable in the restoration of 1896. The meat hall was converted into a hall open up to the roof and, in 1951, it became the Bürgersaal of the town hall.

Town wall: The almost square Oude Stad, and the Nieuwstad which adjoins it in the N., have both retained considerable remains of the medieval town wall. The *Bourgonjetoren*, a gun turret dating from 1457, stands near 's-Gravenhof square, and on its S. side there is a section of town wall. The *Drogenapstoren*, which has four octagonal corner turrets, stands at the end of the Zaadmarkt and was built as a town gate in 1444–6, although after 1465 it was no longer used as such. A water gate, the so-called *Berkelruine* (probably early 15C), stands to the N. of the Hagenpoortplein. Part of the *Oude Nieuwstadspoort* (1536) survives on the N. side of the Nieuwstad; the *Kruittoren* (probably early-15C) stands in the NW corner.

Wijnhuis (Groenmarkt): The Renaissance tower, whose lower part dates from 1618 and upper section from 1637–41, is all that survives of the old 17C wine house.

Houses: The best of the many buildings of medieval origin include the *former provost's house of St.-Walburg* (2 Proosdijsteeg) from the first half of the 13C, the houses at *65–67 Beukerstraat* (possibly 14C), *101 Zaadmarkt* and *42–44 Markt* (probably *c.* 1300). There are also: the *former coin-mint* of Zutphen (10–14 Rodetorenstraat) from the early 14C. The houses at *109 Zaadmarkt* (1549) and *44 Beukerstraat* (1557) are also interesting. Beautiful *Renaissance façades* can be seen at *70 Houtmarkt, 3 Lange Hofstraat* and *5–9 Groenmarkt*. The houses at *11 Kuiperstraat, 6 's-Gravenhof* and *88 Zaadmarkt* are 17&18C. A number of *town houses* on the *IJsselkade* were built in the third quarter of the 19C.

Museums: Apart from the museums already mentioned (Stedelijk Museum and Library of the St.-Walburgskerk), there is also the *Museum of*

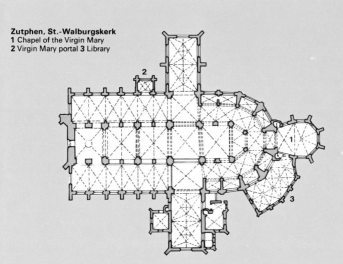

Zutphen, St.-Walburgskerk
1 Chapel of the Virgin Mary
2 Virgin Mary portal 3 Library

Henriette Polak at 88 Zaadmarkt, with a collection of modern art. Opening times: Tue.–Fri.: 10 a.m.–12 noon & 2–5 p.m., Sat. 10 a.m.–12.30 p.m., Sun. 3–5 p.m.; closed on Good Friday, Ascension Day, 1 January & 30 April. There is a collection of tin soldiers in the Kruittoren.

Environs: Bronkhorst (8 km. S.): This attractive village with timber-framed farmhouses was built around a castle of which nothing has survived. The small 15C *brick church* was comprehensively restored in 1960–1. *Huis Ophemert* (1633), a tall house, belongs to a farm.
Brummen (7 km. SW): The 15C *Dutch Reform church* has a somewhat older tower. In the choir there are two tombstones in the wall, commemorating Johanna van Heeckeren (d. 1652) and her husband Conraad van Hoost. *Engelenburg*, a 17C country house, was altered in the 19C. Only part of *Laag-Helbergen*, a 16C noblemen's house, survives.
Lochem (14 km. E.): This formerly fortified small town has a late Gothic hall church with a tower (1478) half of

which is included in the main structure. The *town hall* (1634–40) was built to the plans of Edmond Hellenraet; today's façade dates from 1741.

Zwolle
Overijssel   p.287☐M 4

History: Zwolle, the main town of the province of Overijssel, lies between the rivers Vecht and IJssel on the Zwarte Water in the old glacial valley which became marsh, high moors, sand and heaths. The name *Suol* first occurred in 1040, and in 1230 the place was granted a charter and was fortified for the first time. Zwolle became a member of the Hanseatic League in 1407, at which time it was experiencing a peak period of prosperity. At this time it was also a cultural centre, thanks to the Devotio Moderna (a religious revival movement headed by Geert Groote) and the Latin school of Johan Cele. Zwolle later declined in significance owing to a reduction in the volume of trade and the rise of other towns such as Amsterdam.

Zwolle, Sassenpoort

Religious buildings

Grote Kerk or **St.-Michaelskerk:** This large Dutch Reform hall church with a nave and two aisles was begun in the second half of the 14C on the site of an older structure and completed sometime after the middle of the 15C. A very tall tower, begun in 1406 on the W. side, collapsed in 1682 after a fire, whereupon a consistory building was erected on its site. There is a very ornate early-16C portal on the N. side. Most of the decorative *vault paintings* (probably second half of 16C) inside have been restored. Paintings on walls and pillars have been severely damaged. The choir screen (1597) is the work of Sweer Kistemaker in the style of Vredeman de Vries; the magnificent *pulpit* (1617–22) is by Adam Straes from Weilburg in Nassau. The splendid *organ* (1719–21) is by Johann Georg and Franz Caspar Schnitger from Hamburg, while the organ casing was designed by Jurriaan Westerman from Amsterdam. A painting (1691) by Hendrik ten Oever, of the preachers of Zwolle, is to be found in the consistory building (1688).

Bethlehemsekerk: This Dutch Reform church with two aisles was originally the church of a monastery founded in 1309 and belonging to the Augustinian Canons Bethlehem or Belhem. The oldest section, probably from the first half of the 15C, is the choir, while the other parts of this hall church were built in the course of the 15C.

Broerenkerk: This Dutch Reform church was previously built for the Dominican monastery founded in 1465. It was rebuilt as a large hall church with two aisles in *c.* 1500 and consecrated in 1512.

St.-Michaels church: This modern Roman Catholic church contains the reliquary of Thomas à Kempis (1379–1471), donated by the Prince Elector of Cologne.

Onze-Lieve-Vrouwekerk: This late-Gothic Roman Catholic church was built in *c.* 1463. The tower, begun in 1478, increased in height in 1538–40 and given a dome in 1828, has dominated the town's appearance ever

Zwolle, Old and New Town Hall

since the Grote Kerk's tower collapsed. Low aisles of simple design were added to the church in 1887–9.

Waalse Kerk: This fine single-aisled chapel was built in *c*. 1500 as the chapel of the St.-Geertruiden convent (founded in *c*. 1390). Staircase turret beside the attractive façade.

Secular buildings

Hoofdwacht: This picturesque Renaissance building (1614) designed by Thomas Berendsz, an architect from Kampen, stands on the N. side of the Grote Kerk. Sculpture by Adam Straes from Weilburg.

Sassenpoort: This gate, which probably dates from 1409, is an impressive remnant of the fortifications. The corner towers on the outside stand on a round ground plan which becomes octagonal higher up. The gate has polygonal bartizans on the side facing the town.

Stadhuis: The mid-15C town hall in Sassenstraat was much modernized in 1821 and thereafter. A new section was added in 1973–5. The old *council chamber* (1448) is a large and elegant room with a timber ceiling, a Gothic fireplace, a 'Last Judgement' (1606) by an unknown painter, and four recesses in the walls with small carved doors. Opening times: Mon.–Fri. 10 a.m.–5 p.m.

'De Passiebloem' windmill (1 Vondelkade): An octagonal upright mill (1776).

Museums

Provinciaal Overijssels Museum (41 Melkmarkt):This museum, which is housed in an early-16C building modernized in rococo style in the 18C, has 17&18C silver and other objects of widely varying types ranging in period from Gothic to Art Nouveau. Opening times: Tue.–Sat. 10 a.m.–5 p.m., Sun. 2–5 p.m.

Natuurmuseum West Overijssel (32–34 Voostraat): Exhibits concerned with the geology and natural history of West-Overijssel and Salland. Opening times: Tue.–Sat. 10 a.m.–5p.m., Sun. 2–5 p.m.

Also worth seeing: The neoclassical *Gerechtshof* (1840–1) is by E.L. de Coninck. The *Vrouwenhuis* (*c*. 1640) at 53 Melkmarkt has a warden's room with 17C paintings. The *railway building* (1863) is eclectic in style. The *Karel V-huis* at *33 Sassenstraat* has a magnificent early-Renaissance pilastered façade (1571).

Environs: Agnietenberg (3 km. N.): A memorial stone commemorates the fact that Thomas a Kempis lived and died here. Tradition has it that he wrote the 'Imitatio Christi' here.

Heino (14 km. SE): The plain tower of the *Dutch Reform church* is probably 15C. *Het Nijenhuis*, an elegant country house is probably late medieval. Its present regular form dates from the 17C. The tower-like annexes at the back are 19C.

Mastenbroek (7.5 km. NW): The single-aisled *Dutch Reform church* is late Gothic. The tower was replaced by a new tower in 1845.

Wijhe (13 km. S.): This very old settlement was mentioned in 960 in a document of Otto I. The *Dutch Reform church,* with its nave and two aisles, has a late-Romanesque tower which was increased in height in Gothic style. The nave and N. aisle are 13/14C, while the S. aisle probably dates from *c*. 1500. There are two richly designed tombs inside the church.

Windesheim (6 km. SE): All that survives of the famous Windesheim *monastery,* founded in 1387, is a tall, plain building which—so tradition has it—has been a brewery since time immemorial. Since the 17C, the lower storey of this building has been a Dutch Reform church. Octagonal *windmill* (1748).

Index of places referred to in the guide

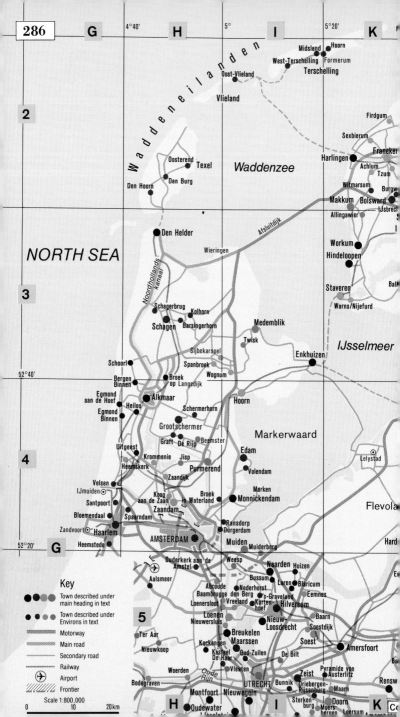

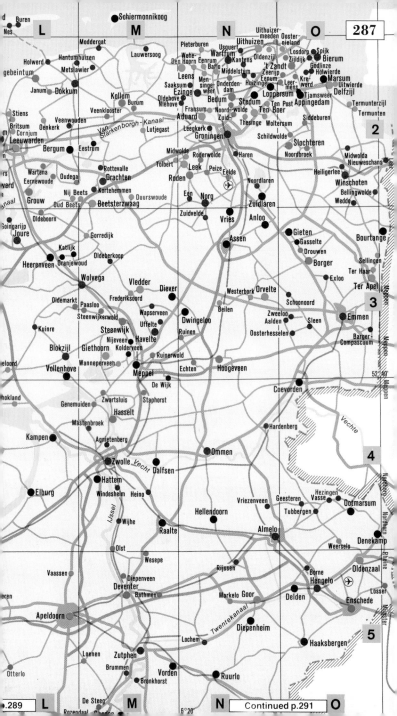

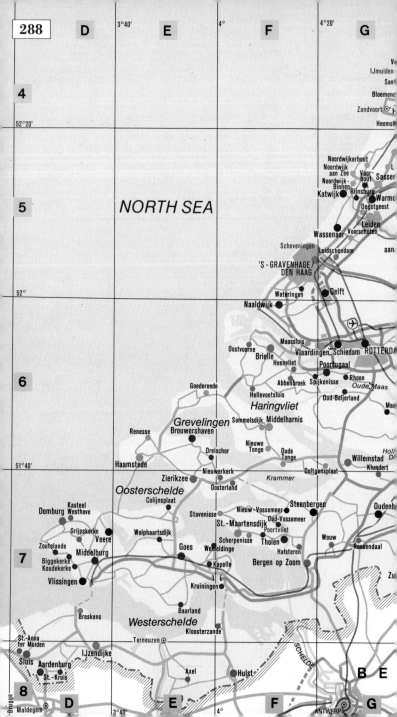

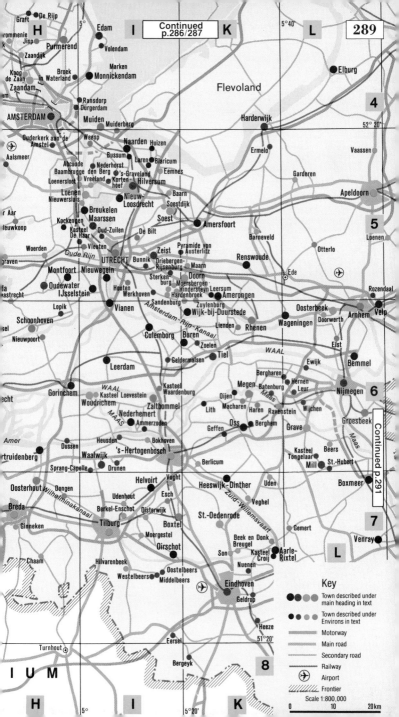

Graft
De Rijp
rommenie
Jisp
k
Zaandijk
Kaog
de Zaan
Zaandam
am
Aalsmeer

H
Purmerend

5°

Edam
Volendam

Marken
Monnickendam

I

K

L

Elburg

Flevoland

5°40'

Broek
in Waterland

AMSTERDAM

Ransdorp
Durgerdam
Muiden
Muiderberg

Muiden

Harderwijk

Ouderkerk aan de
Amstel

Weesp
Naarden
Huizen

r Aar
ieuwkoop

Abcoude
Baambrugge den Berg
Loenersloot
Loenen
Nieuwersluis

Breukelen

Woerden

Kockengen
Kasteel
De Haar
Vleuten

Bussum
Nederhorst
Vreeland
Korten-
hoef
's-Graveland
Hilversum

Laren
Blaricum
Eemnes

Ermelo

Vaassen

Garderen

Apeldoorn

Baarn
Soestdijk

Nieuw-
Loosdrecht

Maarssen
Oud-Zuilen

De Bilt

Soest

Amersfoort

Barneveld

Loenen

Montfoort
graven
Nieuwegein
Oudewater
la
IJsselstein
aastrecht

UTRECHT
Oude Rijn

Lopik
Schoonhoven
sel
Nieuwpoort

Vianen

Bunnik

Zeist
Pyramide von
Austerlitz

Driebergen-
Rijsenburg
Sterken-
burg
Doorn
Moersbergen
Hindersteyn Leersum
Hardenbroek
Sandenburg
Zuylenburg
Amerongen

Maarn

Renswoude

Ede

Otterlo

Rozendaal

Houten
Werkhoven

Wijk-bij-Duurstede

Oosterbeek

Velp
Arnhem

Culemborg

Amsterdam-Rijn-Kanaal

Buren
Zoelen

Lienden
Rhenen

Wageningen
Doorwerth

Elst

Leerdam

Geldermalsen
Tiel

WAAL

Ewijk

Bemmel

Gorinchem
WAAL
Kasteel Loevestein
Woudrichem

Kasteel
Waardenburg

Bergharen
Megen
Batenburg
Hernen
Leur

Nijmegen

Nederhemert
Zaltbommel
Ammerzoden

Oijen
Lith
Macharen
Haren

MAAS

Ravenstein
Wijchen

Groesbeek

Geffen
Oss
Berghem
Grave

Amer
Dussen
Heusden
Bokhoven

Waalwijk
Drunen

's-Hertogenbosch

Berlicum

rtruidenberg
Sprang-Capelle

Oosterhout
Dongen

Breda
Udenhout

Ginneken

Chaam

Helvoirt
Vught

Esch
Berkel-Enschot
Oisterwijk

Tilburg

Moergestel

Hilvarenbeek

Heeswijk-Dinther

Uden

St.-Oedenrode

Boxtel

Oirschot

Son

Westelbeers
Oostelbeers
Middelbeers

Veghel

Beek en Donk
Breugel

Kasteel
Croij
Aarle-
Rixtel

Nuenen

Eindhoven

Geldrop

Heeze

Eersel

Bergeyk

Kasteel
Tongelaar
Mill

Beers
St.-Hubert

Boxmeer

MAAS

Gemert

Venray

Turnhout

IUM

H

5°

I

5°20'

K

Continued p.291

L

Key

Town described under
main heading in text

Town described under
Environs in text

Motorway

Main road

Secondary road

Railway

Airport

Frontier

Scale 1:800,000

0   10   20km

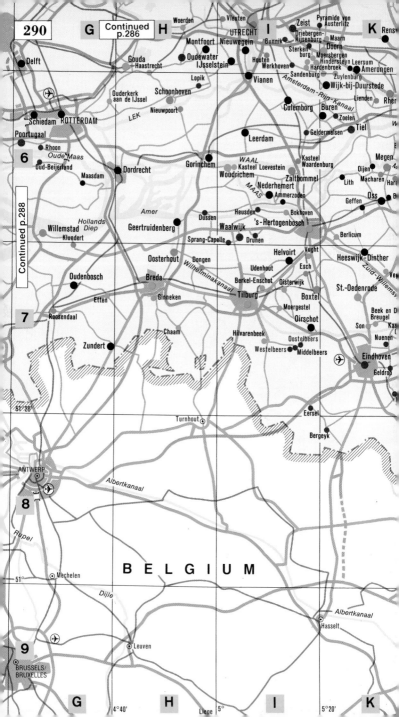